"Wanderjahre of a Revolutionist"
and Other Essays on American Music

Arthur Farwell
Photo taken by Charles F. Lummis for the *Bulletin of the Southwest Society of the Archaeological Institute of America 2* (1905);
courtesy of The Southwest Museum, Los Angeles
Photo No. 42036

"Wanderjahre of a Revolutionist" and Other Essays on American Music

by

Arthur Farwell

Edited by Thomas Stoner

University of Rochester Press

First published 1995
University of Rochester Press
34-36 Administration Building, University of Rochester
Rochester, New York, 14627, USA
and at P.O. Box 9, Woodbridge, Suffolk IP12 3DF, UK

Library of Congress Cataloging-in-Publication Data

Farwell, Arthur, 1872–1952.
    [Literary works. Selections]
    Wanderjahre of a revolutionist and other essays on American music
/ by Arthur Farwell ; edited by Thomas Stoner.
        p.   cm. — (Eastman studies in music ; 4)
    Includes bibliographical references and index.
    Contents: Wanderjahre of a revolutionist : memoirs at age thirty-
seven—Toward American music—Society and American music—
National work vs. nationalism—A glance at present musical
problems in America—Individual advancement—The new gospel of
music—Community music-drama—Evolution of new forms foreseen
for America's music.
    ISBN 1–878822–48–9
    1. Farwell, Arthur, 1872–1952. 2. Composers—United States—
Biography. 3. Music—United States—History and criticism.
II. Title. III. Series.
ML410.F228A3 1995
780'.92—dc20
    [B]   95-31528
                                                                              CIP

British Library Cataloguing-in-Publication Data

A catalogue record for this book is available from the British Library

This publication is printed on acid-free paper
Printed in the United States of America
Designed and Typeset by Cornerstone Composition Services

To
M.L.M.S.

Eastman Studies in Music

*The Poetic Debussy: A Collection of His Song Texts and
Selected Letters (Revised Second Edition)*
Edited by Margaret G. Cobb

*Concert Music, Rock, and Jazz since 1945:
Essays and Analytical Studies*
Edited by Elizabeth West Marvin and Richard Hermann

*Music and the Occult: French Musical Philosophies,
1750-1950*
Joscelyn Godwin

*"Wanderjahre of a Revolutionist" and
Other Essays on American Music*
Arthur Farwell, edited by Thomas Stoner

French Organ Music from the Revolution to Franck and Widor
Edited by Lawrence Archbold and William J. Peterson

Contents

"Wanderjahre of a Revolutionist [Memoirs at Age Thirty-Seven]"

1889-95: The Student Years
Farwell's "discovery" of music in the summer of 1889. Student years at MIT, with the "revivifying Grail" of the Boston Symphony Orchestra. Farwell drawn further into the pursuit of music through the influence of a mysterious pianist named Rudolph Gott. Serious musical study undertaken in Boston after graduation with Homer Norris, George Chadwick, and Edward MacDowell.

1895-96: Bohemian Years in Boston
Years of study, composing, and absorbing the musical life of Boston. An appetite for Wagnerian music drama is whetted by the visiting Metropolitan Opera and Walter Damrosch's German Opera. Meets the famous Wagnerian conductor Anton Seidl, who gives a reading of one of Farwell's first orchestral works. Thomas Mott Osborne offers to send Farwell abroad for study.

Illustrations

An asterisk (*) indicates that the illustration appeared in the original "Wanderjahre" series, published in Musical America.

Preface

Art is a pathway from this world to the Land of Dreams . . .
The true artist must find the way to his Land of Dreams . . .
When the dream calls . . . there is no refusing . . .
nor, however dim it may become through the years,
can he ever wholly forsake it.

These fervent words come from a remarkable visionary by the name of Arthur Farwell (1872–1952), whose particular dream called him to an extraordinary mission for American music. His mission, which took place in the first quarter of this century, began shortly after Farwell had returned from study abroad in 1899. Farwell, who was then in his late twenties and hoping to pursue a career in musical composition, soon made the unhappy discovery that American composers, those of concert music at least, had little status in their own country. As Farwell put it, the idea of "American composer" was almost nonexistent in the United States; works of serious aspiration by Americans rarely received performances and were even more rarely published. The circumstance did not deter someone of Farwell's optimistic bent. Indeed, the climate of confidence and idealism so prevalent in America in the years before the Great War seemed only to stimulate Farwell's sense of cause. He was determined not only to compose, but to change the environment for the American composer. The mission was to include a closely related issue, the development of a national style of music that would "speak" to the American people.

Farwell's voice in his day was truly an original one. He was, in fact, revolutionary in proposing audacious changes that were bound to collide head-on with the practices of the musical establishment, creating detractors along the way. He was also a beacon of hope for many struggling musicians. As the music critic Olin Downes wrote in 1918, "association with the energy and idealism of Arthur Farwell was important for anyone engaged those days in the pursuit of such a derided affair as American music."[1] From today's perspective, Farwell's vision often ap-

---

[1]Olin Downes, "An American Composer," *Musical Quarterly* 4 (January 1918): 27.

pears unusually farsighted. An avid student of history keenly interested in the growth and demise of cultures throughout the ages, he was forever attempting to look into America's future. He was impassioned in his belief that the United States, founded on new ideals of freedom, offered unusual possibilities for a fresh artistic life. On the other hand, he foresaw that *this* land of dreams could only become the next artistic leader of the world if it awoke to its possibilities as a democratic nation. He predicted that if there were no changes in the musical life of America of the sort he was proposing, such a life, rooted as it was in European aristocratic thinking, would eventually fade into oblivion. The prophecy has a particularly poignant ring at the close of this century, as concert managers and symphony boards in all quarters of the United States face the problem of dwindling audiences.

If Farwell was a visionary, he was a man of action as well. His ideas and activities go hand in hand, one inspiring the other. This is made evident in the significantly large body of writing that Farwell published concerning his mission.[2] His philosophical essays and articles on his activities appeared both in conjunction with publications from the Wa-Wan Press—a firm he had begun in 1901 to publish works of American composers—as well as in numerous other magazines and newspapers of the day. Except for the items in the Wa-Wan Press issues, which have been reprinted,[3] most of his writings are not easily accessible. Though Farwell's activities for American music have been generally recognized by historians, his essays as a whole are generally unknown and the scope of his vision thus cannot be appreciated.[4] It is hoped that this anthology,

---

[2] An incomplete list of Farwell's writings appears in Edgar Lee Kirk, "Toward American Music: A Study of the Life and Music of Arthur George Farwell" (Ph.D. diss., Eastman School of Music, University of Rochester, 1958), 261–65. I am preparing an updated list for future publication.   [3] All extant issues, which were published originally as a subscription series, appear in Vera Brodsky Lawrence, ed., the *Wa-Wan Press: 1901–1911*, 5 vols. (New York: Arno Press and the *New York Times*, 1970). Farwell wrote opinion pieces as Introductions for twenty-three issues that came out between 1901 and 1906 (reprinted in volumes 1–3 of Lawrence). From March 1907 through February 1908 Farwell published twelve issues of *The Wa-Wan Press Monthly*, the organ for the Wa-Wan Society of America, which he helped to organize in 1907. Essays by Farwell are contained in each of these monthlies, which are reprinted in volumes 4–5 of Lawrence.   [4] Farwell's contributions are discussed in the standard historical works on American music, including Gilbert Chase, *America's Music*, 3rd ed. (Urbana: University of Illinois Press, 1987), 353–56; Charles Hamm, *Music in the New World* (New York: W. W. Norton, 1983), 417–19; H. Wiley Hitchcock, *Music in the United States: A Historical Introduction*, 3rd ed. (Englewood Cliffs, NJ: Prentice Hall, 1988), 156; Daniel Kingman, *American Music: A Panorama*, 2nd ed. (New York: Schirmer Books, 1990), 443–46; and *The New Grove Dictionary of American Music* (1986; article on Farwell by Gilbert Chase and Neely Bruce). It should be noted that Gilbert Chase was by no means oblivious to Farwell's message. In the Introduction to his ground-breaking first edition of *America's Music* (1955), he indeed acknowledged that Farwell had "more than half a century ago formulated the principle

comprising some of his best, most representative, and most significant prose, will place Farwell's thought into fuller view, so that the individual ideas can find their broader perspective. At the same time, the articles are valuable documents of the historical period, revealing information about many composers who are little known today, a rare picture of musical life from coast to coast, and colorful personal observations on America's cultural life in general and some of the individuals who helped to shape it.

Of the writings brought together here, twenty-five articles, entitled collectively *Wanderjahre of a Revolutionist*, were first published by *Musical America* in 1909. An autobiographical account covering the twenty years from 1889 to 1909, Farwell presents an engaging story of his student years as well as the first decade of his American campaign— years that indeed involved a good deal of "wandering," throughout Europe and from one American coast to the other.[5] An additional eight articles, published between 1904 and 1927, provide a representative sampling of several key issues that Farwell addressed in his writings, including the following: 1. America's need to recognize its composers; 2. nationalism; 3. the place of music in a democratic society; and 4. spiritual aspects of music. In the Introduction I have attempted to provide a biographical sketch in which the context for these issues might be better understood. In order to aid the reader in finding passages of

upon which my bias [as a historian] rests." Chase was particularly struck by *Music in America* (1914), a volume that Farwell had edited along with W. Dermot Darby and for which he had provided the Introduction and two chapters. Farwell's ardent concern for music as a specifically *American* development color- ed by democratic ideals—not simply an outgrowth and continu-ation of European ideals—was particularly influential on Chase, whose book devoted more space to folk and popular musics than any of the histories of American music that had preceded. Richard Crawford, in a recent overview of American musical historiography, draws attention to Farwell's importance to historians from later in the century. In his *The American Musical Landscape* (Berkeley: University of California Press, 1993), Crawford makes a case for there having developed two general categories of histories, what he calls the "cosmopolitan" and the "provincial"; historians of the former type have "been inclined to find European hegemony inevitable, or healthy, or both," while those of the latter persuasion reject "Europe as a musical model for America" (7). The provincialists, Crawford points out, began to make their mark beginning in the 1950s with Chase, and that point of view has since flourished, most notably in the work of Charles Hamm. The implication is that Farwell seeded a historical outlook which is still vital at the close of this century.   [5]According to Farwell, the music publisher G. Schirmer of New York was to publish as a book the combined installments of "Wanderjahre of a Revolutionist" (see letter of Farwell to Arne Oldberg, 6 January 1911, Arne Oldberg Collection, Music Division, Library of Congress), though, for whatever reason, this never occurred. The "Wanderjahre" series is obviously a valuable source of information on Farwell's early years and is used substantially by Evelyn Davis Culbertson in her recent biography, *He Heard America Singing: Arthur Farwell: Composer and Crusading Music Educator* (Metuchen, NJ: Scarecrow Press, 1992).

particular interest on a given topic, I have included in the Table of Contents a summary of the main topics touched on in each of Farwell's articles reprinted here. This edition includes nine of thirty-seven illustrations that appeared in the original "Wanderjahre" series; these are specified on pages xiii-xiv.

Regarding annotations, I have succeeded in identifying nearly all of the persons Farwell has cited and have added information on his relationship to that individual which is not obvious from the article. Proper names that were misspelled in the original publication are noted, though I have corrected, without explanation, obvious typographical errors. In general, conventions of punctuation and like matters of style are retained as in the original article. I make exception, though, for such cases as opera titles that were in quotation marks, rather than italics, and for foreign words where capitalization did not conform with today's practices (e. g., the opera "Der Arme Heinrich" in the original article is changed here to *Der arme Heinrich*).

I am indebted to many individuals for their share in bringing this book to completion: to Evelyn Davis Culbertson who graciously gave me access to her rich collection of Farwell papers (since donated to Eastman School of Music); to John Koegel for providing information on Charles F. Lummis from works awaiting publication and for putting me in touch with Farwell files in California; to Catherine Parsons Smith for her help in tracking down certain individuals in the Los Angeles area; and to Barney Childs for supplying a copy of a Farwell letter to A. Walter Kramer. Thanks also go to Connecticut College for the funds provided through the R. Francis Johnson Fund for Faculty Development to travel to various collections and to help with other costs of this project; to Carolyn Johnson and June Ingram of the College's Greer Music Library for their invaluable help in securing needed materials; and to colleagues Paul Althouse and Michael Burlingame for reading the manuscript and suggesting helpful changes. I greatly appreciate the assistance given by the following institutions in identifying less well-known individuals who came within Farwell's sphere: Detroit Public Library; Goshen (Indiana) Public Library; Grand Rapids (Michigan) Public Library; Evanston (Illinois) Historical Society; University of Kansas Library; Memphis (Tennessee) Shelby County Public Library and Information Center; Pikes Peak (Colorado) Library District; Rochester (New York) Historical Society and Rochester Public Library; St. Joseph (Missouri) Museum; and, in Salt Lake City, the City Library, the Utah State Historical Society, and the Historical Department of The Church of Jesus Christ of Latter-Day Saints. Citations in this book from the correspondence of Arthur

Farwell and Charles F. Lummis are made through the courtesy of the Southwest Museum, Los Angeles (Braun Research Library, MS.1.1.1388A and MS. 1.1.1388B). A special word of thanks goes to my editor Ralph P. Locke whose enthusiasm and helpful direction from the beginning has greatly eased the project to its conclusion. Finally, to my wife Mary Lou, for her expeditious assistance at various libraries during the early stages of research, for her careful reading of the introduction, and above all, for her steadfast encouragement, I offer my affectionate gratitude.

T. S.
Fall 1994

Abbreviations

AF Collection   Arthur Farwell Collection, Sibley Music Library, Eastman School of Music, University of Rochester, Rochester, New York

AF Scrapbook   Scrapbook entitled "Clippings and Some Programs Describing the Career of Mr. [Arthur] Farwell from 1903–1911," microfilm copy, New York Public Library at Lincoln Center

AM   Arthur Farwell and W. Dermot Darby, eds., *Music in America*. Vol. 4 of *The Art of Music*, general editor Daniel Gregory Mason. New York: The National Society of Music, 1915

AO Collection   Arne Oldberg Collection, Music Division, Library of Congress, Washington, D. C.

AS Papers   Arthur Shepherd Papers, Marriott Library, University of Utah, Salt Lake City, Utah

CFL Collection   Charles F. Lummis Collection, Braun Research Library, MS.1.1.1388A and MS. 1.1.1388B, Southwest Museum, Los Angeles, California

MA   *Musical America*

WP   Vera Brodsky Lawrence, ed., *The Wa-Wan Press: 1901–1911*, 5 vols. (New York: Arno Press and the *New York Times*, 1970)

Editor's Introduction

Farwell the Democrat, Composer, and Mystic Seer

The America into which Arthur Farwell was born in 1872 was coming of age musically. In that year the great Russian pianist Anton Rubinstein had begun a triumphant concert tour of the United States, playing 215 recitals that netted $40,000. Rubinstein's success can be viewed as a sort of barometric reading for the growing musical sophistication taking place in America at the time. Unlike pianists who typically appealed to audiences with less demanding fare—variations on "Yankee Doodle," opera potpourris, and the like—the Russian visitor won respect with programs drawn solely from European masters. The appetite for "serious music" in America is seen also in the growth of professional orchestras. Between 1881 and 1900, symphonies were founded in Boston, Chicago, Cincinnati, Pittsburgh, and Philadelphia, each committed to high standards of the orchestral repertory. America's premier orchestra, the New York Philharmonic (organized in 1842), took a great leap forward in this period when it hired in 1877 Theodore Thomas, its first conductor of stature and a disciplinarian adamant about the need for performing European masterworks. Opera was also part of the mushrooming of European cultivated music in America, signalled notably by the opening of New York's Metropolitan Opera House in 1883. By the end of the century, it looked as though the United States was beginning to shake loose its image of being, as one European had sniffed some years before, "excellent for electric railroads but not for art."[1]

One might have thought that such an advance in the status of serious music was a promising sign for American composers, who were

---

[1] Cited in H. Wiley Hitchcock, *Music in the United States: A Historical Introduction*, 3rd ed. (Englewood Cliffs, NJ: Prentice Hall, 1988), 58.

increasing in number at this same time. But the native sons and daughters had to resign themselves to the disappointing fact that their compositions were only occasionally heard in concerts. The situation was
to be expected, considering that the performers and conductors were
primarily of European extraction who favored works from their own
long-established tradition. It made little difference that most American
composers were affected by that tradition and wrote in a style that
intentionally imitated their European, particularly German, counter-
parts. So strong was this Germanic dominance that there were few
composers who showed an inclination to create any sort of national
imprint in their works. As one historian recently put it, "the American
frontier, a wellspring of imagery in American novels, plays, and paintings,
seemed less transportable into its concert halls and opera houses."[2]

Farwell himself could easily have been swept under by the Germanic
pull that overtook American music in the late nineteenth century. He
had, in fact, drunk at the fount of wisdom, having returned in 1899 from
a year and a half of study in Germany and France. His first-hand
experience of the firmly grounded musical life abroad had indeed made
him long for similar riches in the United States. He recognized that this
was a propitious moment in the country's artistic development, but he
quickly determined that it was essential to cultivate an "American idea
in music" rather than to foster European traditions. For a quarter
century Farwell was to champion such an American idea in a remarkable
number of ways—as composer, publisher, lecturer, builder of organizations to promote American composers and their works, community
music leader, teacher, and, not least, as a writer.

In his writings we see Farwell clearly as a product of the fervent
idealism flourishing in the United States in the years before World War I.
His articles began appearing in various publications early in the century
and continued well into the 1940s, the greatest number being produced
in the second decade, when he was on the staff of *Musical America*. In
this era of Progressive thought and social reform that had spawned many
causes, he viewed his campaign above all as a societal issue. He believed
music was a democratic phenomenon that should involve the people as
a whole, not some elite group. His more polemical essays, in fact, often
targetted the wider public, rather than the musical establishment. He
hoped that interested lay people would catch the urgency of his vision
and lead the cause for American music in their own communities.

---

[2]Joseph Horowitz, *Understanding Toscanini: How He Became an American Culture-God and
Helped Create a New Audience for Old Music* (New York: Alfred A. Knopf, 1987), 17.

Farwell called into question the whole musical superstructure that was inherited from Europe—the commerciality of the concert system, the training of musicians, and the genres of composition that were "aristocratic" in origin—exposing reasons for its perpetuation, including ignorance, snobbery, profit, or politics. Farwell's controversial ideas were too rebellious to attract the musical establishment, as he acknowledged by entitling his autobiographical piece "Wanderjahre of a Revolutionist." At the same time, Farwell knew he could not ignore the musical institutions that for better or worse had begun to take shape. So the self-proclaimed "revolutionist," bent on changing the prevailing attitudes toward music in America, attempted to steer a course that aimed for his dream while pursuing a musical career in a world that confounded the dream at every turn.

From Wagnerian to Indianist

Farwell's attraction to music came relatively late in his life. First drawn to a career in electrical engineering, he planned to enroll at the Massachusetts Institute of Technology in the fall of 1889. In the preceding summer, however, the seventeen-year-old from St. Paul, Minnesota, made his "discovery" of music, a revelation that came with all the impact of a religious conversion. The sudden lure of the newfound art must have brought with it a certain confusion, but for the moment the original plans were not to be abandoned. The commitment to music grew steadily during his student years at MIT, being continually kindled by the array of concerts and operas offered in Boston, so that at some time during this period he decided to dedicate his life to composing. After graduation in 1893 he stayed on in Boston to commence serious musical study. The theorist Homer Norris provided formal tutoring, while the composers George W. Chadwick, then at the New England Conservatory, and Edward MacDowell, in the years just prior to his becoming the first chair of Columbia's music department, became his informal mentors. Any American living in this period who was serious about a musical career generally went to Europe, most likely Germany, for private or conservatory study. Such an opportunity fell into Farwell's hands fortuitously. Thomas Mott Osborne, a family friend and wealthy industrialist from Auburn, New York, took Farwell on a European tour in the summer of 1897, and then arranged for the young composer to stay abroad for another twenty months, during which time he studied with the German composers Engelbert Humperdinck and Hans

Pfitzner, and with Alexandre Guilmant, the renowned pedagogue of counterpoint and master organist at the Church of the Trinité in Paris. The years in Germany were especially vital in shaping the composer's musical and philosophical views, and the origins of his nationalistic thinking can be traced to this period. There was first of all Engelbert Humperdinck, Farwell's beloved teacher and one-time member of the Bayreuth circle, who had become arguably the most successful German to carry on the tradition of the music drama. In Berlin Farwell came under the sway of the ardent German nationalist opera composer Hans Pfitzner and moved in a social and intellectual circle that included, besides Pfitzner, the composers Siegfried Wagner and Eugen d'Albert and the publisher Max Brockhaus, all working to advance the cause of German opera. But none had a greater impact than James Grun, an obscure poet and somewhat eccentric socialist who was the librettist for two of Pfitzner's early operas. According to Farwell, it was Grun who first brought to his attention the importance of folk sources in creating a national art. The imprint of Grun's high regard for Wagner is clearly seen in Farwell's belief that Wagnerian principles could be used in developing a distinctive American music: "[Wagner] was more of an American than many of our own composers, for he worked with the primal forces of man and nature, and not with the over-refined and predigested delicacies of a decadent culture."[3] Farwell was ever to look longingly over his shoulder at Wagner's accomplishment, finding inspiration there for new musical direction in the United States.

Farwell was brought home from Europe in the spring of 1899 by an invitation from Cornell University to lecture on Wagner. While at Cornell he gave a series of lectures on the history of music that included the topic of American music. Such an inclusion was rare at this time, and it is one of the earliest indications of what would soon become his lifelong pursuit.

Farwell's aspirations for nurturing a music with an American stamp were brought to focus about this same time, when he came across the newly published *Indian Story and Song from North America* by the ethnologist Alice Fletcher. Moved and fascinated by the melodies and myths encountered in the book, he began to make harmonizations of the tunes, attempting to capture their spirit as revealed by Fletcher's commentary. Farwell claimed that in the beginning he had no nationalistic aim in making these settings; he was simply drawn to the melodies and their potential for fresh inspiration. He soon discovered, however,

---

[3]Arthur Farwell, "The Struggle toward a National Music," the *North American Review* 186 (December 1907): 569.

that his experiments with this music rooted in American soil offered rich possibilities for creating a distinctly national spirit which he thought was every bit as valid as that found in works of European composers. Farwell, to be sure, was not the only composer in this period to advance such a development—in the 1890s the Bohemian composer Antonín Dvořák had urged American composers to look at homegrown sources of music for their composition—but he was without a doubt its most vocal proponent. He began to lecture in the Boston area and New York on Indian music, playing as well selections from the sizeable number of "Indianist" pieces for piano he had written in these years. Encouraged by the response in the East, Farwell decided to make his message more broadly known, taking four cross-country tours between 1903 and 1907 to present his lecture-recitals.

The growing interest in the Native American that had begun to flourish at the turn of the century, particularly the scholarly work being done in the field, helped to convince Farwell of the timeliness of Indianist composition. He was to gain first-hand experience in studying Indian music after meeting on his initial trip West in 1904 Charles F. Lummis, that indomitable Americanist, writer on the Southwest, and archaeologist, who had just begun a project of recording on wax cylinders songs of Native and Spanish Americans of the Southwest. Through the auspices of the Archaeological Institute of America, Lummis was to hire Farwell to transcribe several hundred of the songs over the next two years. Farwell had also befriended the ethnologist Alice Fletcher and knew as well the work of others in the field, including that of Theodore Baker, Frank Hamilton Cushing, Natalie Curtis, A. F. Bandelier, and Frances Densmore. During his Western sojourns he met the artists Maynard Dixon and William Keith, whose works with Native American subjects made a strong impression. In Seattle he visited the studio of Edward S. Curtis, the photographer whose monumental work on the American Indian was published over the next twenty-five years.

Farwell believed that it was a democratic obligation of Americans of European origin to try to understand the Indians, to preserve something of their vanishing civilization, and to heal the rift that had grown between the Indians and themselves, the vanquishers. Farwell's Indianist pieces reflect this need for bringing the Native Americans into the democratic fold, for he believed that in them the Indian melodies had been rendered more acceptable to non-Indians, without violating their original purpose. Behind this was Farwell's metaphysical view that there existed an *animus* of the Indian "race spirit" which could be absorbed by non-Indians who were attuned to it.[4] He perceptively and even-hand-edly set forth the importance of music in bringing about such an under-standing of the Native American in a Wa-Wan publication from 1904:

> We have tried four methods of approach to the Indian. First, by fighting him; second, by seeking to convert him; third, by treating him as a scientific specimen; fourth, by offering him the hand of fellowship. By the first way we have received in turn wounds, torture and death, and the material for a little superficial romance. Through the second method we have given him something he did not want and received nothing in return, being prevented by bigotry from receiving what he had to give us. . . . By the third process we have filled the shelves of great museums with rare and valuable objects, all carefully labeled, and the museum libraries with books learnedly written by scientists for scientists. It is wonderful work, but there is an aristocracy, a free-masonry about it all, that constitutes an almost impassible barrier between it and the American people. Finally, in the fourth way, the only way wholly compatible with democratic ideals, we have gained that which is to bring—which brings—the American people as a whole into a sympathetic relation with the Indian. For through his simple, direct, poetic expression, in ritual, story and song, which he is willing to communicate to one who approaches him as a fellow man, we are to recognize, once for all, his humanity and the wealth of interest and significance which it offers for the enrichment of our own lives.[5]

Charles Lummis and Edward Curtis seem to have shared with Farwell this need for reconciliation. Lummis's Pueblo stories, published in 1894 as *The Man Who Marries the Moon and Other Pueblo Indian Folk-Stories*, were not literal translations; rather, Lummis "tried to capture the 'exact Indian spirit' in which they were told."[6] In the same manner, Curtis's photos of Native Americans frequently are not so much documents of Indian life as they are idealized impressions that evoke within the viewer a reverence for the subject.[7] Whatever shortcomings their views of the Indian may reveal from today's perspective, Farwell, Lummis, and Curtis each attempted to translate the inner voice of Native Americans and to make it more widely understood in America.

Farwell's belief in the importance of developing a national style, particularly through the use of Indian melodies, drew frequent criticism

---

[4]*WP* 2:66.   [5]*WP* 2:51.   [6]Robert E. Fleming, *Charles F. Lummis* (Boise, Idaho: Boise State University, 1981), 44.   [7]Vine Deloria, Jr. takes this view in his "Introduction" to Christopher M. Lyman, *The Vanishing Race and Other Illusions: Photographs of Indians by Edward S. Curtis* (Washington: Smithsonian Institution Press, 1982).

during the first decade of the twentieth century. Many of his detractors claimed that he insisted that Indianist music was the only path to be taken by the American composer. That this was untrue is shown in one of his earliest articles, "Toward American Music" (p. 185), published in 1904. Here he asserted that the nation's music could not fully mature "until it has assimilated every phase of musical life, however primitive, existing within America's borders," citing, in addition to Indian song, various types of folk music. His concern was that unless composers developed an art that was American in spirit, the country's musical life would eventually cease to exist. It was this conviction that gave him the confidence to stand pat when a critic called him an "excited patriot," responding that he had great respect for the works of Bach, Beethoven, and Brahms, but that "these works do not say the last word for America, any more than do the British articles of constitution" ("National Work vs. Nationalism," p. 198). While the development of a national style continued to preoccupy Farwell in the 1910s and '20s, the focus in this later period is less on the use of folk music. The emphasis was (as we shall see) instead on types of musical performances that were appropriate for a democratic society—specifically, the community chorus, pageants and pageant-like works.

Fighting for the American Composer

Besides lecturing and writing on the need for a national music, Farwell also took up the "fight" for the American composer. When he had returned from study abroad in 1899, he found the environment generally hostile toward native-born composers. Despite the isolated success of a few Americans such as Edward MacDowell, the national consensus seemed to be that there were virtually no composers from the homeland who could be taken seriously. This predicament was made clear to Farwell when he discovered that it was nearly impossible for American composers to find a publisher for any of their substantial works. With the strong will that was to drive him again and again over obstacles, Farwell decided to meet this problem head-on with a daring move. In 1901 he initiated his own firm, the Wa-Wan Press, to publish "the most progressive, characteristic, and serious works of American composers, known or unknown," for the benefit of all who wished to enjoy "the increasing ripeness of the composer's art in this country."[8] With the help of his father George Farwell and the composer Henry Gilbert, the

---

[8]*WP* 1:124.

business operated out of the family home in Newton Center, Massachusetts, where Farwell's parents had recently moved from Minnesota. The greatest share of the responsibility was Farwell's; from letters it is evident that he gave countless hours both to editorial duties and to promotional activities to keep the business afloat. Despite the inevitable burden on Farwell's time and finances—the Press was continually in debt—the firm lasted until 1912, when the rights of publication were transferred to G. Schirmer of New York.

Farwell found very soon that his campaign could not be led from Newton Center. During the summer of 1903 he decided to make a tour of the Western states, not only to lecture on Indian music but also to assess the musical conditions of the country and to meet composers who might have works ready for publication. In addition to the three other cross-country tours that Farwell subsequently made, there were several treks to the Midwest as well as numerous shorter jaunts throughout the Northeast taken in the five years between 1903 and 1908. Though these journeys were taken at considerable cost to Farwell's physical and mental well-being, his selfless sense of duty did not waver: "It is no whim, but deep *need* that has driven me into this work—need of a place in American life for an American composer," he explained to a friend. "This *need* that I speak of I do not feel to be a personal thing,—I believe only that I am the first one to feel it with sufficient intensity to act upon it, and that in doing so, I am responding to a need arising in many others,—however much or little its full force has yet dawned upon them." [9]

Farwell was elated by the developing musical life he witnessed on his trips. After reaching Los Angeles in 1904, he recalled: in Rochester, New York, there was "a symphony orchestra managed by men of energy, ideals, and independence of thought"; a musical club in Columbus, Ohio, that went from seventy members to 700 in three months due to the energy of one woman; in Minneapolis an organization that sponsored a concert of local composers' orchestral works; and in Columbia, Missouri, a composer "who for daring and for psychological refinement of expression might be matched against any modern composer." [10] So impressed by the number of composers he had met in his travels, with some satisfaction he warned the Eastern musical establishment: "The Great Word of the West has not yet been spoken in art,—when it arises, many traditions must fall." [11] But Farwell had no wish to cultivate divisiveness. In an article published in *Out West* shortly

---

[9] Arthur Farwell to Arthur Shepherd, 20 November [1907], AS Papers.   [10] *WP* 2:107.   [11] *WP* 2:105.

after he returned home from his first cross-country trip, he lamented that composers from the East and West knew so little of each other's work (see p. 189). He believed that this was the time when significant strides for the American composer could take place, if a unified effort were made. He acknowledged the difficulty of bringing about such unity: "the immense proportions of America and the greater diversity of its human elements make our problem more difficult to grasp and slower to develop." Still, he argued, there was already in place a "significant American musical art" that simply needed to be brought to a higher level.[12]

Farwell saw the composer's primary problem in America as one of "social attitude," asserting bluntly: "The cultured American public generally, through force of habit, and especially through the fiat of fashion, does not want American composers' names upon the programs which represent its fashionable musical doings."[13] He complained that America was so habituated to imported music "that it cannot believe that there is any other source of this art than Europe" ("Society and American Music," p. 191). As he made his way over the country lecturing, he found people dismally unaware of the music of their own country's composers. Determined to correct the situation, Farwell threw himself into setting up organizations that would present concerts of American composers' works, as well as inform the people about this music.

In the spring of 1905 Farwell gave a talk on composers he had met on his Western trips to the Twentieth Century Club of Boston. It generated an enthusiastic response, out of which was immediately initiated an organization called the American Music Society; Farwell was charged with arranging the programs for the organization's regularly scheduled concerts of American music. A more ambitious undertaking was begun in 1907 when the Wa-Wan Society, an adjunct of the Wa-Wan Press, was organized. With the goal of making American composers known through a national grass-roots effort, local centers were established in cities across the country, including Detroit, Colorado Springs, Salt Lake City, Buffalo, and Springfield, Illinois. Here members could learn of the work of American composers through study, discussion, and performances. Some idea of the educational outreach that was projected is seen in issues of the Society's official organ, the *Wa-Wan Press Monthly*,[14] which provided lists of American composers and their works, as well as articles on featured composers. In this same period Farwell helped to launch yet a third organization, the New Music Society in New York, aimed at presenting new orchestral works by

---

[12]*WP* 3:5.   [13]*WP* 4:146.   [14]These are reprinted in *WP*.

Americans. Although it turned out to be short-lived, the Society's two concerts in the spring season of 1906 featured several composers published by the Wa-Wan Press. In 1908 the Wa-Wan Society was merged with the American Music Society in Boston; the new organization, taking the name of the Boston society, established around the same time a very active local center in New York City, which seemed to signal a bright future for the national association.

Early in 1909 an invitation for Farwell to join the staff of the New York-based *Musical America*, a weekly with national circulation and numerous foreign correspondents, brought with it an unusual opportunity to promote the new Society as well as to disseminate more widely his growing vision for American music. His first major piece of writing for the paper was the serialized autobiographical essay "Wanderjahre of a Revolutionist," which appeared each week for the first six months of 1909. Along with the account of his activities on behalf of American music in the first decade, he gives special place in the "Wanderjahre" to the American Music Society by providing a complete text of the organization's constitution. But despite the promise that the American Music Society seemed to hold, after 1909 we hear very little of the group in Farwell's writings. We know from letters of Farwell that the organizational work had nearly exhausted him physically, and that he saw the need to step back from what had become a monumental task. Perhaps Farwell felt that he had done all that he possibly could for this organization to promote the American composer and that it must now seek to thrive on its own.

Farwell often felt himself a loner in his mission. Though the American composer was not entirely bereft of advocates at this time, the evidence of this was so sporadic that one could scarcely speak of a movement for American music. There are a few noteworthy examples of backing for the American composer in the years before Farwell became actively involved. Among these, the Music Teachers National Association, founded in 1876, took the unusual position to further American composition and arranged concerts for national meetings during the 1880s and 1890s that programmed American works. American compositions were also included in a series of "Novelty Concerts" produced by the composer Frank Van der Stucken at Steinway Hall in New York during 1884. In 1889, the Manuscript Society of New York, an organization comprised of composers, was established to find performances for new American compositions.[15]

---

[15]Information on the activities of the Music Teachers National Association, Van der Stucken's Novelty Concerts, and The Manuscript Society is provided in Barbara Zuck, *A History of Musical Americanism* (Ann Arbor: UMI Research Press, 1980), 41–55.

Support for the American composer came from various other corners at the turn of the century. Rupert Hughes had published in 1900 his pioneering *Contemporary American Composers*. While more of a laudatory accounting of composers than a critical assessment, the work is significant in bringing to light individuals and their works in a systematic way. Lawrence Gilman, music critic for *Harper's Weekly*, was particularly supportive of the American composer and wrote enthusiastically of the Wa-Wan Press and the American Music Society. Much of the critical opinion concerning American compositions was conditional. Writing in 1896, James G. Huneker echoed what many critics believed, that American composers had not yet come into their own and that this would not happen for several generations. He was not smug, however: "Heaven forbid that I should be considered insular or parochial in this matter, but I do long for an American art, by American artists, for the American people."[16] Performers who supported American composers existed, but they were also few and far between. The German émigré conductor (and devoted Wagnerian) Anton Seidl was more than willing to conduct works by Americans, and in an article of his published in 1892 entitled "The Development of Music in America" he praised the music of John Knowles Paine, Chadwick, and, notably, MacDowell, "whose compositions seem to me to be superior to those of Brahms."[17] It was Farwell's opinion that by and large performers avoided American compositions: "most artists, even those who are enthusiastically interested in certain works of American composers, are afraid to place them upon their programs, for fear of losing prestige and support."[18] One who did not fit this description was the American operatic baritone and recitalist David Bispham. Bispham, who was more than willing to program songs of Americans, was warmly sympathetic to Farwell's cause and became the first president of the New York City center of the American Music Society.

New York and California Years: Community Sings and Pageants

Farwell's move to New York was pivotal. The experiences gained in the previous decade brought a clearer sense of purpose, and Farwell now moved forward with a new agenda for American music. For the

---

[16]Quoted in Arnold T. Schwab, ed., *Americans in the Arts—1890–1920: Critiques by James Gibbons Huneker* (New York: AMS Press, 1985), xxxv.   [17]Anton Seidl, "The Development of Music in America," *Forum* 13 (May 1892): 392.   [18]*WP* 4:146.

next fifteen years—first in New York and then in California—Farwell
was to give his greatest efforts to the community music movement. He
was convinced that in a democracy the populace's need for art had to
be met. In accord with the apostles of social betterment active in the
United States in these years, he thought music should be available for
the uplift of the people. He did not think that a composer had to make
artistic compromises in writing for the populace. Rather, music of the
highest aspiration could be written that would still reach the feelings of
the lay person, if its composer were truly in touch with the people. But
such music would more than likely not spring from the European
tradition, Farwell suggests: "Perhaps the masses are, all unconsciously,
waiting for . . . some other means of the presentation of music than the
conventional ones of concert, recital, or opera" ("A Glance at Present
Musical Problems in America," p. 204). Farwell's confidence in the
sensitivity of the populace to artistic expression was latent when he
worked to found the American Music Society, and he was doubtlessly
encouraged in his populist ideas by the spirited response he received
lecturing to people from all walks of life up and down the country. "Have
you ever met a man whose soul is overflowing with enthusiasm?" asked
an excited reporter in the Fishkill (New York) *Evening Journal* who had
heard one of the talks. "A man in whom there glows that spark of divine
energy which rouses you from your lethargy to clamber over glaring
obstacles up to the true realm of human endeavor? Arthur Farwell is
such a man."[19]

Farwell seems to have first seen the possibilities of community
music when, in addition to his work at *Musical America*, he took on the
responsibility of Supervisor of Municipal Music in the Parks and Recrea-
tional Areas of New York. In the four seasons that he held the position
between 1910 and 1913, he was particularly moved by the audience's
rapt attention at the free orchestral concerts given during the summer
months. This was enough to assure him that the common people were
a force to be reckoned with in the country's musical life. A couple of
years later, Farwell and a charismatic community song leader by the
name of Harry Barnhart took this venture in the parks one step further
by instigating the New York Community Chorus, which was open to all
who wished to join, without audition. Community "sings," where
crowds would gather to raise their voices in favorite songs, were events
of growing popularity in these days, often stirring up patriotic fervor in
face of the impending war. For Farwell and Barnhart, the idea of the

---

[19]From a newspaper clipping (dated by hand: "c. 1905") in AF Scrapbook.

community chorus was to build on the spirit generated at a sing, at the same time to gain greater artistic results through rehearsals and through performing more demanding music. Audience and chorus might both participate at a sing, as was the case at a stupendous gathering that Farwell helped to organize, held in Central Park in September 1916, shortly before the United States entered the European conflict. Called the "Song and Light Festival," crowds estimated at 30,000 for each of two evenings massed around the park's lake, while at one end the chorus and an orchestra performed from a stage lit by geometrically shaped lanterns that were specially designed by the architect Claude Bragdon, giving the whole a mystical aura, according to Farwell. He thought such events as this, tinged with the ceremonial, had great potential for creating new types of performance that were in tune with democratic principles. Farwell would experiment more with the community chorus and with compositions involving audience participation in the 1920s when he was in California.

Before moving West, Farwell was to turn to democratic compositions that more heavily emphasized not only the ceremonial, but his long-standing interest in combining drama and music. Pageants had become a popular type of community effort during these years. Farwell seems to have been first drawn to the form after attending *The Pageant of Thetford* [Vermont] in the summer of 1911.

> None of the things shown or done on this outdoor stage were extraordinary or wonder-provoking in themselves . . . or anything beyond what any American town or country community could do proportionately to its own size. And yet these things brought together and put into a certain order were capable of gripping the attention of several thousand persons for two hours and a half, and of producing in the multitude one of the most powerfully exalting and humanly moving emotions which life can afford ("Community Music Drama," p. 227).

The director of the Thetford production was William Chauncy Langdon, who had become one of the most sought-after leaders of pageants. Farwell got the chance to work with this pageant "master" during the following summer in Vermont as musical adviser for *The Pageant of St. Johnsbury*, which Langdon directed. In the next summer, Farwell became even more fully involved with pageantry, as he wrote and directed the music for two pageants produced by Langdon, the *Pageant of Meriden* [New Hampshire] and the *Pageant of Darien* [Connecticut]. During his New York years between 1913 and 1917 he was to write altogether music for five pageants and pageant-like works. The largest of this type, involving 1500 performers, was *Caliban by the Yellow Sands*, a masque with text by Percy MacKaye produced in May 1916 at New York's Lewisohn Stadium for the Shakespeare Tercentenary.

Farwell had stopped writing reviews for *Musical America* by 1912, as the demands of community music began to increase, though he continued to contribute opinion pieces regularly through 1915. The largest number of articles on various issues of American music, including his vision for community music, appears between 1912 and 1915, primarily in *Musical America*. After 1915, when he succeeded David Mannes as director of the Third Street Music School Settlement, his output of published writings decreased notably.[20] Farwell seems to have felt that his efforts for the next ten years, between 1915 and 1925, should best be directed toward bringing to fruition the vision of which he had long been writing; for the most part, this was to take place in California.

Ever since his cross-country trips in the first decade, Farwell had found the West attractive as a place where people were open to new ideas in building a musical life. The musical life in urban areas of the East may have been more sophisticated, but it forced Farwell to deal with a concert establishment that he saw as insensitive to the needs of a democratic society. The hectic pace of New York City was also apparently wearying to Farwell, who frequently needed to remove himself to some natural setting for rejuvenation. It is no surprise, then, to find that he accepted an offer to come to Los Angeles in 1918 to teach in the summer session at the University of California. In the same summer, he organized and directed a community chorus in the city.[21] Having traveled there with his new wife, the former Gertrude Brice, whom he had married the previous year, and a recently born infant son, he had planned to stay for just the summer. But as it turned out, a temporary position opened up that fall in Berkeley where he was hired to be the acting head

---

[20] It is not precisely clear when Farwell gave up his staff position at *Musical America*. Although he had a few articles published by the paper after 1915, it seems fairly sure that he did not continue there on a regular basis after taking his new position at the settlement house in 1915, but he may have left sooner. According to a letter that Farwell wrote to his friend Arne Oldberg, he had curtailed his duties with the paper as early as 1911: "*I have retired from criticism*, i. e., going to concerts for that purpose, though I am likely to write articles of a general critical nature. I retain my connection with the paper and contribute editorials, special articles, occasional reviews of music, etc. . . . I get less money for this—but about twenty five hours a week to myself that I did not have before—and shall much more than make it up on serious articles for magazines" (Farwell to Arne Oldberg, 6 January 1911, AO Collection).   [21] This is revealed in a letter of J. F. Tucker to Charles C. Moore, no date, but from the contents of the letter, written in the late summer of 1918; President's Files, University of California Archives, Berkeley.

of the music department at the University, while the young musicologist Charles Seeger was on leave. Farwell was never inclined toward teaching, feeling that such work interfered too much with composing. Likely the real reason he took the year's position was its apparent promise for developing community music at Berkeley. The singing movement had gained even greater momentum with America's involvement in the war, and one of Farwell's duties at the university was to lead group singing for the Students' Army Training Corps. In addition, he organized the Berkeley Municipal Community Chorus, consisting of students and townspeople. Two pageant-like works resulted from his time there, the masque *California*, presented in the spring of 1919 by the music department, and *Chant of Victory*, involving the Berkeley Community Chorus, produced that summer to celebrate the end of the war. Both productions were presented at the University's newly built outdoor Greek Theater.

Though there was no possibility for the renewal of a position at the University,[22] Farwell decided to remain in California, likely because of the great promise he foresaw there for community music. In the next eight years he threw himself relentlessly into realizing his conviction that the community music movement could give birth to a new and legitimate national art form. Farwell saw three avenues of approach as important in this regard: the community chorus, the use of singing by an audience, and what he called "the community music drama." Sometimes these elements were combined in Farwell's works; most often they were tied in with some significant local or national function in which a kind of ceremonial, reverential tone was the aim. Preferable, but not altogether necessary, was an outdoor performance locale that was thought to contribute to a more elevated atmosphere and would allow for a larger audience, in keeping with the democratic principle.

After his work at the Berkeley campus ended in the summer of 1919, Farwell moved quickly to organize another community chorus in Santa Barbara, an organization that soon grew to 3,000 members.[23] During the following spring, the chorus took part in the outdoor community pageant-drama *La Primavera*, for which Farwell wrote the music. Santa

---

[22]The *Oakland Tribune* of 25 May 1919 reports that Farwell had been "'dropped' from the teaching staff," suggesting that he was not reinstated because he had refused to give up some of his "new ideas in [community] music." In a letter of 26 May Farwell emphatically denies the suggestion. Both the newspaper clipping and a copy of Farwell's letter are in the President's Files, University of California Archives, Berkeley.   [23]According to a brief article on a Christmas concert given in Santa Barbara in 1919 (*MA* 31 [24 January 1920]: 13).

Barbara must have looked to Farwell like a place where the arts could thrive in a unique way. For some years he dreamed of a community where professional and amateur artists could work together to produce music dramas of high quality. He was drawn to the then recent work of the English composer and Wagner enthusiast Rutland Boughton, who had attempted to build such a community around a festival in Glastonbury.[24] This seems to have been behind Farwell's effort to establish a School of the Arts in Santa Barbara. But these were difficult times for Farwell, whose financial responsibilties had grown with the addition of two more children to his family. So, when in late 1920 there came a commision from the wealthy arts patroness Christine Wetherill Stevenson to write music for her dramatization of the life of Christ, the *Pilgrimage Play*, he had to abandon any hopes he might have had for an arts colony in Santa Barbara.

Another factor explains Farwell's departure from Santa Barbara. In the summer of 1921, word came that he was to be the first recipient of the Composer's Fellowship of the Pasadena Music and Arts Association, an award that would be reinstated for the next three years. With his family he moved to Pasadena, where presumably there would be more time for composing. But here, too, Farwell took on yet another community music project, the Pasadena Community Music Meetings, which he instituted in 1922. Characteristic of the high purpose of all Farwell's ventures, the Meetings had a melioristic intent: "to establish centers of good will" where people of all levels of society could unite through singing together—"We can not sing the great songs and choruses of the world without feeling our common humanity," stated a prospectus of the Meetings.[25] The sings were the centerpiece of the weekly gatherings, which included talks by Farwell as well as the performance of other music. Surviving song sheets compiled for the meetings attest to the musical diversity he was seeking to introduce, as Schubert Lieder appear shoulder to shoulder with cowboy tunes in a mix of unison and four-part arrangements that he himself made. While it is true that Farwell placed a high priority on the social benefit of community sings, he believed equally that such efforts had great *musical* benefit and could eventually lead to the creation of a new art. During his time at Pasadena he composed two works—*Symphonic Hymn on March! March!* (1921) and *Symphonic Song on Old Black Joe* (1923)—that

---

[24]Farwell to Bernhard Hoffmann, 9 January 1933, AF Collection.   [25]The prospectus is headed "Pasadena Community Music Meetings/Founded December, 1922/A Statement of Some of Their/Objects and Principles" (AF Collection).

call for the insertion of audience singing, thereby enveloping the community sing within the folds of an orchestral work.[26]

Farwell's culminating effort in community music was his "Theater of the Stars," an outdoor amphitheater located in a magnificent canyon setting in the San Bernardino Mountains at Fawnskin, on Big Bear Lake. Farwell was barely able to contain his exuberance in contemplating the possibilities for his new "temple built without hands": "Here music and drama will find again the conditions for the manifestation of their fullest power, in beauty, in mystery and wonder."[27] Though the season in the summer of 1925 was devoted mainly to the presentation of twenty-four concerts, Farwell's ultimate aim was to develop a summer festival for producing what he considered to be "a new type of music drama for America and the American people, in which high universal and spiritual conceptions shall be expressed."[28] Wagnerian music drama always stood as a sort of model for Farwell, but the idea of an American Bayreuth perhaps first occurred to him after seeing in 1904 one of the outdoor Grove Plays given annually by the Bohemian Club of San Francisco. This high-quality semi-professional production with original music and drama was greatly reinforced by the superb staging and spectacular setting in a redwood forest. It constituted an unforgettable inspiration to Farwell, who now foresaw the development at Fawnskin of an annual festival that "holds the possibility of becoming the greatest creative artistic center and expression of America."[29] But the great hopes for the Theater of the Stars were sadly dashed when financial backers decided not to fund a second season. The closest he came to realizing an American music drama there was with *The March of Man*, a brief work with both text and music by Farwell, presented prior to each of the final four concerts of the season in early September.[30]

Farwell's ten years in California cannot be characterized as a suc-

---

[26] A typed list, compiled by Farwell, of twenty works he composed, partially composed, or revised from earlier works during the four years he held the Pasadena Music and Art Association Fellowship is located in the Special Collections of the University Research Library, University of California at Los Angeles. [27] From "The Theater of the Stars," first published in *Fawnskin Folks* and reprinted in Brice Farwell, ed., *A Guide to the Music of Arthur Farwell* (Briarcliff Manor, NY: published by the editor, 1972): 86–88. [28] From Farwell's sixteen-page typed "Report on the Inauguration and Artistic Activities of the Theater of the Stars: First Season - 1925," 6 (Special Collections, University of California at Los Angeles). For more on the Theater of the Stars, see Charles H. Gabriel, Jr., "Music and Colored Lighting Glorify Natural Theater," *MA* 43 (21 November 1925): 3, 10. [29] Ibid., 7. [30] A synopsis of *The March of Man*, along with a listing of the cast, appears in Farwell's report on the Theater of the Stars (see n. 28 above). The report also notes that some of the music for *The March of Man* was composed by the

cessful period, particularly in regard to his goals for community music. Part of the problem was financial, made more acute as his family had grown to five children in these years. Had Farwell been able to pursue his aims for a longer time at either Santa Barbara or Pasadena, the final story might have been different. But, as it was, providing for a large family made it necessary that he move on to a position offering more financial stability. In addition, Farwell's intense idealism apparently caused him difficulty. An account given by Gertrude Farwell, a few years after Arthur's death, sheds light on the matter:

> His quality of creativity was very dictatorial in these personal human relations. . . . This pattern is repeated so many times in his life it is as if he became only a stimulating agent for this dream of beauty for America. Wherever he went, and when the task was done, the project in a community on a fair way to being realized, the same energy that used him to create and build, then would use him to destroy his usefulness with the group and send him elsewhere.[31]

Whether or not this sort of hubris brought the demise of Farwell's last effort in community music, the Theater of the Stars, is unclear, but in any case it seems that Farwell probably sensed that his dreams for a democratic music were not be to realized in the near future, when he published in 1927 his "Evolution of New Forms Foreseen for America's Music" (p. 235). Here, in one of the last articles expressing his national aims, Farwell recognized that the country's pre-war exuberance, which had fostered community sings and pageants, had since cooled, though he leaves no doubt about his hope of rekindling the fervor. But despite the message, Farwell's personal involvement with the movement would have to be abandoned in order to improve his financial circumstances.

Teaching and Composing in East Lansing

In 1927 Farwell left the West Coast to accept an invitation to head the theory-composition wing of the newly organized music department of the Michigan Agricultural College (presently Michigan State University)

Swiss-born Ernest Bloch (1880–1959). No further information can be given on Farwell's association with Bloch; the two may have met in New York when Bloch came to the United States in 1916, the year he began teaching at Mannes School of Music.   [31]From a typed manuscript in the AF Collection having the following hand-written heading (in an unknown hand): "Gertrude Farwell's Memories/Presented by Brice [Farwell] 12/54."

in East Lansing. Putting bitter memories of California behind, Farwell wrote Gertrude (who had been detained in the West with the children), "You have seen amply how impossible California is to me—except perhaps to go out and carry out some commission or special work," whereas in Michigan there are "new paths opening out in important directions."[32] These new paths likely point to his pursuit of music along more traditional lines. It is true that Farwell had never stopped writing pieces in the standard genres, even in the busy years of pursuing community music between 1910 and 1925. Interspersed with the pageants, choruses, and experimental works deriving from democratic ideals were piano pieces, a sizeable group of songs, an important string quartet called *The Hako* (1922), and incidental music for four plays. But with the move to the structured life of a college professor and the need to put aside the unfulfilled ideals of the past fifteen years, Farwell's output now included more chamber works—solo works for violin and for cello, and a piano quintet—a full-blown symphony, as well as a greater number of songs and pieces for piano. Even in the East Lansing years, however, he could not give up completely the vision for musical-dramatic works that were spiritual in tone and would appeal to the larger public. There is evidence, for example, that he was thinking of proposing for the Chicago World's Fair (1933–34) a music drama based on the life of Christ[33] and for the New York World's Fair (1939–40) a revised version of his pageant *God and Man*, first composed in 1913.[34] Also from this period is *Mountain Song*, subtitled "A Symphonic Song Ceremony of the High Sierras in Five Movements for Orchestra with Occasional Choruses."

Another of Farwell's ideals resurfaced in East Lansing, the publishing of music. But unlike the Wa-Wan Press venture, the purpose this time was both to disseminate his own works and to experiment with the printing process. Having purchased a lithographic press with a small inheritance, Farwell printed works for which he had both drawn the notation and designed the covers. "My first object," as he explained in one of his publications, " . . . is to be free to give out my works when and as I wish, without the restrictions which must necessarily condition the activities of publishers."[35] Farwell always had a certain distrust of the commercial aspects of musical life, and was especially disturbed that such matters were so often a deterrent in bringing music to the public. His lithographic

---

[32]Farwell to Gertrude Farwell, 5 April 1928, AF Collection.   [33]Farwell to Noble Kreider, 29 November 1931, AF Collection.   [34]Farwell to Olin Downes, 13 March 1938, AF Collection. [35]Afterword to Arthur Farwell, *Two Songs on Poems by William Blake* (East Lansing: Arthur Farwell, 1931).

publications were a sort of mild protest to a "world [that] has never been excessively hospitable to the quiet search for beauty"[36] and at the same time an attempt to reach a public sympathetic to his quest. Perhaps the efforts to disseminate his music salved a disillusionment over the low ebb to which he thought American musical life had sunk in these days:

> Radio and automobile have cut sheet music sales down to next to nothing, and the former has terribly cheapened the musical idea generally. The conditions are pretty rotten—and I am not out to try to fight and overcome them, but to try to live as enjoyable a musical life as possible in a cock-eyed world, to compose, and to make it not impossible for people to get my works if they are interested.[37]

In the end, Farwell produced only six works from his lithographic press, though each is a handsomely wrought testament to the composer's ideal.

1939 brought momentous changes. In that year Farwell left his teaching post in Michigan, being forced out by a newly instituted college policy that required retirement at age 65—Farwell was then 67. In the same year, his marriage of some twenty years which had produced six children (the last born in East Lansing) ended in divorce and he moved to New York that summer. In September he married Betty Richardson, a former student of his, then in her twenties.[38] Whatever personal upheaval Farwell may have experienced at this time did not seem to affect his productivity as a composer during his last years in New York.

The compositions from these years, most of which were unpublished in Farwell's lifetime, include some thirty songs on Emily Dickinson texts, an orchestral work entitled *The Heroic Breed*, dedicated to the memory of General George S. Patton, Jr., a three-act "Operatic Fantasy of Music in America" called *Cartoon, or Once Upon a Time Recently*, and his last large-scale composition, finished in 1950, a sonata for cello and piano. In addition, there were some important items for piano: a one-movement sonata (1949) and twenty-three *Polytonal Studies*. These latter pieces seem on one hand a curious departure from Farwell's typical musical conservatism, of which he once wrote:

> You see I am not at all an ultra-modern, and am a rather close adherent of the general scheme established by Wagner and Tschaikowsky (no

---

[36] Afterword to Arthur Farwell, *Land of Luthany: Poem for Violoncello and Piano* (East Lansing: Arthur Farwell, 1933).   [37] Farwell to Dr. H. G. Bull, 21 June 1937, AF Collection.   [38] Evelyn Davis Culbertson, *He Heard America Singing: Arthur Farwell: Composer and Crusading Music Educator* (Metuchen, NJ: Scarecrow Press, 1992), 314.

invidious comparisons intended!), and am vehemently looked down
upon by my younger colleagues, as a hopeless reactionary, harking
back to the 19th Century, which they all despise.[39]

But Farwell was hardly a "hopeless reactionary," as is shown by the
Polytonal Studies composed between 1940 and the year of his death in 1952.
His willingness to test a new musical style late in life is, on the contrary,
more likely an indication of Farwell's strong belief in the importance of a
"creative musical evolution"—a phrase closely tied to Farwell's beliefs
recognizing the spiritual qualities of music. His main quarrel with the music
of his day, be it modern or conservative, was that it was spiritually
bankrupt; for him, style was always secondary to transcendent message.

Music and Spirituality: The Larger Scheme

It is not possible to consider fully Farwell's career, and certainly not his
writings, without including the man's deeply spiritual nature. His emphasis on music as a divine art and on the composer as a prophet
delivering a divine message clearly echoes feelings held by the German
Romantics, and was probably nurtured to some extent by his European
stay. But the sources for Farwell's spiritual credo include, actually, a
diverse array of religious and metaphysical ideas. Never orthodox in any
religious sense, his writings show a knowledge of Christian mystics, the
Cabala, religious scriptures of the East, as well as new spiritual paths
attempting to wed science and mysticism that had come into being in
his own day—especially the "New Thought" writings of Thomas
Troward.[40] In addition, Farwell's spiritual inclinations were enriched by
the works of various literary figures. Sprinkled throughout his writings
are references to a wide array of poets and dramatists with mystical
leanings, including William Blake, W. B. Yeats, Walt Whitman, Gerhart
Hauptmann, and Maurice Maeterlinck.

As a young man he had been drawn to astrology, a more than casual
interest of his mother that coupled with her own spiritual searches
involving Theosophy and Hinduism. Ever sensitive to the deep strain in

---

[39]Farwell to Keith Merrill, 26 March 1949, AF Collection.   [40]The English writer Thomas Troward
(1844–1916) was one of the foremost representatives of New Thought, a "mind-curist" spiritual
path that began in New England during the middle of the last century and is thought to have
originated with Phineas P. Quimby (1802–66; see Charles S. Braden, *Spirits in Rebellion: The
Rise and Development of New Thought* [Dallas: Southern Methodist University Press, 1963], 4). Three
of Troward's works that Farwell notes as influential are: *Edinburgh Lectures on Mental Science*
(1906), *Bible Mystery and Bible Meaning* (1907), and *The Creative Process in the Individual* (1911).

Arthur's character, Sara Farwell noted in her diary with pleasure what the "class prophet" said of her admired son at the MIT Class Day of May 29, 1893: "There is Farwell—you know him—the astrologer—I see him using his astrology in his business & then he has to come down to earth again."[41] The prophecy had more truth than its author could have known. For if Farwell's life was grounded in the metaphysical, he was always a pragmatist with a need to work in the everyday world. Sara Farwell was a model for her son in reconciling things of the spirit with day-to-day affairs. A distant cousin of Ralph Waldo Emerson, she turned to Transcendentalist ideas as a way of living a more harmonious life in the here and now and enjoyed a career as a lecturer on these ideals.

Farwell described in "Wanderjahre" his encounter with music in the summer of 1889 as a sort of mystical revelation. While performing music with friends during a vacation in the White Mountains of New Hampshire, it was the strains of Schubert that "sped through my nerves like liquid fire," revealing itself as a channel of communication on a divine plane. Though his attunement to the metaphysical had apparently begun earlier in life, suddenly it was the music of Schubert that communicated the ineffable and set this would-be engineer on a new path.

Though only hinted at in "Wanderjahre," his spiritual views are evident in his letters and other articles of the first decade and are increasingly a part of his writings thereafter. In an introductory essay to a Wa-Wan Press publication of 1905, he distinguished between two types of music—one which places emphasis on music as an art, the other which regards as paramount its spiritual message. The former deals with "music as the perfect technical expression," the latter with music's role in the "expansion of the human spirit."[42] Two years before, he had written of a music that could be used "for inducing exalted states of mind" and which could create a new "religion . . . of art" in the country. Here he spelled out America's unique mission, to create a music that was not modeled on Europe's, but rather one grounded in the spirit of a new place and time that could lift mankind to a higher level of consciousness. He called on composers, performers, and the people of America to "join forces to build up a national artistic life," sharing in "the divine joys" of such a music.[43]

Farwell further pursued the idea of a transcendent music in the second decade. In a series of articles published in late 1913 entitled

---

[41]Diary of Sara G. Farwell, 23 February 1892 to 22 June 1893, AF Collection. [42]WP 3:107.
[43]Farwell, "Music in the Abstract," Musical World 3 (1903): 93–95.

"Individual Advancement" (p. 211), he spoke of being at "the threshold of a new era of musical life" which "will arise from the special development of the individual, from a higher knowledge and use of his individual powers." Farwell was speaking here of the intuitive mind, a phenomenon that had caught his interest when he was a student. In "Wanderjahre" he tells of his wayward friend Rudolph Gott, an apparently gifted pianist whose improvisations lifted the impressionable Farwell to another realm. Some years later in New York, he corresponded with and eventually met the English-born American essayist Francis Grierson, who had attracted much interest especially in Europe as an untrained pianist performing recitals of improvisations.[44] Farwell became more vitally interested in the topic of intuition after discovering in 1910 the writings of Troward, whose so-called "mental science" merged mysticism with scientific thought. Troward's ideas spoke compellingly to Farwell, the spiritually inclined artist trained as an engineer, who saw all phenomena, whether scientific or artistic, as subject to the same universal laws. From Troward, Farwell found that through certain meditative states a person's intuitive mind could connect the individual with a universal source of creative power which was to be used for the good of all mankind. Farwell opined that composers in touch with this divine force of creativity and at the same time attuned to the needs of the people would create new forms of music consonant with the "new time-spirit." Such music would not be "for the few"; rather it would appeal to the people as a whole through what Farwell calls "mass appreciation"—a spiritual and psychological condition inherent in everyone that draws together an audience in collective appreciation of a musical work ("The New Gospel of Music," p. 222). Farwell reasoned that as all "creative cultural epochs are the spiritual flowerings of particular racial or national groups," the dawning of a new age of music in America was simply mirroring what had happened again and again in history.

While Farwell's efforts for American music decreased in his last years after leaving California, his ideals for human betterment had not diminished. During the final period of his life in New York he advanced these ideals through further work with intuition, giving lectures on the topic that included lantern-slide projections of drawings of his own

---

[44]Francis Grierson was the pen name of Benjamin Henry Jesse Francis Shepherd (1848–1927), whose books include *Modern Mysticism and Other Essays* (1889) and *Abraham Lincoln, The Practical Mystic* (1921). Farwell wrote two articles on Grierson for *MA*: "Francis Grierson—Musical Liberator" (19 [13 December 1913]: 19): and "The Improvisations of Francis Grierson" (19 [17 January 1914]: 12).

intuitive visions; and in 1948 he completed "Intuition in the World-Making," a book-length explication begun in the East Lansing days, though never published. In one of his last articles, "A Hidden Race,"[45] he again takes up the theme of hope for spiritual evolution, but here that hope is not in reference to a new musical life in America, but rather to a "world order really superior to the present one."

Farwell had a profound belief in the possibilities for a higher evolution of mankind, an outlook that no doubt reflected his interest in Eastern-based spiritual practices. A letter to a friend written a few years before he died shows his straightforwardness on the matter:

> Man would be nothing if he were an automatic well-acting puppet, made good from the beginning. To reach his godhead and be conscious of it, he has got to be permitted to work it out while getting there. But he will continually err according to whatever ignorance remains in him, until he learns better by experience. But he will carry himself through hell doing it![46]

The quest for a higher consciousness, indeed, appears to have given direction to Farwell's life. The many facets of his career were the means "to work it out," not the true objects of his quest. By keeping in sight the real goal, Farwell could retain a certain detachment when the lesser aims were not to be reached, and yet be ready to take up other projects with renewed energy: "We [dreamers] burn the bridges behind us without a regret. . . . We start continually upon quests of which we cannot see the end, and launch unnumbered ships to unguessed ports" (p. 178).

Farwell's "land of dreams" was a vision born of a spiritual outlook that gave each of his efforts a higher purpose. The writings which follow in this collection reveal something of the "divine adventure" of a man whose own inner development intersected intentionally with his worldly work. His idealistic message may compel us in these turbulent years of the waning century to remember an era in America when it was not uncommon to voice high hopes for the future, no matter how grim the prospects. For some, the message may even be an invitation to follow in the path of Farwell and other dreamers like him who lived "to turn belief into manifestation—vision into fact."[47]

---

[45]Arthur Farwell, "A Hidden Race," *Tomorrow* 2 (August 1943): 41–42.   [46]Farwell to Ivan Narodny, 18 November 1948, AF Collection.   [47]Arthur Farwell, "An Eleven Years' Adventure," *MA* 16 (14 September 1912): 9.

Wanderjahre of a Revolutionist
[Memoirs at Age 37]

CHAPTER 1

1889–1895
Student Years[1]

What sensation is more glorious than that with which a young man comes to the realization that now at last mere studies for life are over, that he is done with the business of staring around him in the world to see where he is, and of having things crammed into his brain by others and that henceforth he is to look within himself—to his own powers, for the realization and upbuilding of his independent manhood! And this great awakening which comes once for all to each man, comes also to nations of men, not only in their political life, as it came to the United States in 1776, but in their intellectual, and at last in their artistic life, as it is coming to the United States now.

Twenty years ago America looked eastward, across the Atlantic, for all that concerned her musical development. To-day, for that development, she looks within her own borders. Do we realize in what a time we are living, the time of the artistic awakening of our own land!—the time of a face-about, a reversal of viewpoint that can come to a nation but once in its history, and which now has come to ours. The moment—for these few decades which have brought this change about are as a moment in the national life—is dramatic. Systems, institutions, men, based upon the facts of the earlier régime, dwindle

---

[1] The titles, including the dates, for this and the remaining articles of "Wanderjahre" have been added by the editor as a reference aid. The word "Wanderjahre" refers in German to a young man's years and travels as an apprentice. Farwell's use of a foreign term may seem curious in the title of a series of pieces that deal so forthrightly with the development of a national musical life in the United States. On the other hand, Farwell was not a chauvinist, and his openness in acknowledging the musical debt America owed to Europe is perhaps indirectly reflected in this title. Indeed, Farwell's own considerable maturing as a musician took place during his period of study and "wanderings" in Germany and France (as is clear from these articles). This chapter first appeared in *MA* 9 (23 January 1909): 5.

WANDERJAHRE

OF A

REVOLUTIONIST

By
ARTHUR FARWELL.

Heading for Farwell's "Wanderjahre" series, published weekly in
Musical America, 23 January–10 July 1909

and fall; new enterprises, new men, arise, on the foundation of the truths and facts of to-day. The "young men see visions"—and fight and labor that they may come true.

We are so close to the event, which has been enacted over so vast a length and breadth of the earth's space, and by so great an army of players, that it is not strange that no chronicler has yet arisen to gather into a single vivid and consecutive drama these scattered scenes of the establishment of national artistic, and especially of national musical, independence. Nor would it be profitable to set about it in formal and academic fashion. But, as a single drop of water may reflect clearly in miniature the whole visible universe, so it may be that the experience of one who has been caught up in—has been a part of—these evolutions, may in some complete way, in however miniature a fashion, reflect them and reveal their collective significance. Especially may this be so where the youth and awakening of that one, a striver for artistic ends, appears to have exactly coincided with the psychological moment (vague and unscientific term!) of the nation's musical awakening. The present narrative, however, would fail of its object, did it not strike its roots back into the days of enthusiastic ignorance, of blind acceptance of circumstances, of cheerful nescience. Only in the spectacle of the dawn scattering the darkness, do we appreciate the dawn. With this apology for what is to follow, let us offer up our prayers of the Deity who presides over the destinies of American art, and make the mad plunge.

It all began in the Summer of 1889, when among the inspiring scenes of the New Hampshire Mountains, I first made the discovery of music. And what a world to discover! I had come from the then Ultima Thule of Minnesota, a state of pioneers, young cities, wheat, and Indians, and was to enter the Massachusetts Institute of Technology as a student of electrical engineering in the Fall. But before this step could occur I was to be accorded a vision, splendid and auroral, of the tyrannical mistress whose slave I should ever henceforth be. I found myself among a group of musical people. Some one brought forth an arrangement of the *Unfinished* Symphony of Schubert, for piano, four hands, violin and 'cello. I took the violin part, having fiddled assiduously for seven years, having no more idea than a backwoodsman of what music was. But now, with this divine Schubert, a revelation was at hand. Was music this! Did the world contain the means of speaking of *these* things! And was *music* that means? Why, I had known all about that all my life, in one continuous golden dream by day and by night; that was I *myself* but in my wildest dreams I had not imagined that there was any language for speaking it. And here it had been at hand all these years, and I had not known it. I did not have time to feel defrauded. The heavenly Schubert sped through my nerves like liquid fire. I trod the dazzling regions of the air, and made intimate companions of the sun, moon and stars. The mysteries of nature, of life, of creation were revealed to me. Like Tiresias of old, the heaven being opened to me, I became blind to the things of earth. I was lost—and I was saved.

Here was a startling and secret realization—but what to do about it? Nothing, I thought at last, but to proceed on schedule and await developments. I was going to Boston, and there I could look about and see what this miracle meant with relation to the world, upon which, somewhat to my surprise, I still found myself to be.

The institute was entered in due order, but the shrine of all knowledge for me was the old music hall,[2] where, under Nikisch, that very year new to America,[3] the symphony concerts were given. Saturday night always found me there as a "standee," and often Friday afternoon as well. There, weekly, was the vivifying Grail unveiled. Most musical educations begin early, and proceed in an orderly manner. Mine came late and all in a jumble. Still a babe at the breast, musically, I fed on the *Liebestod*, the symphonies of Beethoven, Schubert and Haydn, the

---

[2]This is a reference to the first home of the Boston Symphony Orchestra, the Boston Music Hall (built in 1852), where the orchestra played its inaugural concert on 22 October 1881. The orchestra stayed there until 1900 when it moved to its present home, Symphony Hall, where it began the season on 15 September.   [3]The Austro-Hungarian conductor Arthur Nikisch (1855–1922) led the Boston Symphony for four years, making his debut on 11 October 1889.

"Magic Fire" and Bach, classicals and radicals heaped together, Pelion on Ossa, without knowing which was which, nor caring.

The four years of engineering studies may be taken at a leap. Not that I loved electricity less, but that I loved music more. The demands of the course were severe; and working day and night, rising for weeks at a time at four and five in the morning, and grinding more frequently than not until after midnight, I was still not certain until the end that I should not be dropped. But interested as I was in this work for its own sake, the lathes and engines whirred music, the dynamos buzzed music, and the imaginary quantities of zero and infinity, in the higher mathematics, whirled one off into the regions where one heard the music of the spheres. I have often heard an innocent-looking dynamo doing the Allegretto of Brahms's Second Symphony, or a ponderous flywheel beating out the measure of Beethoven's Seventh. I remember whistling Raff's Lenore[4] to the time of a great Corliss "triple-expansion" during an engine test, and finally bringing down upon myself the ire of an instructor who had searched fifteen minutes to locate the squeak in the machinery. I longed for the day when I could throw off the restraint of the absolute and inviolable laws which bound scientific deductions, and unfettered and unrestrained, drive recklessly upon the roadways of the dawn in the phaeton-chariot of music. During the last two Summer vacations I studied harmony by myself, from Richter's awful and labyrinthine book.[5]

One experience of these years should not be overlooked. Up to this time, music, a distant goddess, had been an abstraction, an emanation, issuing from the tones of the orchestra, or from those produced by some great artist, himself remote as Arcturus from the sphere of my own life. But now I was to find a friend, in whom the genius of music was incarnate, a man in whom music was a consuming and torrential passion.

Inspirational, unbridled, his musical utterances, in composition and performance—for he was a phenomenal pianist—were of a kind to whirl an impressionable nature to the rim of the universe, and beyond—to summon genii, and invoke visions of angels. I was no longer dependent, for such empyrean transportation, upon a great mysterious system of orchestras and concert halls, a world outside my daily life. As often as I wished, my friend would transport me to any or all of the seven heavens. The mysterious powers of music were transferred from the soul of the

---

[4]Joachim Raff's (1822–82) Symphony No. 5 (1872), subtitled Lenore, after Gottfried August Bürger's ballad.   [5]Probably Ernst Friedrich Richter's (1808–79) popular Lehrbuch der Harmonie (1853; English trans., 1864).

Rudolph Gott
Farwell's unnamed
friend who introduced
him to music's
deeper mysteries.

distant Goddess to the soul of *my friend*! Music, heretofore divine, and divine only, had become human. I beheld the primal creative impulse at its human source, ungoverned, volcanic, it might be, but overwhelmingly real. Not Schubert, Beethoven only—distant spirits they were to me— might smite the strings. One's friend, oneself, mortal and profane, might presume to lay a hand upon the lyre. The effect of this revelation was indescribable. The earlier vision had been no delusion—here was the gleam again, unswervingly to be followed, for reasons both human and divine. And who was this strange man, and what part did Fate reserve for him? That is "another story," to be told, perhaps, some day.[6]

---

[6]The friend was Rudolph Gott about whom Farwell was to write in "The Rudolph Gott Story," a serialized piece appearing weekly in *MA* between 14 August and 2 October 1915. Farwell tells that he had been introduced to Gott by a fellow student at MIT ("who knew that I was going mad about music") in January of 1892. That Gott remained an inspiration in Farwell's later life is evident by his *Rudolph Gott Symphony*, Op. 95 (1932–34), a work in which Farwell used a fragment of an unfinished symphony by Gott as the opening of the first movement. In 1903, Farwell's Wa-Wan Press published one of Gott's works, *Landscape* for oboe and piano, reprinted in *WP* 2:54–58.

At last one Spring day, in 1893, about fifty ghosts, myself among them, were graduated, from an entering class of three hundred and fifty flesh and blood boys. I had, during the last year of my course, completed what I supposed to be a sonata for violin and piano, and a couple of songs. The day after graduation I made an appointment, and took these, with fear and trembling, to Mr. George W. Chadwick. He turned the pages of the violin work slowly, while I sat by, the blood congealing in my veins, and a benumbing frost creeping into the centers of my brain. After an aeon of agony, he spoke the never-to-be-forgotten words: "Of course you know, Mr. Farwell, that this is not really a sonata at all." Oh yes, I knew—or knew that I should set myself to know, and know why. With the songs it went better. I drew enough encouragement from his words to determine to begin musical studies in Boston in the Fall.[7]

After spending the Summer at home in the West, I returned to Boston, where I now also met Mr. MacDowell, whose kindly suggestion, together with that of Mr. Chadwick, set me in progressive paths of study.[8] I reviewed harmony, and began counterpoint with Mr. Homer

---

[7]George Whitefield Chadwick (1854–1931) had been on the faculty at Boston's New England Conservatory since 1882 and was its director from 1897 to 1930. Farwell elaborates on this encounter with Chadwick some months later in an 22 August 1893 entry of his diary (in AF Collection): "[Chadwick] explained that he would much rather have me show him something original like the sonata—not having studied—than to take him something technically perfect—but resembling Mendelssohn or other composers—having studied their works. [']I suppose you know what you have to do—' 'Work?' I asked. 'Begin at the bottom like everyone else.' I told him I expected that but I did not tell him that I expected to climb on a rapid action extension ladder—we will see. Five dollars an hour—can I do it? I asked him on leaving how much of his time I had used up—and he said—'don[']t charge anything for advice—I am glad to see anyone who is promising.' He advised me to learn the piano as fast as possible. Oh—I forgot about the Song. He saw that after the sonata—and glancing at it a moment—said 'well, why didn't you show me this first? This has evidence of form about it.' Then he criticised severely and justly—the modulations which he described excellently as 'ineffective.' I felt quite encouraged—though—for he committed himself by the word 'promising.' " Though Farwell implies in the next paragraph that his study with Chadwick was rather informal and sporadic, apparently the older man regarded him to be among his "advanced composition students," to whom Chadwick assigned "much of his teaching" after 1897 (see The New Grove Dictionary of American Music, s. v. "Chadwick, George Whitefield").   [8]Farwell's diary indicates that he left Minnesota for the East in mid-September, stopping in Chicago for two days (23–24 September) at the Columbian Exposition, and in New York City to see friends before finally arriving in Boston about a month later. A 22 October 1893 diary entry gives details of the first meeting with Edward MacDowell (1861–1908), who lived and taught in Boston for eight years (1888–1896) before moving to New York to take the post as the first chair of music at Columbia University in 1896: "Among other things I said—'Is there anything in orchestration or harmony or kin-

Norris,[9] and made a belated beginning at the piano with Mr. Thomas P. Currier.[10] The two happy years which followed—and perhaps too happy—were uneventful, except for the inward alternate hopes and despairs of the student. I showed my work to Mr. Chadwick from time to time for criticsm, and occasionally on Sunday mornings, his receiving time, exposed it to the fire of Mr. MacDowell's devastating criticism. These visits to MacDowell are also never to be forgotten. I have never gone before an audience, even one of cowboys, Comanches or Bostonians, with more insidious qualms than those which preceded these occasions. MacDowell, while at heart the kindliest of beings, was, when I saw him, always savage and breathless. I never knew at just what particular moment he would, critically speaking, carve out my heart. Restless, mobile, eager, nervous, omnivorous of notes, he seemed never to know a moment of repose. He expressed himself continuously, immediately, without reflection, without reserve. His very nature was expression. I have always been grateful for the slashings and lashings I received at his hands.[11]

But now, after two years of music-study, the protecting hand of kindly

---

dred subjects that I cannot learn alone?' 'No' he said[,] 'but you can learn many things quicker with a teacher.' He asked me what I knew about form—orchestral coloring—balancing of instruments etc. 'Only what I know from intuition' was my answer. Well he recommended some good teachers. I had said that I had but little money to spend and wished to get the most out of it. He said that his own prices would be too high for me and that there was considerable elementary work that any one could put me through easily, then he said come up occassionally [*sic*] and I will look over your work and correct it and help you out and it will not cost you anything. He was extremely kind to me and I felt much drawn to him."   [9]Homer Albert Norris (1860–1920) was a prominent organist, composer and pedagogue in Boston who published two theoretical texts, *Practical Harmony on a French Basis* (1896) and *The Art of Counterpoint* (1899). As Farwell gained in musical sophistication he regarded Norris, who had spent four years at the Paris Conservatory, as one of the first Americans to promulgate the use of modern French harmonies in composing. (See *AM*, 437f.) Norris doubtlessly influenced Farwell's later belief that the new French harmonies offered a starting point from which American composers could create a national style of their own (see, for example, Farwell's "Overtones and Sanity," *MA* 17 [3 May 1913]: 26). It may have been Norris's work with Alexandre Guilmant that led Farwell to seek out the French organ master for contrapuntal study when in Paris in 1899.   [10]Thomas Parker Currier (1855–1929), after study in Europe with Theodor Leschetizky and others, returned to Boston where he studied with MacDowell and taught piano. A critic and writer on music, his close association with MacDowell during the latter's Boston years is recounted in "Edward MacDowell as I Knew Him," *Musical Quarterly* 1 (1915): 17–51.   [11]A letter of 5 April 1895, from MacDowell in AF Collection provides another anecdote regarding Farwell's encounter with the older composer. On the envelope, a note written by Farwell and dated "Apr. [?] 1949" states: "Letter from Edward MacDowell during, obviously, my callow period. I had been after him so much on his 'Sunday mornings for American composers' that

fortune was to be removed for a time, and I must shift for myself. Still unequipped for any serious professional start along my chosen path, I determined to stay in the occidental Athens and carry the day one way or another.

I didn't want to go again just then, so I wrote him, not realizing what a lot of unnecessary questions I was pestering him with. He himself had picked out from some 17 or 18 early pieces the 14 or so that I put in 'Tone Pictures after Pastels in Prose' [Op. 7, privately printed; see Brice Farwell, ed., A Guide to the Music of Arthur Farwell (Briarcliff Manor, NY: published by the editor, 1972), 7], and I wanted his further guidance in seeing the work through. We hung on his every word in those days (1895)." In the letter, MacDowell responds to Farwell's questions on mechanics, closing with: "For Heavens' [sic] sake man use your thinker . . . I am not an Intelligence Bureau. Working hard all day makes me savage you see—All of which is meant in a kindly spirit by Yours Truly E MacDowell." A few years after MacDowell's mental breakdown and subsequent death, Farwell noted with touching respect: "He remained a wanderer on the borderlands of spirit, never coming to his spiritual home, and at the end his mind itself wandered never to return in this life. But he struck a telling blow for American musical art, and placed the nation upon a new musical footing" (AM, 365).

1895–1896
Bohemian Years in Boston[1]

O BOHEMIA! Happy thy children! The hour of joy is upon them, and the yoke of a weary world knows them not. Freedom is theirs, if in powerlessness. Triumph of conquest, if but amid the cohorts of the clouds. Sacred Bohemia! Many the sins committed against thy immaculate name! Many the polluted hours of stupid prodigality offered up in futile sacrifice to thee! Idle debauchees and hedonists behold not thy face. For those who tread the steep foothills of knowledge, buoyant of heart, and with eyes upon the distant gleaming peaks—for these is thy veil withdrawn, thy gracious smile reserved!

Not a term of student life in Germany, not a sojourn in the "Quartier Latin" of Paris, to an American who has early striven, against odds, in the world of art—not even these delectable experiences can be wafted back to the recollection on so authentic, so balmy an air from the real Bohemia, as the first days of aspiration and struggle among his own people. The two years from 1895 to 1897, in Boston, were for me that true Bohemia which Murger characterizes for the Parisian as the "vestibule which leads to the Academy [of Fine Arts], the Hotel Dieu [i.e., hospital], or the Morgue."[2] The world still fresh and dewy, the struggle hard, but not sordid, the responsibilities of life and the meaning of the history of art not yet realized, these were Elysian years.

An Athos and a Porthos are indispensable to happiness in such an experience, nor were they wanting in this instance.[3] What shall we call

---

[1]From *MA* 9 (30 January 1909): 11.   [2]The French writer Henri Murger (1822–61) is known for *Scènes de la Vie de Bohème* (published serially in 1848), colorful depictions of artists' lives in nineteenth-century Paris that were the basis for the libretto of Giacomo Puccini's *La Bohème*. [3]Farwell alludes to two characters belonging to a famous trio of friends who appear in *The Three*

them? One was a Prince; so let us call the other the Pauper.[4] Of course we were all paupers, in reality, but even a pauper can be princely if he be born under the proper star for it, and be incapable of realizing that he is a pauper. The Pauper and I took a modest room together somewhere up near the sky, in one of those byways of Boston that makes it the Londoner's favorite American city. The landlady was a good Methodist, and we must promise not to play operatic or other profane music on Sundays—a promise only indifferently kept. We learned that the good lady did not know an opera from a jig, but had only heard that it was something very wicked.

Why the Prince took up his abode with us cannot be said in a word. First of all, we wanted him; then, our habitation was much nearer "Mechanic's Building," where the Abbey and Grau opera was shortly to be ensconced,[5] than to the psychological laboratory in Cambridge; and despite his high marks he had excellent reasons for having lost interest in the future of his college course. And he possessed the obvious advantage of being opera mad, in addition to being an authority on all matters of philosophy, psychology, literature, and art; which latter circumstance enabled the Pauper and myself to derive, in the course of our daily life, many of the benefits of a classical education.[6]

Walter Damrosch now began a short season of German opera at the Boston Theater, among his principle singers being Alvary, Klafsky and Ternina. There, rushing up the long stairs with the rabble, on

---

Musketeers (1844), the swashbuckling historical romance of Alexandre Dumas (1802–70). In addition to Athos, who is quiet and gallant, and Porthos, who is brawny but short on wit, there is the serious minded Aramis, who looks forward to an eventual cloistered life. Though he does not mention this character, one might wonder whether Farwell, with his mystical bent and wish for a more tranquil life (see pp. 116 and 118), perhaps sees something of Aramis in himself.   [4]The reference here is to the novel *The Prince and the Pauper* (1881) by the American writer and lecturer, Mark Twain (1835–1910).   [5]Farwell refers to New York's Metropolitan Opera which regularly presented a brief season in Boston. The company was managed in the 1890s by Henry Eugene Abbey (1846–1896), Maurice Grau (1849–1907), and John B. Schoeffel (1846–1918); Schoeffel is not mentioned by Farwell probably because the former had only recently joined the management.   [6]Farwell never reveals the names of either of his friends in "Wanderjahre," though other sources provide the identity of the "Prince" as Winslow Mallery. Mallery, two years Farwell's junior, left Harvard after his sophomore year (in 1896) for a career in business, first in Chicago and then in New York from 1904 to his death in 1926 (see [Secretary's] *Report* for the Class of 1898 published by Harvard University in 1904, 1913, and 1928). Farwell kept in touch with Mallery at least through the period covered by "Wanderjahre," even moving in with Mallery for a time in New York toward the end of 1907 (see p. 155). The Prince's identity is provided by the return address of a letter Farwell has written from this period to the composer Arne Oldberg: "C[are]/o[f] Winslow Mallery/Nat'l Arts Club/119 E. 19th St./New York City, N. Y." (14 January 1908, AO Collection). In another letter of considerably later date Farwell speaks of Mallery as a friend of his "Boston Bohemian days" (Farwell to L. A. Freedman, 10 June 1940, Special Manuscript Collection: L. A. Freedman, Butler Library, Columbia University). The identifi-

"admissions," but finally enthroned as gods in the gallery, we witnessed the *Ring*. There, intoxicated with tone, I first saw the fires flame up around Brunhilde's rock, and, in a trance of epic gloom, watched the slain Siegfried borne off by the huntsmen. There I first went down in the tonal maelstrom of *Tristan*, and there learned of fine old Hans Sachs at his cobbler's bench, things good to know.[7]

These weeks of opera over, another season, even more stellar, opened at Mechanic's Building with Anton Seidl and Mancinelli as conductors—Anton Seidl, "der grosse Schweiger" [the great silent one], as he was known at Bayreuth, where this record will later find

cation of the "Pauper" is less certain, though evidence in Farwell's diary (in AF Collection) points to John Marshall, whose association with Farwell during the Boston years surfaces in ensuing chapters of the "Wanderjahre" series. An entry of 19 June 1896, mentions a small group of family and friends who had attended a Boston Promenade concert at which were played two of Farwell's works (orchestrated pieces from the piano album *Tone Pictures after Pastels in Prose*; the whereabouts of the orchestral versions is unknown). Among the friends Farwell names are Winslow Mallery and John Marshall. Marshall, a musician five years younger than Farwell, studied with some of the same teachers as did Farwell—Chadwick, MacDowell, and Norris (*Baker's Biographical Dictionary of Musicians*, 4th ed., s. v. "Marshall, John"). During their student days, a Boston critic singled them out as two of Norris's pupils "making names for themselves" as composers ("Boston Music Notes," *Musical Courier* 33 [18 November 1896]: 15). The likelihood of Marshall being the "Pauper" is strengthened by a diary entry of 22 September 1896, written after Farwell had returned to Boston following a summer in upstate New York. Here, though not stated directly, a close mutual friendship between the three is implied: "I have seen John and we dined together and talked over 'old times' which means last winter. It seems preposterous that it should already be old times. Winslow I have seen but for a moment." John Patton Marshall (1877–1941) became professor of music at Boston University in 1902, where he founded and became dean of the College of Music in 1928, remaining in that position to his death. Over the years he served as organist for several churches in Boston as well as the Boston Symphony Orchestra (1909–18), and authored several college textbooks on music.

[7] The conductor Walter Damrosch (1862–1950) organized his opera company in 1894 comprised of German singers and mainly German repertory; it gave performances in New York and throughout the country for the next five years. If Farwell is recalling one particular season between 1895 and 1897 when the Damrosch company appeared in Boston, the most likely is that of 3 to 15 February 1896, when the German tenor Max Alvary (1856–98), the Hungarian soprano Katharina Klavsky (1855–96), and the Croatian soprano Milka Ternina (1863–1941) all sang. Neither Klavsky nor Ternina appear in the cast lists of the *Boston Globe* for the 1895 season, and since Klavsky died in September, 1896, it does not appear that Farwell is referring to the 1897 season, even though this was the only one of the three seasons when the entire *Ring* cycle was performed. An impressive array of seven Wagnerian operas were offered in the two weeks of 1896, including *Lohengrin*, *Tannhäuser* (with Ternina), *Tristan und Isolde* (performed twice, with the role of Isolde being taken once by Klavsky and once by Ternina; Alvary appeared as Tristan), *Die Walküre*, *Siegfried* (with Alvary and Ternina), *Götterdämmerung* (with Alvary and Klavsky), and *Die Meistersinger*. In addition, there were performances of *Freischütz*, *Fidelio*, and one work from outside the German repertory, Damrosch's own *The Scarlet Letter*. Hans Sachs, the central character of Wagner's *Die Meistersinger*, was based on the sixteenth-century German poet, dramatist and mastersinger, a shoemaker by trade.

him conducting the magnificent production of *Parsifal*, which was the crowning achievement of his life.[8]

The serious occupation of our lives now was "suping" [serving as a supernumerary] at the opera. Nightly, the Prince, the Pauper, and I drank air out of tin cups at the inn in *Carmen*, paraded as nobles of Brabant, or cringed as Egyptian slaves. Thrice happy were we when we could carry Russitano in on a palanquin, or Melba in a sedan chair.[9] For such service the "super-master" was supposed to pay each "supe" 50 cents an evening, and it had formerly been the custom to do so. But the suping fever now became epidemic at Harvard, and so thickly the students crowded at the door before the performance, seeking engagements, that the supe-master found it profitable, instead of paying them 50 cents each, to charge them that amount, thus deriving both an external and an internal revenue. Here was a fatal blow at our meager exchequer! What were we to do in this dilemma! A happy thought struck the resourceful Prince—he would join the opera company. Through his regularity of attendance and familiarity with the super's functions and répertoire, he had become valuable to the supe-master. The Pauper and I never knew the precise nature of his understanding with his superiors, but we never again paid for the vast privilege of wearing dirty and ill-fitting costumes and being kicked about by the stage hands—or more accurately, the stage *feet*. Indeed, from now on we had the best places on the stage, where we could witness the triumphs of the giants of those days, the de Reszkes, Maurel, Tamagno, Plançon, Melba, Calvé, Nordica, Eames, and their colleagues. Scalchi, of many registers, and the faithful Bauermeister, were among them.[10] Evenings, after the performance, we even attained to

---

[8] In recalling the performances of the Metropolitan Opera, Farwell appears to have conflated two seasons, those of 1895 (25 February to 9 March, with a return engagement from 9 to 14 April) and 1896 (17 to 29 February). Of the artists Farwell mentions, the conductor Anton Seidl (1850–1898) and the French soprano Emma Calvé (1858–1942) appeared, according to the *Boston Globe*, in the 1896 season but not in 1895. On the other hand, the conductor Luigi Mancinelli (1848–1921), the American soprano Emma Eames (1865–1952), and the Italian tenor Francesco Tamagno (1850–1905), whom Farwell mentions, appear in the 1895 season but not in 1896, according to the *Globe*. All of the other artists mentioned by Farwell performed in both the 1895 and 1896 seasons.   [9] The Italian baritone Giuseppe Russitano sang two seasons with the Metropolitan Opera, 1894–96; in Boston he appeared in the production of *Lucia di Lammermoor*. Dame Nellie Melba (1861–1931), famous Australian soprano, appeared both in *Faust* and *Lucia*.   [10] Of the singers Farwell cites, the Polish brothers, tenor Jean de Reszke (1850–1925) and bass Edouard de Reszke (1853–1917) both appeared in Boston in *Faust*, *Les Huguenots*, and *Tristan*; Francesco Tamagno sang in *Otello* and *Il Trovatore*; Victor Maurel (1848–1923), the French baritone who created roles for Verdi's *Otello* and *Falstaff*, sang in

Anton Seidl

eat a late Welsh rarebit, occasionally, at a near-by café, with certain of the petty officers of the company. Such ecstatic evenings well over, we sought out the altitudes of our abode. The Prince slept on the floor, the Pauper and I providing him with one of the pillows and a portion of the bedding, to which he added overcoats *ad lib*. In the morning, when the Pauper and I arose, the Prince would sleepily crawl up over the edge of our abandoned couch of repose, like the Nickelman over the well's edge in the *Sunken Bell*,'' and thus more securely fortified in comfort, would re-enter the misty mid-region of dreams. Our lusty piano practicing seemed only to enhance the virginal quality of his slumber. About noon he would rise, and going to a neighboring and unpretentious lunch room, would make a belated breakfast of ice cream and cake.

Faust and *Les Huguenots*; Pol Plançon (1851–1914), French bass, sang in *Faust* and *Les Huguenots*; Emma Calvé sang in *Carmen* and *Cavalleria Rusticana*; Lillian Nordica (1857–1914), American soprano, appeared in *Les Huguenots* and *Tristan*; Emma Eames sang in *Falstaff*; Sofia Scalchi (1850–1922), Italian contralto whose range was reputedly two octaves and a half—from f to b''—appeared in *Faust* and *Les Huguenots*; and Mathilde Bauermeister (1849–1926)—given as "Baumeister" in the original text—German soprano known for her wide repertory of almost 100 roles, sang in four operas: *Faust, Carmen, Lucia,* and *Cavalleria Rusticana*.
''A verse play completed in 1896 by the German dramatist Gerhart Hauptmann (1862–1946).

But these operatic enterprises did not contribute materially to the incidental industry of earning bread. There was a tentative pupil or two, but they fell away for one cause or another. The Prince mortgaged his books, but that did not answer our needs for long, especially as the Prince himself insisted in riding in cabs upon the least provocation. For him to see a cab was to take it. A fortune of seventy-five cents, that should have lasted us for three days, would vanish in a trice if fate, to the terror of the Pauper and myself, sent the dread Jehu around the corner into the Prince's view at the wrong moment. The times bore hard upon us in many ways. To add to our perplexities, the kingdom of our hats was divided, like "all Gaul, into three parts." We had one soft hat, one derby, and one silk hat. When the first two were in use, the unfortunate third of us was compelled to go forth arrayed like Solomon in all his glory, even if it were only to buy a needed package of shredded wheat at seven o'clock in the morning. For state events, such as studio receptions, where we hoped for a few macaroons and a cup of tea at the least, we had two frock coats, one of which was usually in pawn. When my two companions were off on one Quixotic errand or another, of a day's duration or more, five cents worth of dates, or three doughnuts at that price, one for breakfast, one for lunch, and one for supper, were my daily fare. I wandered aimlessly about Copley Square, unable to work, looking at that great monument of culture, the Boston Public Library, with its famous Allen Brown library of musical scores,[12] which I had seen arise stone by stone. I thought what excellent use I could make of the small fortune that had gone into a single one of those granite blocks.

The unrelenting stress of circumstances finally made it necessary for us to call a session, and discuss seriously, action for the present and possibilities for the future. There seemed only one hope of salvation—the army. And so, from nine o'clock that morning until four o'clock in the afternoon, we debated this question, whether we should try to pull through in our present course, or enlist. Long and hard the debate raged, serious enough, but not without its aspects of humor. The Prince urged that we enlist in the British army, in order to have a Nile trip thrown in. If you had to go into a battle, he argued, you could shoot yourself through the flesh of the arm and get sent to the hospital. But at last, when the Prince and the Pauper had expended all

---

[12]The collection, given in 1894 by Boston business man Allen A. Brown, contained 7,000 volumes, and was added to subsequently by Brown and others; in addition to scores were "historical, theorectical, and critical works" and "unique collections of programs, etc." (Waldo Selden Pratt, ed., *American Supplement, Grove's Dictionary of Music and Musicians*, 3rd edition, s. v., "Brown Musical Library, The Allen A.").

their argumentative force, I maintained that I would stand by the ship of music, come what might. So we said no more of the army.

I had often seen songs published in the Sunday *Herald*, and so next day, in the hope of augmenting our resources, I took down a song to the musical editor, who was no other than Ben Woolf, of "Almighty Dollar" fame. I persuaded the Prince to go with me, in the silk hat, to help in making an impression. The august critic looked at the song, and with a sickly smile told us that the persons whose songs appeared in the paper, paid, or their managers or publishers did, for their appearance there. Thus were the vaudeville songs of the day made popular and profitable.[13]

As we walked sadly up a narrow street paralleling one of the thoroughfares (the Prince wished to avoid the possible embarassment of meeting certain Harvard professors) one of those sudden flashes of clairvoyance overtook me, which I had experienced on several previous occasions, and I made the flat statement, "There is one hundred dollars coming to me through the mail." Farther up the street we parted, as the Prince determined to walk to Cambridge, professor or no professors, and make a brain analysis which was due at the laboratory on that day, and which phase of his work still interested him.

The Pauper was away for two days, and as I went homeward, I pictured to myself, with no glowing anticipation, the lonely and meager evening meal of the remaining doughnut. I toiled up the stairs, entered the room, and listlessly opened a letter which lay on my table. *Mirabile dictu!* there was the check, and one hundred dollars was the amount. By an instinctive impulse I threw open the window, and remembering my baseball days, sent the innocent doughnut which lay on the table, whizzing out into the snowy and darkening spaces of the night. But this was an overhasty action, for now I had nothing to eat, and a check which I could not cash. I bethought me finally of a doctor of my acquaintance, looked him up, and on the evidence of the check, borrowed $15. No amount of reflection could suggest to me a companion in my good fortune. The Prince and the Pauper might not reappear on the scene for hours, or even days. But I must eat, and eat well, and betook me to a good downtown hotel, when after laying in an ample supply of magazines, large and small—it was the day of the ephemeral freak magazines—I encamped at a table and with the air of a captain of

---

[13]Benjamin Edward Woolf (1836–1901)—spelled "Wolff" in the original text—was known for his caustic reviews of music and art in the *Boston Herald* from 1894 to 1901. He was also a composer of operettas and songs, as well as symphonic and chamber music, and enjoyed some success as a dramatist. His comedy *The Mighty Dollar* (not "Almighty Dollar," as cited by Farwell) earned Woolf considerable reputation. See Philip Hale, "In Memoriam B. E. Woolf," *Musical Courier* 42 (13 February 1901): 28–29.

industry ordered broiled live lobster, peach shortcake, and ice cream. Thus intrenched in bliss, I remained into the small hours of the night. The next evening our trip was reassembled and the Prince, now that we were rich, demonstrated in his own way, how such a celebration should be conducted.

From now on, a faint smile was discernable on the face of fortune. I heard of a school in an outlying town that wanted a conductor for a chorus of pupils. Taking what vague recommendations I could get, I went out and arranged the matter. Then, as I was not sure whether I could conduct, never having tried, I took one lesson from dear old Carl Zerrahn, and was thereafter master of twenty dollars a month.[14]

Fortune's smile, like the barometric smile of the Cheshire cat in *Alice in Wonderland*, became still more plain when I was invited to spend the Summer at one of the beautiful lakes in the central part of New York State. My host and benefactor was an ardent lover of music, and together during the Summer months we ransacked the musical climes.[15]

In the Fall Anton Seidl visited, with his orchestra, the city in which my new friend lived, and through the intercession of the latter we were able to hear a new orchestral work—made possible by the leisure which had been so generously accorded me. Thus I learned to know the great gap which exists between how one thinks an orchestral work is going to sound, and how it actually sounds, and better still, I learned to know Anton Seidl, a circumstance not only happy in itself, but which was to mean much at a later time.[16]

---

[14]Farwell notes in his diary for 19 June 1896 that he directed "a little chorus" at Thayer Academy. Carl Zerrahn (1826–1909) was a German-born conductor, well-known in Boston as director of the Handel and Haydn Society from 1854 to 1898 and also the Harvard Musical Association Orchestra from 1866 to 1882. [15]Farwell's friend was Thomas Mott Osborne (1859–1926), a wealthy industrialist from Auburn, New York, where he served as mayor from 1903 to 1905. The two met in June 1896, through Farwell's brother Sydney, who worked for Osborne (Diary, 9 June 1896). An amateur musican of considerable ability himself, Osborne saw promise in the young composer and was generous in helping to launch his career, which Farwell never forgot (see his memorial tribute to Osborne, *New York Times*, 6 March 1927, sec. 8, p. 10). Osborne became known especially for the reforms he instituted while warden at Sing Sing Prison (see Farwell's "Three Days at Musical Sing Sing," *MA* 22 [5 June 1915]: 25). [16]A program in AF Collection indicates that Seidl and his "Metropolitan Permanent Orchestra from New York" included in their performance in Auburn, New York, on 17 October 1896, "Andante from a New Suite" by Farwell. This was the second movement, "Love Song," from Farwell's unfinished *Suite for Grand Orchestra*, (see Brice Farwell, ed., *A Guide to the Music of Arthur Farwell*. [Briarcliff Manor, NY: published by the editor, 1972], 7). Farwell notes that "it was his [Seidl's] performance of one of my earliest orchestral works that had led, unknown to Seidl himself, to my having the opportunity of European study" (Farwell,

Fortune fairly beamed when I learned that after another Winter of struggle I should go to Bayreuth for the Wagner Festival, and perhaps remain in Europe for study.[7] I did not know that I should set sail not only from America, but from my Bohemia as well, in the same ship.

"America's Gain from a Bayreuth Romance: The Mystery of Anton Seidl," *Musical Quarterly* 30 [1944]: 450). There is indication that Seidl gave more than one performance of Farwell's "Love Song": "Upon a recent tour Seidl played at one of his concerts the andante of an unfinished suite by Arthur Farwell, and was so pleased with the work that he will use it in programs this winter" ("Boston Music Notes," *Musical Courier* 33 [18 November 1896]: 15). A number of years after the Auburn performance Farwell related his apprehension at attending a rehearsal of the work in New York. Not having had at that time any training in instrumentation, he feared his first attempt at orchestral writing would turn out a disgrace, so he hid behind a large coat rack during the orchestra's read-through, hoping to remove himself unnoticed if the worst occurred. "The tragedy never happened. It was about half an hour before they got to my work. It really sounded like an orchestra, and nearly bowled me over. I went out, and Seidl was very nice to me, and introduced me to the orchestra players, who clapped!" (Letter to Miss Larabee, 21 March 1939, AF Collection).   [7]"Another Winter of struggle" does not seem to be an accurate description of Farwell's following months. In his diary for 27 August 1896, he tells that Osborne "has secured me a scholarship of two hundred and fifty dollars—originally intended to assist someone at Harvard—but finding not the right person this year, he gives me the amount. The scholarship was founded by Mr. Osborne himself. This will enable me to live in decent quarters next winter with perhaps some kind of a studio." Farwell's circumstances for the next year, indeed, were far from destitute. According to his diary (4 October 1896) he moved into a studio apartment with piano on St. Botolph Street in Boston, and even when that became too expensive he was invited to move in at the comfortable home of Mrs. Ole Bull in Cambridge, where his mother, Sara Farwell, had been staying (Diary, 22 February and 24 March 1897).

1897
The Grand Tour[1]

The certainty of a European journey in prospect—the mere anticipation of a truce in the struggle with the wolf at the door—robbed the second year of Bohemia of somewhat of its authentic flavor. To be wholly itself, must not any particular *régime* be lost within itself, have no past and no future? When we see what we shall be next, we are no longer what we are now! Being thus for the moment not precisely anything, nor caring much in what manner I should bridge the interim, I spent the last five months in a bookstore, collating magazines at a dollar a day. Needing a little leisure to see my friends and adjust a few matters before sailing, three weeks before that happy date I made a flying trip back to my old haunts in the mountains, gave vent to five months' pent-up feelings in a few songs, which, returning to Boston, I sold to grudging publishers for five dollars each.[2]

How many times during many years had I wondered with what wistful feeling, should that day ever come, I should first see my land disappearing behind me, and with what impatient and curious surmise look forward to the strange old world beyond! And now that day, a July day in 1897, had arrived. To be between a new world and an old! Between what old nations had done, and what a new nation was to do! Little enough I thought of it in that light then, a callow and selfish pleasure and enthusiasm in the experience leaving no room for evolutionary reflection.

We landed duly at Southampton, where, at the restaurant at-

[1]From *MA* 9 (6 February 1909): 21.   [2]Brice Farwell (*A Guide to the Music of Arthur Farwell* [Briarcliff Manor, NY: published by the editor, 1972], 7) lists three songs that were brought out by the publisher Oliver Ditson of Boston in 1897: "Blow, Golden Trumpets," "The Message of the Lilies," and "O Ships that Sail." The last Farwell cites in his diary (AF Collection) on 14 November 1896, as being accepted by Ditson.

Thomas Mott Osborne
Wealthy industrialist who
underwrote
Farwell's stay
in Europe.

tached to the steamship landing, I first experienced the sensation of
seeing a barmaid. My friend, on business, and I with him, upon pleasure, now began a kind of informal "grand tour."[3] The story of the great
European cities, their galleries, their opera, has been too often written
to repeat here. I usually sought out the quaint old corners of the cities
we visited to catch their medieval flavor, while my friend, an insatiate
traveler and incorrigible historian, with a penchant for "going to the top
of everything," looked up all the palaces, towers, and mountains of any
consequence, and went to the top of them all.[4] We visited Hamburg,

---

[3]Farwell's unnamed friend is Thomas Mott Osborne, whom he has alluded to at the close of the
preceding chapter (see p. 42, n. 15). Farwell was traveling as a guest of Osborne, who also underwrote
the young composer's year and a half of study in Europe.   [4]According to Farwell's diary, they arrived
in England on 14 July and stayed there for the remainder of the month. Ever an enthusiast of art,
particularly painting, Farwell eagerly drank in the treasures of the London galleries: "I have spent hours in
the National Gallery before the Raphaels and Botticellis and Rubens and Velasquez and Turners! and felt
the spirit of the painting as it is impossible to do from reproductions" (Diary, 17 July 1897).

listened to good music out of doors at the Tivoli in Copenhagen, and spent some days at the Exposition in Stockholm. Being on business, my friend was much entertained, and we thus came into intimate touch with many of the quaint and interesting social customs of the different lands, and learned many national dishes which would not otherwise have come within the range of our attention or our appetite.

Passing through Kiel, Berlin, and Dresden, we at last reached the Mecca of our pilgrimage—Bayreuth. We had with us now a German captain of artillery, a friend of my companion, who was a good violinist.[5] Taking up quarters in a wing of the old palace, we spent two weeks of golden days, with *Hausmusik*, bicycling about the Bavarian roads, afternoons attending the festival, and evening sitting about the cafés and watching the strange cosmopolitan humanity that gathers to witness the attempted realization of the transcendant dreams of Richard Wagner.[6]

It was the year of Anton Seidl's fleeting return, at last, to the scenes of his earlier activities, and the year of his consecrated effort in the masterly conducting of *Parsifal*. It had been determined that I should study in Germany, and I had deferred making plans until I should have the advice of Seidl. So I began a search for him in the village—he was not registered with the police, a ceremony necessary with suspicious characters like ourselves—and at last discovered his lodging, a large medieval-looking house on the outskirts, which I learned had been one of his earlier haunts. He was not at home, but presently came down the road, meditatively and unconcernedly smoking a large cigar. He greeted me cordially, and we spoke of things in general, and in particular of various personages in Bayreuth. I can remember his unstinted laughter when I asked him the identity of a man I had seen—could not well help seeing— parading the terrace between the acts of the performance; a man of large and heavy stature, with face preternaturally pale and framed in masses of coal-black hair and beard, and who wore a pale, yellow flannel summer suit with an embroidered satin waistcoat, a broad-brimmed

---

[5]Farwell identifies in his diary the new traveling companion as Ludwig Klipfel, Captain in the Third Artillery, Brandenburg, noting that he joined them at Hamburg (4 August 1897).   [6]Farwell's diary indicates that they arrived in Bayreuth on 11 August 1897, staying there at least a week. In addition to *Parsifal*, which he witnessed twice, Farwell writes that he saw the entire *Ring*. Excerpts from his diary of 11 to 17 August are indicative of how he was moved by the productions: *Parsifal* at Bayreuth "is like a great and wonderful dream of Heaven . . . Yesterday Rhinegold. The curtain was not up five minutes before I was in tears! I cannot imagine why—except that it was so wonderfully beautiful." After seeing *Die Walküre*: "I am afraid constantly of taking all this good fortune as a matter of course! . . . I have heard it [*Götterdämmerung*] now, five or six times, and enjoyed it today more than ever. It was a pleasure to hear it all—including the parts usually cut out. I came out at the end, limp as a wet rag."

hat, and was accompanied by an equally remarkable looking female. "That," he informed me, "is the Sâr Péladan, who has founded an order of the Holy Grail in Paris." It is this man, I believe, who claims to have discovered a complete arcanum of the ancient mysteries in the songs of the troubadours.[7]

The "Great Silent One" now asked me to take a walk, and we passed along the road until we came to a bridge over a little stream. Here he paused, and, untrue to his Bayreuth name, spoke most eloquently for some time upon the beauty and nobility of the music of *Parsifal*, upon his memories of the earlier Bayreuth, his homesickness there now, and his desire to go back to his beloved New York. No incident of my wanderings has impressed itself more deeply upon my memory than this privileged moment, when the soul of this silent man so simply, so nobly revealed itself. It was the last time that I was ever to see him.[8]

Seidl asked me why I did not study with Engelbert Humperdinck, and I seized upon the idea as precisely the thing. He told me that Humperdinck was then in Bayreuth, and I set out to find him, but he, too, was one of the unregistered, and it was only after some search I discovered him. I was at once impressed by the naturalness and simplicity of this famous man, who received me without a vestige of ceremony. He took some of my work to look over and in a few days it was arranged that in September I should go to Boppard on the Rhine, where he lived, and there begin study.[9]

---

[7] Joséphin Péladan (1858 or '59–1918), self-titled "Sâr Péladan," was the eccentric novelist, art critic, playwright, and founder in 1891 of an occult group in Paris known as the *Rose+Croix du Temple et du Graal*. Péladan claimed in his *Le Théâtre complet de Wagner*, 1895, that while attending a performance of *Parsifal* in the summer of 1888 "he conceived . . . in a single flash" his mystical order based on Rosicrucian doctrine (Robert Pincus-Witten, *Occult Symbolism in France: Joséphin Péladan and the Salons de la Rose-Croix* [New York: Garland, 1976], 68f.). For a while Erik Satie was a member of the organization and set to music Péladan's "Chaldaic pastorale" *Le fils des étoiles* (Carl Dahlhaus, *Nineteenth-Century Music*, trans. J. Bradford Robinson [Berkeley: University of California Press, 1989]: 384). [8] Seven months after Seidl's triumphant return to Bayreuth in the summer of 1897 the musical world was stunned by his death from ptomaine poisoning. An added note to the story is that Farwell was asked by Seidl's wife in 1900 "to assemble and write out the scores of Seidl's own arrangements of excerpts from the Wagner music dramas, from the orchestral parts" (Farwell, "America's Gain from a Bayreuth Romance: The Mystery of Anton Seidl," *Musical Quarterly* 30 [1944]: 453). According to a note in Farwell's hand in AF Collection, "Seidl never had *scores* of them, as he had them in his head . . . I did the work at the old St. Denis Hotel, cor[ner of] 12th St & Broadway in 1900, a year after my return from European study." [9] Farwell's diary entry for 23 August shows his anxiety over the possible reactions Humperdinck might have to his compositions:

Our artillery captain now left us, and heaving a deep sigh for the
passing of this span of richly laden days, we turned southward to
Nuremberg, quaintest of cities, and erstwhile the stamping-ground on
home-made shoes—of old Hans Sachs. Thence we went to Vienna,
visiting the houses and haunts of Beethoven and Schubert, which
reminded me vividly of my earliest enthusiasms.[10]

Even now, eight years after those enthusiasms, I was still ac-
cepting all things naively, without historical comparisons. Music was
still simply music to me. I had not yet apprehended the truth that
living music to-day cannot be produced by imitating even the greatest of the masters, but only by doing something as alive for our day
as their music was for their day. I did not yet appreciate what startling innovators, what inventors, what revolutionists, these early
masters were in their time. They not only felt music, they *thought* it;
thought their way out of the old into the new. And the vigor of that
flaming creative thought keeps their music alive to-day, as a mere
falling back upon their natural musical feeling—their primal emotion—would never have done. These things were still unknown to
me—I had not yet learned to *think*.

A trip over the strange, wild, craggy Semmering brought us down one
evening in Venice. One should always reach Venice by night. Through the
darkness, trunks and all, we sped in a gondola, and ere long were tucking
away various appetizing Italian dishes cooked in olive oil, and a bottle of
Chianti that was real. I thought of Boston and the doughnuts, and pinched
myself to see whether I were dreaming. There are plenty of dreams in
Venice. One is to see St. Mark's, a miracle of conglomerate opalescence,

---

"That same morning [of 19 August] I met Humperdinck on the street—and said 'Ich fürchte
dass Sie haben meine Compositionen sehr schlecht gefunden [I fear that you've found my
compositions poor].' 'O nein, sehr hübsch [Oh no, they're charming]' he replied, and I
breathed again. I had expected torrents of scathing criticism. He told the captain [Ludwig
Klipfel] I had talent, and understood harmony." Engelbert Humperdinck (1854–1921) was
a member of the Wagner circle in the early 1880s, when he spent much of his time in
Bayreuth preparing for the first production of *Parsifal*. Success came for Humperdinck in
1893 with the premiere of his *Hänsel und Gretel*, perhaps the best known German opera
that followed in the train of Wagner's influence. Farwell's meeting with Humperdinck
occurred shortly after the latter had moved from Frankfurt, where he had taught at the
Hoch Conservatory, to Boppard to devote himself fully to composition, and, apparently,
to take on a few private students.   [10]Though Farwell spent only a couple of days in
Vienna he was ready to claim it "the best city in Europe! . . . and [I] should like to live
here." He was awed by the paintings of the Gallerie Rubens and saw for the first time *Don
Giovanni*, which he enjoyed, though the "orchestration sounded like nothing, after
Bayreuth" (Diary, 23 August 1897).

gleaming in the morning sun. One feels sure that some Parsifal with a Klingsor spear will level the vision to dust in another moment."

Verona with its perfect coliseum, Milan with its gingerbread cathedral, were visited in turn, and crossing the St. Gothard by night, we awoke to the splendor of the Alps. After a glance at Lucerne, we sped on to Interlaken, and to Murren, high up on the cliff in the Lauterbrunnen valley. There, across the great chasm, we watched the first light of day touch the still and awful summit of the Jungfrau, and listened to the music of its distant avalanches as they thundered down the lower ravines. These are the sights and sounds to prepare one for a hearing of the *Manfred* symphony of Tschaikowsky!

"Arriving in Venice on 25 August, Farwell writes: "I cannot wonder that Wagner and Browning and Byron and Poe were enslaved by the beauties of Venice. I hope to live there some time" (Diary, 27 August 1897).

1897
Study with Humperdinck[1]

A week in Paris brought our Summer wanderings to an end—a week in which I saw more of the sights of the city as a tourist sees them, from Maxim's to the Opéra, than in all of the Winter which I passed there at a later time, for study.[2] I returned with my friend to London whence he took passage for home, and I braved once more the notorious perils of the Channel. A confusion of continental sleepers, garlic-reeking Frenchmen, and penny whistles—O those continental train whistles!—brought me to Cologne. I inquired of a guard the hour of departure of the Boppard train. Not understanding him clearly, I inquired of another, who gave me a different answer. So I asked still a third, with a like result. In despair I added the three together, struck an average, looked at my watch, and fled to the platform just in time to break the laws of Germany and leap aboard the train which was already pulling out.

Boppard, on my arrival, presented a discouragingly gloomy appearance. I spent my first thoroughly lonesome hour since leaving America. A cold and steady afternoon drizzle of rain fell from the low-hanging clouds into the little cobble-stoned alleyways that passed for streets. The summer hotels along the Rhine were closed and the only quarters I could find were such as to redouble my sense of dreariness. But as quickly as possible I hunted out Villa Humperdinck, on the hill back

---

[1]From *MA* 9 (13 February 1909): 21–22.   [2]Among highlights of Farwell's five days in Paris were the Louvre—where he "was lost in admirations of the Venus, which make all other sculptures utterly unbeautiful"—an evening at the Folies Bergère, another at the Cirque d'Été, *Tannhäuser* at the Opéra, and poster shopping on the Rue Bonaparte. He left Paris with an impression "of greatness and of rottenness and beauty and ugliness" (Diary, 5–9 September 1897; AF Collection).

Engelbert Humper-
dinck

from the Rhine. I found myself at last before a great ironwork gate in a high wall. I pressed a button, and click! the lock rattled, just as in a New York apartment house. I afterwards learned that Humperdinck's hobby is inventions, electrical and other mechanical appliances, especially those which constitute modern improvements in the household econ-omy. Passing through the gate and up a winding path which led among trees and flower beds now despoiled by approaching Winter, I came to the villa. This was a large house of three stories commanding a far and beautiful view of the windings of the sleepy Rhine.

Once the hospitable lord of this cheerful domain had greeted me, all nostalgia fled, and I felt happy and at home. I was presented to Frau Humperdinck, who is as natural and unceremonious as her husband,

and to Wolfram and Edith, the Hänsel and Gretel of the household. The third child, little Irmgard, was already abed. Herr Humperdinck showed me through the beautifully furnished house—his study, with a little seat in the window by the piano, where Frau Humperdinck usually sat reading or working while he composed—the tower, its walls covered with "Hänsel and Gretel" wall paper. I then made the acquaintance of the goat, the rabbits, the doves, and last, but not least, the little dog Loki, "ein Feuerhund,"[3] his master said.

After looking about the extensive grounds, with their fruit orchards and vegetable gardens, Herr Humperdinck took me for a little walk in the village, with its quaint half-timbered houses, and showed me its fragments of the old Roman wall-towers and arches buried to half their height in the centuries' silt of the Rhine. For, centuries before, this had been the walled town of Baudobriga. Then we returned to a savory dinner of larded hare, *Rotkohl mit Kastanien* [red cabbage with chestnuts], Rhine wine and other excellent dishes of the land. Boppard was not such a cheerless place after all. After dinner there was *Bowle* [punch], not the *Maibowle* of the spring, but made with Rhine wine, sugar, and crushed peaches. When I said good night and descended the garden path, the electrical gate, operated from the house, for some reason refused to open. Not wanting to retrace my steps to the villa, I calculated my chances of exit, and climbing up the ironwork, squeezed between the high iron pikes and the under surface of the stone arch, landing safely at last in the road below—an ungraceful maneuver, of which I never informed my kind host.

A season's stay in a German "small town" is an experience unknown to most Americans who go to Europe for study, an experience brimming with interest. I soon found comfortable lodgings in a good *Pension*, and quickly became accustomed to feather beds, *familienkaffee* [coffee with the family] and the exclusive use of the German tongue. Such a small town in the valley of the Rhine is unaware of the existence of an outer world. So long have these little villages lived within themselves—nurtured their own traditions—that although they are but three or four miles apart along the Rhine, each has its own recognizable dialect of the mother tongue! The inhabitants think and speak of Americans as impossible beings, but as they know only the species *tourist*, they may readily be forgiven. To have every one speak to me of the Americans as demons, ruffians, and scalp-takers, and to

---

[3]Literally, a "dog of fire"; supposedly a reference to Loki, the god of fire in Norse mythology.

Sketch by Farwell of half-timbered houses in Boppard, Germany

be treated at the same time with the utmost consideration and hospitality, was a phenomenon that long perplexed me. I concluded at last that I must be regarded as one who had been caught young and civilized on the continent. These were the days of the first scenes of the Spanish war, which brought forth such an outburst of slumbering German feeling against the United States, a feeling undoubtedly arising from commercial rivalry.

The time passed like a dream. Walking along the lazy Rhine under the shadow of the hilly vineyards, with their old ruined fortresses above, or back into the sleepy valleys where one would sometimes meet a forester with a feather in his green cap, or an old woman straight out of Grimm's fairy tales, with a bundle of faggots on her bent back—I often rubbed my eyes to see if I were really awake.[4] Then there were study lessons, and the evenings up at Villa Humperdinck. The lessons were informal: I went up whenever I had sufficient work to show. We would spend several hours over it, and my teacher-host would usually serve coffee and cigars, and sometimes a glass of yellow Marsala. Sometimes Herr Humperdinck would take me out for a walk, on which occasions he would seldom speak a word, except to point out something of especial interest here or there that I might

---

[4]Farwell notes in his diary on 19 October that he "sketch[es] for amusement, when I go on afternoon walks. There is a never failing source of subjects in the quaint corners of this old town." One of his drawings of Boppard appears on this page.

otherwise miss. I am certain that the processes of composition never ceased in his mind during these strolls.[5]

On those evenings which I spent at the villa, after dinner we would congregate in his study, where Herr Humperdinck would usually read, smoking a pipe which reached to the floor, while I would engage in a battle at chess with Frau Humperdinck, who is a good player and would usually win. "Which do you like best, chess or counter-point?" Humperdinck would ask. Sometimes Frau Humperdinck would read a letter from Frau Wagner, reporting Siegfried's progress with the *Bärenhäuter*, and giving other Bayreuth news.[6]

Humperdinck was at this time composing the overture to the *Koenigskinder*, which he had just completed as a spoken drama—text by Frau Bernstein[7] of Leipzig—with orchestral accompaniment throughout. The original proof sheets of this overture with his signature, a gift from the composer, I still treasure. Humperdinck took me to Frankfort to hear the play, which was being given without the overture.

---

[5]Farwell's study with Humperdinck lasted at most eighteen weeks, from late September to the close of the following February; for over five weeks in November and December Farwell was in Bonn unable to study, being treated for a "catarrh of the middle ear" as well as a knee ailment (Diary, entries for 25 November 1897 and 2 January 1898). At his first session with Humperdinck on 19 September they spent the entire time on Farwell's *Death of Virginia*—referred to by Farwell variously as an orchestral tone poem and a suite—begun in the summer of 1893, just after he graduated from MIT (holograph in AF Collection). Humperdinck found the work "rather too bold and risky in modulation, not enought [*sic*] development of the themes, but had little to criticize in the orchestration" (Diary, 24 September 1897). A month later Farwell writes of setting texts by Johanna Ambrosius and of Humperdinck's saying that he had a very great talent for Lieder. Farwell thought that one of the Ambrosius songs, "Dahin," was "in many respects the best thing I have done" (Diary, 19 October 1897). This along with three other Ambrosius songs were published in 1898 as *Mädchenlieder* by H. B. Stevens of Boston and given praise by James G. Huneker in one of the earliest reviews of Farwell's music (*Musical Courier* 40 [24 January 1900]: 28). The kindness of Humperdinck to his young student is indicated by a note Farwell appended to a receipt for payment for a lesson, dated 15 October 1897: "This [is from] early in my season of study with Humperdinck. First payment. He never could accept another, and taught me all winter free of charge" (AF Collection). Farwell gives a more extended appreciation of Humperdinck in "A Musical Poet of Childhood: Engelbert Humperdinck, the Composer of 'Hänsel und Gretel,'" *The Outlook*, 23 December 1905: 1007–9.   [6]Siegfried Wagner (1869–1930), only son of Cosima von Bülow and Richard Wagner, became a conductor at Bayreuth in 1894 and general supervisor of the festival in 1909. He also was a composer and had studied with Humperdinck. *Der Bärenhäuter*, completed in 1898, was his first of several operas and was premiered at Munich the following year.   [7]In the original text, a question mark appears after "Frau Bernstein." Perhaps this indicates that Farwell could neither recall the full name of the author of *Die Königskinder*, which was Elsa Bernstein-Porges, nor the pseudonymn she used, "Ernst Rosmer."

Beautiful and idealistic as this musically-aureoled fairy play was, it was never regarded as a wholly successful experiment. But it contains some of its composer's best music, and this he is probably retaining in his present opera of the same name. Certain extremely high pianissimos in the strings, Humperdinck asked me if I could hear. His slight deafness made them wholly inaudible to him.[8]

To hear the new overture we made a trip to Heidelberg, where the composer conducted this joyous and delightful work at a concert of the Bach-Verein, of which Herr Wolfrum is the director. In Heidelberg we were royally entertained for several days at Villa Beausejour by the charming Frau Daniela Thode, the daughter of Hans von Bülow. We heard the concert from the greenroom. When Frau Thode spoke of three songs by Liszt, which occurred on the program, as "drei Lieder von Grosspapa," I felt near to the royal family indeed. On the return trip to Boppard, Humperdinck went ahead to friends in Frankfort, while I spent a frigid night between ice cold sheets in an unheated chamber of the quaint house of the hospitable Conductor Mendelssohn on the outskirts of Darmstadt.[9]

---

[8]*Die Königskinder*, referred to as a "fairy tale" by Bernstein-Porges, was originally set as a new type of melodrama with recitations having prescribed rhythms and pitch inflections. Farwell heard the final rehearsal of the work in Berlin (Diary, 11 March 1898) and was enthralled: "From the first to the last bar is *Idealization*." Despite its apparent success—it received over 100 performances in various theaters—controversy arose over its melodramatic setting and Humperdinck eventually withdrew the work (see Edward F. Kravitt, "The Joining of Words and Music in Late Romantic Melodrama," *Musical Quarterly* 62 [1976]: 571–90). Humperdinck recast the piece as an opera, which was first performed at New York's Metropolitan Opera in 1910. Farwell reviewed the performance in *MA* ("The Music of Humperdinck's New Opera," 13 [31 December 1910]: 1, 4–5), where he praised Humperdinck for not stooping to the recent rage for Straussian realism. A brief interview of Humperdinck by Farwell that took place when the German composer was in the United States for the operatic premiere, appears in "Likes His Königskinder Best," *MA* 13 (17 December 1910): 6. [9]The excursion to Frankfurt and Heidelberg took place in early February 1898, according to Farwell's diary. Phillipp Wolfrum (1854–1919), conductor, musicologist, and friend of Humperdinck since their student days at the Königliche Musikschule in Munich, was at the University of Heidelberg and director there of the Bachverein since 1884. Farwell notes in his diary (22 February 1898) that the hospitality of Daniela Thode, daughter of pianist and conductor Hans von Bülow and Cosima von Bülow Wagner and granddaughter of Franz Liszt, made perhaps his most delightful day in Europe. Over forty years after meeting Thode, Farwell published an unusual story about a romantic attachment between her and Anton Seidl which Farwell believed eventually resulted in Seidl's leaving Europe for America in 1885 (see Farwell, "America's Gain from a Bayreuth Romance: The Mystery of Anton Seidl," *Musical Quarterly* 30 [1944]: 448–57). The conductor and composer Arnold Mendelssohn (1855–1933), another member of Humperdinck's circle of friends, was at the time a professor at Darmstadt Conservatory.

Most amazing of Boppard experiences was my plunge into its social whirl. Let any jaded American in need of amusement, excitement, and wholly new sensations generally, seek out a small German town and identify himself with the life of its inhabitants. The most usual social habits of the glorious bird of freedom make the rural German eagle turn pale with apprehension. The villagers throw up their hands when they see their traditional gods of custom falling in ruins at their feet. They wonder at what moment you will dash over the limits of mere social terrorization and begin shooting them up in earnest. They waver between fear of their lives and joy in the common possession of a new and thrilling topic of conversation.

1898
Berlin[1]

*I*nterspersed with the vivacious recreations of the Rhinelanders, who are far more like the Latins than like North Germans, these dream-like study days flew by. Herr Humperdinck had no other pupil than myself at this time, as he had just withdrawn from his active life as a teacher in Frankfort, and I happened to be first to hunt him out and disturb him in his new retreat. While other periods of my European life were more strenuous and exciting, the picturesque environment of this sojourn and the whole-souled friendliness and hospitality of the family Humperdinck made this the most delightful of my European experiences. And I profited greatly by the sympathetic and suggestive instruction which I received.

But Boppard, with its old towers and quaint half-timbered houses, was to be left toward the end of the winter. Humperdinck was to spend some time in Berlin preparing and conducting the first perform-ances of the *Koenigskinder.* A month or more after Christmas—to know what Christmas is, one must spend one in rural Germany—we bid farewell to Father Rhine and went to the Powerful City of Ger-many.

Here, again, my experience was one far from the usual experience of Americans studying in Europe. Meeting only Herr Humperdinck's friends, I fell into the heart of a purely German circumstance of art life, a circumstance of intense reality and struggle, through the modern Teutonic atmosphere of which the life of the Americans in Berlin, with whom I never came in contact, looked hazy and far away. What they looked into, I looked out from. A *Stammtisch* [a regular gathering of cronies] on the very evening of our arrival brought me in contact with the two men who were in the main to represent Berlin, and much more, to me for a number of months. Such a mixture of ages, sexes, professions as this *Stammtisch* brought together is seldom seen in America. There were composers, publishers (the lion and the lamb lying down together), actors, sculptors, bankers, elderly ladies—and younger, no girls, of course (this being Germany), architects and dignitaries with various kinds of *hofs* and *raths* attached to their names. Siegfried Wagner was there; Max Brockhaus, the publisher; Hans Pfitzner, the composer, and James Grun, the poet. The conversation was prolonged and brilliant, and when finally the *Kellner* went around this vast table, and each guest in turn paid his own reckoning, I first realized the meaning of a "Dutch treat."[2]

The owls who outsat the rest were Pfitzner, Grun, and myself. Grun spoke English as well as German, and both superlatively well; his birth and early training had been in England. He was the intimate friend of Pfitzner, and as Humperdinck had designated the latter as my musical mentor in Berlin, I fell at once into a closer relation with them than with any of the others whom I met. I took a room near Pfitzner's abode, out by the barracks.

Life now became strenuous—physically, socially, and intellectually. I lived three lives at once: social, as I wished to learn something of the nature of German society; operatic, I haunted the opera; and the life of study. I had a nice room with a balcony, with breakfast, at 27 marks a month, and my landlady's piano free for giving her little daughter lessons.

My point of contact with the life in which I was now plunged was Grun. His Anglo-Saxon half gave us a life in common, and his Teutonic half enabled him to initiate me into the deeper aspects of the German life about us. Grun was a personality. In February or March, 1898,

---

[2] Farwell's diary (AF Collection) indicates that after arriving in Berlin on 5 March he went to the house of two elderly maiden ladies by the name of Ebeling where Humperdinck was staying. He was invited thereafter to social gatherings that were hosted by the sisters each Monday evening. Wolfram Humperdinck in his biography *Engelbert Humperdinck: Das Leben meines Vaters* [Frankfurt am Main: Verlag Waldemar Kramer, 1965] mentions (p. 244) the writer Elisabeth Ebeling as a friend of Humperdinck living in Berlin, but does not mention the other sister. Max Brockhaus (1867–1957) in 1893 founded his music publishing firm in Leipzig which especially promoted contemporary operas, including those of Humperdinck, Pfitzner, and Siegfried Wagner. Hans Pfitzner (1869–1949), best known in the United States for his opera *Palestrina* (1912–15), had in 1897 been appointed concurrently to two Berlin posts: a teacher at the Stern'schen Conservatorium der Musik and Conductor at the Oper des Westens.

when I met him, he was about one-third through with the composition
of the poem of *Die Rose vom Liebesgarten* for Pfitzner's opera. To write
this colossal poem he had thrown up what odd jobs he had in London,
where he had been living, and absolutely without a pfennig had come
to spend a Winter in Berlin at the task. He had what is the German
equivalent for a "hall bedroom," and his entire worldly possessions
beyond the clothes which he wore consisted of a small black satchel
containing an extra shirt, a toothbrush, a pen and a bottle of ink. Being
a socialist he was somewhat under surveilance, but as the officers of
the law had no overt act wherewith to charge him, they conceived that
at least they could worry him with taxations. To this end the police
made him frequent visits, to look over and evaluate his property. But
the peaceful proprietor of a toothbrush and a pen was never taxed.
(The worst the police could do to me was to oblige me to send back to
Boppard and get a certificate of good conduct—a *Führungsatteste*—
from the Burgomeister, which with great generosity he at once sent to
me.)

Grun when I first met him was earning the few crumbs which
served him for meals by translating for a German socialistic paper
certain laws of the State of Illinois referring to the rights of women.
The last job in which I ever knew him to be engaged was the conveying
of lunatics from their homes to the asylum. For years he had done, and
taken a kind of ironical delight in doing, such odd tasks as a humorous
Providence assigned to him, while pouring the whole energy of his fiery
spirit, and the light of a transcendent vision into poetic works, of which
we shall certainly hear more in the course of time. Never had I known
a nature in which simple and burning humanity, practicality even to
sophistication, humor and common sense, went hand in hand with
prophetic and consuming vision and the uttermost of world forgetful-
ness as it did in the strange crucible of this man's heart and mind. Early
thrown homeless upon the world, he had nevertheless received the
major part of an excellent English education. But the grim and rugged
reality of his experiences had given him a profound sympathy and a
startling directness in his relations with others, which took one by
storm. Although of rather delicate mould physically—in strange con-
trast to his volcanic mentality—he had worked as a stoker in London,
and had done other equally rough work. At that time he was sharing a
room with, I believe, a butcher and a bus driver, and writing his poetry
nights, on the kitchen sink for a table, after the family of the house had
gone to bed. His education he finally completed himself by gaining

access to the library of William T. Stead. Presenting himself before Mr. Stead in his office one day, he told the famous editor that he had come to work for him. "But I have no job for you," said Mr. Stead. "I didn't say that I wanted a job," Grun replied, "I said I had come to work for you." And work he did, job or no job, earning his living by other work evenings, but now having access to the coveted books. In London slum work for Mr. Stead, Grun came in daily contact with degraded humanity at its very worst, and his socialistic labors were in behalf of these wretched beings of the underworld.[3]

An episode of these earlier years, however, had been Grun's short sojourn at Mainz, where he had first met Hans Pfitzner. In Grun, Pfitzner found his poet, and Grun his musican in Pfitzner. These two men were artistic complementaries in a remarkable degree. Pfitzner's poignant and intense utterance was precisely what Grun required for the musical expression of his conceptions. Shortly after their meeting they produced *Der arme Heinrich*, which was given its first representation in Mainz, and at once lifted its composer out of oblivion and ended the period of his greatest hardships.[4]

And, now, some years after these occurrences I was watching the growth, page by page, of *Die Rose vom Liebesgarten*, romantic opera in two acts, prelude and postlude—virtually four acts. Grun had been a prodigious student of Wagner, and of dramatic construction generally. In our long nocturnal wanderings about Berlin and its environs, Grun outlined to me the scheme of *Die Rose*, and *motif* of which had been suggested to him by a painting by Hans Thoma—*The Guardian of the Garden of Love*.[5] The far- and deep-reaching ideas and suggestions in this *Welt-gedicht* [universal poem] of Grun's led us on to the ransacking of all the climes of thought and existence, and in these unforgetable expeditions he made me the sharer of the results of a vast amount of study and thought, and far more valuable, of real and deep experience.

In short, my association with Grun was an intellectual and spiritual shaking up, such as I have never experienced before or since. Pleasant dreaming was over forever for me. Grun was a natural disturber. Wher-

---

[3]The English journalist and editor William Thomas Stead (1849–1912), founder of the noted periodical *Review of Reviews* (1890), was known for his work on behalf of social as well as international causes.   [4]Completed in 1893, the opera was premiered two years later. [5]Hans Thoma (1839–1924), born in the Black Forest region of Germany, is known for his landscapes, as well as paintings involving symbolic and religious ideas. Farwell had the opportunity to admire the paintings in Thoma's studio through the intervention of Daniela Thode (Diary, 22 February 1898). See p. 64 for Thoma's sketch of James Grun.

ever he went there was a row. He challenged every conventional or
outworn idea, every tradition or custom, every suspicious or impeach-
able motive that arose within the range of his watchful consciousness.
Woe to the unhappy wretch who presumed to go against him with a
word or a deed that did not ring true.[6]

---

[6]James Grun (1866–1928), born of an English mother and German father, had been a fellow
student with Pfitzner at the Frankfurt Conservatory. As we have seen, Farwell does not
mention Grun's musical background, perhaps with good reason. Pfitzner described Grun as
"a man who attended the Conservatory out of love of music 'without music loving him in
return,'" though he obviously had great respect for Grun's mind. Further insight into Grun is
provided by Pfitzner: "Grun was an individual character and intellect. His education was very
patchy and he stood on bad terms with the German language; but he had nevertheless
acquired a certain educational background from reading and from his frank outlook on the
world. His mind sought out everything great and significant in the areas which interested him,
art, religion, and socialism." (See John Williamson, *The Music of Hans Pfitzner*, [Oxford:
Clarendon Press, 1992], 12–13.) Further information regarding this man whom Farwell saw as
such an important influence on his thinking has been difficult to come by. Among Farwell's
papers there is the detached cover of a book of poems by Grun entitled *Glocken von Eisen und
von Gold*, Frankfurt a. M.: Mahlau & Waldschmidt, 1893. Also among Farwell's papers are
three pages of notes, likely in Grun's hand, with the heading: "*Advice*, (to be taken with free
discretion,) *from an old bird* (not to be caught by chaff) *to a callow American eaglet* (about to
take wing,) *London Nov. 98*." Farwell was apparently in England at this time staying with
Grun, for in AF Collection is a letter dated 23 November 1898, from Hedwig Humperdinck,
wife of the composer, addressed to Farwell, care of "Mr. James Grun, 8 Bridge Rd West,
Battersea, London S. W., England." The notes are suggestions concerning what seems to be
a musical drama called "Springs of Youth" which Farwell anticipated composing, though to
my knowledge no such work exists. Farwell had highest regard for the collaborative efforts of
Grun and Pfitzner, writing that "Since Wagner, we know of but one voice in modern music
that has unequivocally called us back to this standpoint . . . . It is the composite voice, that of
Hans Pfitzner . . . and James Grun . . . whose lyrical drama *Der arme Heinrich* was proclaimed by a modern German master, 'the most important art-work since Wagner,' and
whose later *Liebesgarten* surpasses the first work in largeness of conception and breadth of
outlook upon life" (*WP*:1:181). Other writers have been less positive about Grun as a librettist.
Edward J. Dent believes that the text of *Der arme Heinrich* "is unsuited to the dramatic
handling of a story," that the characters are not clearly drawn, and that "the poet loses himself
in poetic phrases." Dent finds the plot of *Die Rose vom Liebesgarten* "inextricably confused,"
resulting in "a work that is too incorporeal and imaginative for the practical conditions of the
stage" ("Hans Pfitzner," *Music and Letters* 4 (1923): 125. More recently, Carl Dahlhaus speaks
of Grun's libretto for *Der arme Heinrich* as being "of dubious poetic value" (Dahlhaus,
Nineteenth-Century Music, trans. J. Bradford Robinson [Berkeley: University of California
Press, 1989], 342).

1898
James Grun[1]

Many of us in this life are apt to go pleasantly on—more or less pleasantly—taking a great number of things on faith. Only when the creative spark in some new and startling manifestation flashes before us, do we see that the old existing order is not the only possible order. They of Mozart's day believed that the symphony had found the apex of its development in Mozart. And so it had, until another should arise powerful and daring enough to snatch from heaven another spark of the true Promethean fire wherewith to create anew.

Suppose that we are not creators ourselves. In our most impressionable years we are saturated with the great works of the past, by an educational system that must keep a reputation for safety and respectability. We are taught what's what, and the knowledge is clinched and sealed. The years of actual study pass. Nothing is any longer given to us with the august authority of the schools. What crumbs of knowledge we pick up, especially concerning contemporary ideas in art, we mistrust. Unless we have become thorough and persistent students by nature, the authority of our own understanding does not suffice us. The old fellows were great; we were told so from the beginning. The knowledge has become part of our very nature. The new fellows—well, we don't know. They have the presumption to tell us that something else is the right thing to-day. The very authorities which shaped our minds, perhaps, tell us that the upstarts are wrong. To what an unequal pressure of opposing forces are these average minds of ours subjected! Is it to be wondered at that nine hundred and ninety-nine times out of a thousand the distracted scale, so unequally weighted,

---

[1]From *MA* 9 (27 February 1909): 28.

tips at once to the comfort of conservatism? Yet this proportion may be the ideally perfect devising of a divine Providence. If the spark which creates the new were more than a spark—if it were a running fire—it would be a world-destroying conflagration.

If conservatism and radicalism existed in some divinely ordered proportion in each person, we would be close upon the millennium. The trouble is that some persons surrender themselves wholly to the one tendency or to the other. Your hopeless conservative builds a definite and limited airtight world for himself in his youth, and never gets outside of it. And your extreme radical drives his Phaeton-chariot into the sun and is burned up—usually still in his youth. For Joachim to repudiate Wagner and all music after Beethoven may have been heroic, but it was also fatal to his development into a great modern man.[2] It is more swiftly fatal to take the opposite course and recognize no bounds to anything.

And what have these speculations to do with these Wanderjahre? Well, they are reflections aroused by the thought of James Grun, poet, with whose divinely ordained rôle of inquisitor and disturber we are already familiar. Certainly if anything is more real than our wanderings among the scenes and people of the world, it is our wanderings among the thoughts of the world. And in the five months of my association with Grun I had to think, and think hard. If I presented a thought to him which was not alive—fairly wriggling with life—I became conscious of it at once by a sharp crack on the head, so to speak, from his mental shillalah. And these rude awakenings had much to do, later on, with my attitude toward work and toward developments and controversies in the field of American music.

Grun insisted on a knowledge of musical history, that we should be alive to the point which we have reached in musical development, and to the process of getting there. He insisted on form—not any existing conventional or crystallized form, but the *idea* of form—that a musical work should have recognizable internal proportions making it a logical organism. He insisted on the value of folksongs, those melodies sifted and tested by time, which are the "old wine" of melody, deceptive in their simplicity and not easily to be equaled to-day. He urged Parry's great dictum, that whenever the musical art of a country becomes weakened through over-refinement, it derives new strength from the

---

[2]Joseph Joachim (1831–1907) was a noted Austro-Hungarian violinist of the last century, as well as a conductor and composer,

simple melodies of the people.[3] And he particularly insisted upon dramatic truth in the musical setting of a given text. If the text says dark or deep, the music must be convincingly dark or deep—the music must tell no lies.

Under Grun's friendly but sharply critical tutelage, music rapidly lost the static quality which it had heretofore seemed to me to have, and became in my thought what it really is, a continuous, living development. Its flux and change in accordance with the spirit of the time became plain to me, and for the first time I saw clearly the folly of attempting to duplicate the style or manner of any composer of the

---

[3]The musical scholar and composer Sir Charles Hubert Hastings Parry (1848–1918) contributed to the first *Grove's Dictionary of Music and Musicians* (1878–89) and published in 1893 a highly regarded history of music entitled *The Art of Music*. The latter is often cited by Farwell for elucidating what he sees as a basic problem with much music of his time, its "over-refine-

past. However great the men of the older time, I saw that imitation of their manner could be but a vain effort to revive the conditions and forces of an epoch which, with its own particular modes of expression, had passed from the world forever. I learned how the love of the classics must not blind us to the different needs of to-day, in expression—learned the great gulf which necessarily stands between the best older music usually heard to-day and such music of to-day's making as is alive to the time. I saw that no progressive and creative thinker of the past could make progress without giving shocks to the ultra-conservative, and that without shocking that same comfortable worthy we can make no progress to-day. Also Grun introduced me to Walt Whitman.

Day in and day out, and more especially night in and night out, I wandered with Grun about the streets and environs of Berlin, or recreated with billiards, coffee and the weekly *Illustrierters* in the cafés. In fact, we made no particular division of the twenty-four hours into day and night, at least for sleeping and waking purposes. When we were tired we slept, and when we were hungry we ate, whether it was the gray dawn or noontide. The first time I mentioned these prolonged nocturnal rambles to Pfitzner, an immeasurable distress animated his voice as he exclaimed, "The very greatest favor, the one above all others, that you can do me is not to keep Grun out nights!" For Pfitzner expected a certain number of pages each day of the nascent *Rose vom Liebesgarten* from Grun's potent pen.

One of these nights I remember with particular glee. On a certain morning I went into Grun's room which was about the size and shape of a coffin. He was sleepily rubbing his eyes, considering the wisdom of getting up. But the object which caught my eye was upon the broad sill of his one window. It was nothing less than a great circular basket inwoven with gay ribbons, and groaningly taxed to its uttermost capacity with a great load of "delicatessen" of every description. There were some of those wonderful German creations to which the name of sausage seems an insult; there were jars of jelly, of preserved meats, cakes, and bottles of wine. I finally succeeded in communicating my

---

ment." The matter is hinted at here but is stated more forthrightly elsewhere by Farwell; see, for example, "The Relation of Folksong to American Musical Development," *Studies in Musical Education: History and Aesthetics. Papers and Proceedings of the Music Teachers National Association*, Series 2 (1907): 202, and "The National Movement for American Music," *American Review of Reviews* 38 (1908): 721. Farwell's regard for Parry as a historian is seen at a later period, too, when he rates the Englishman's history as one of the few important works of its type (Farwell to E. J. B. Walsh, 6 March 1936, AF Collection).

amazed curiosity to Grun. "Wait," he said; "Pfitzner's away to-day; to-morrow night we'll have a feast."

Several weeks before, Eugen d'Albert had asked Grun as a favor to write him a poem for an aria he was to compose for his wife, Hermine Finck, to sing at a London concert. This was "Die kleine Seejungfrau," based on the old legend.[4] The feast was merely a little acknowledgment of this favor, but made the basis of a great event in Pfitzner's quarters the next evening. I remember that Pfitzner had *Tristan* on his mind that night. Some friend had presented him with the full orchestral score, and from this he played through the entire first act with an intensity and passion that I have seldom seen realized on the operatic stage. The vocal parts he sang throughout with a "composer's voice," but one vastly expressive.

Grun and I withdrew finally, ostensibly to retire for the night, but in reality to adjourn to a friendly café near by, where the cheer and the coffee were good. When we finally went out into the night we saw a lurid glow in the distance, and I would have started at once for the fire had not Grun suggested that it was the sun. A dawn which gave such glorious promise was not to be missed, so we walked to the wooded hills on the outskirts of town, providing ourselves on the way with milk and rolls at an early bakery. The nightingale in the depth of the wood ceased her song, the cuckoos struck up, and the sun rose in splendor. Then we went home for breakfast, a morning of good sleep, and an afternoon of good work.

It is not to be supposed that Pfitzner was averse to the nocturnal life of the cafés. But the noises of the day were such that most of his composition had to be done by night. Besides, he was not a care-free student, or a vagabond poet, but a highly respectable citizen with a position in the Stern'schen Conservatorium. When we could get him out he was the brilliant star of the occasion, his thought as trenchant and flashing as the lightning strokes of his composition.

---

[4]Eugen d'Albert (1864–1932), composer and celebrated pianist was wedded to the singer Hermine Finck (misspelled as "Fink" in the original text) in 1895, the second of six marriages. The d'Albert composition to which Farwell refers was published, circa 1898, by Brockhaus as *Seejungfräulein*, Op. 15.

CHAPTER 7

1898
Study with Hans Pfitzner[1]

*H*ans Pfitzner is one of those geniuses who seems to carry about his neck a fate of hardship, of undue struggle, of insufficient appreciation. Born in Russia, of German and musical parentage, he became familiar with orchestral music at a very early age. Like the Japanese Hokusai,[2] the "old man mad about painting," Pfitzner became the young man mad about music. He left the ordinary means of success as a musician untouched, and endured many hardships, after his removal to Mainz, in order to throw himself wholly and ardently into composition. But the tragic part was that these musical works, when finished, were not of a sort either on the one hand to make a general appeal, or on the other to find their way quickly into the ranks of the serious accepted works of the day.

His one-act opera, *Der arme Heinrich*, made a startling and profound impression when first given at Mainz. Auditors were either won to intense admiration or baffled into rejection. There was no middle ground. The deadly earnestness of the work militated against its continuance or its ready acceptance by other opera houses. Moreover, the music was, to many, hopelessly incomprehensible. When it came to rehearsal, the *Vorspiel* seemed such an impossible jargon of wretched sounds that the players burst out laughing and could not proceed for the shaking of their sides. This prelude depicts the misery of the wounded knight of the "golden legend" upon which the opera is based, and it must be said, very successfully. The modern tendency to prefer inviolable dramatic truth to mere external beauty, Pfitzner pushes farther,

---

[1] From *MA* 9 (6 March 1909): 23.   [2] The painter and woodblock artist Katsushika Hokusai (1760–1849) has had a notable influence on Western artists.

perhaps, than any living composer—at least any living composer who refrains from the employment of extravagant and sensational means.

Grun's completion of the poem of *Die Rose vom Liebesgarten*, while I was still in Berlin, marked the occasion of a joyful celebration by the *Stammtisch* of which Pfitzner was a member, and I frequently a guest, as on this evening. We sat long in the café after dinner, sending *Ansichts-karten* [picture postcards] heralding the glad news to Humperdinck, d'Albert, Brockhaus, and other friends throughout Germany. But it was long before the music was finished, and longer still before the opera came to its first performance, which finally took place at Prague, I think in 1905.[3] As with the earlier opera, the new one made ardent friends and bitter enemies. Since returning to America I have seen an announcement that the production of *Die Rose* was being awaited in Berlin with *Spannung*—that is, with tense interest; but I believe that it has not yet been given there entire. It has, however, been heard in Vienna and Munich.

To study with Pfitzner was not an easy thing. Having such an appallingly definite knowledge of his own mind, and being so intensely absorbed in his own views of musical art, it was not easy for him to find the patience necessary to sympathize with the undevelopment or the different viewpoint of another. I would no sooner put out a poor little shoot of composition than he would lop it off here, or there, in a trice; and while his trenchantly expressed reasons for doing so have been of great value since, they were more than disconcerting at the time—they were annihilatory. It is an art to know how to study with Pfitzner, and I should lay down as its first principle: Finish a work before showing it to him. To disregard this rule is to fly in the face of Providence and nervous prostration. When I once showed him a theme upon which I intended to write a set of variations, he sat back as if he had been struck in the face. When he recovered from his astonishment and was able to speak, he exclaimed, "Ich *spanne* mich—ich *spanne* mich, den letzten Vari-ation zu sehen!" [I cannot *wait* to see the last variation!] "This theme," he continued, "is more complicated than you could dream of making the last variation!" Needless to say, I did not come far with the vari-ations. He was certainly right, and I was wrong—not to have first finished the variations. Pfitzner's nature, his heart, is kindly and simple as a child's; but his brain is a whirlwind full of lightning strokes. He is

---

[3]The opera was completed in 1900 and had its premiere in 1901 at Elberfeld (*New Grove Dictionary of Music and Musicians*, s. v. "Pfitzner, Hans").

more full of surprises than Pandora's box. I remember that once to demonstrate a particular point, he brought forward as a supreme model of perfect *form* in music—the orchestral prelude to *Die Walküre*, the last thing to which one would ordinarily look for such a purpose.

One exclamation of Pfitzner's in particular I have never forgotten, especially as I had at different times heard certain not over-great musicans and composers refer to Beethoven as a primitive whom any child nowadays could understand. It was in regard to this same matter of form. And here was Pfitzner, a *master*, who had staggered me with his overture to the *Fest auf Solhaug*,[4] and with great scenes from *Die Rose*, saying, "At *last*—at *last*, I understand Beethoven." He went on to say that he perceived now Beethoven's reasons for the duration of the different portions or episodes of his works, why this or that section is precisely as long as it is, and neither a bar shorter nor a bar longer. The deep impression which this remark of Pfitzner made, has never left me. It is something which facile musical impressionists of the present day might well ponder.

The Berlin days were rich with memorable experiences. Hugo Lederer, the sculptor who has since won fame and presumably fortune, was among Pfitzner's closest friends.[5] Many the beautiful spring evenings we sat out on the veranda back of his studio out at the *Thiergarten Bahnhof* [railroad station], or lay on the grass, watching the moon rise over the little river. One amusing incident of those days comes to mind. I had gone out to Lederer's alone, and together we started back to the Café Bauer. The drive through the *Thiergarten* seemed uncommonly long, and emerging from our absorbing conversation and taking our bearing for a few moments we found that the shrewd driver, taking advantage of his opportunity, was, and had been for half an hour, driving round and round in a circle and running up the meter to a figure more nearly resembling a Naperian logarithm than the price of a cab. The cabby that night had drinks not only for himself, but presumably for all of his friends.

The days in Berlin came to an end all too soon, and in early Summer I went back to Boppard for a two weeks' visit at Villa Humperdinck, and then to England for the Summer, where I promptly fell ill as the result of too strenuous a life in Berlin. After a summer of

---

[4]Pfitzner wrote, between 1889 and 1890, incidental music for a production of Ibsen's *Gildet på Solhang* (*Das Fest auf Solhaug*), which premiered in Mainz, November 1895.   [5]Among the sculptures of Austrian born Hugo Lederer (1871–1931) are the Bismarck Monument (1901–06) in Hamburg and the *Allegory of Labor* (1912) in Essen.

recovery and study of Italian, among the soft landscapes of Surrey, I started for Naples, where the Humperdincks were expecting to Winter, and where I was to continue studies. Arriving in Paris, I received word that circumstances prevented the Humperdincks from carrying out their plan, and finding myself in the reputed center of the world's art, I determined to spend the Winter there.

A study of strict counterpoint seemed to be my chief need, so I applied to that master of contrapuntal technic, Alexandre Guilmant, and began work.[6] Having little French, I decided to fraternize with the English-speaking population of the Latin Quarter, and thus the second of my two early dreams came true. For I had always wished and prayed for two experiences—student life in Germany, and the life of the "Quarter."

After the *gemüthlichkeit* of the Fatherland, it was lonely enough at first, even in the gayest of gay towns. I took lodgings at the Hotel Foyot, in the neighborhood of Balzac's early labors, and discovered on the Boulevard St. Germain a café bearing the, to me, attractive title "Au Bord du Rhin." At least I could get good sausage and sauerkraut there, and there I repaired daily for lunch, until I made friends, taking with me Schopenhauer's *Will in Nature*, and burying myself in its absorbing pages until three or four o'clock in the afternoon. Thus I became weaned from Germany, and gradually accustomed to the so different life of Paris.

The fascination of Paris proved to be as real as it is proverbial. Who can explain it—who describe! The very air of its obscurest alley is surcharged with a subtle and tantalizing essence which enthralls the dreams of day and the dreams of night. One wants to live there, and to die there—there, where the great traditions of history and of art, of science and of learning, of virtue and of vice, distil from the alembic of a mighty past and penetrate to the marrow of the sensibilities. Elsewhere one is burdened with aspirations. There, one is content merely to be—to be nothing, if one may but breathe this dream air which comes out of the shadowy past. It is poison, but it is potent.

---

[6]Alexandre Guilmant (1837–1911), noted organist at Ste. Trinité in Paris, taught at the Schola Cantorum which he helped to found in 1894.

1899

Paris[1]

As far as studies were concerned, the Winter in Paris was uneventful.
Twice a week I crossed the river, subjected my counterpoint excercises
to the critical scrutiny of Guilmant, and returned to the sacred precincts
of the Quarter.[2] Sometimes on Sunday mornings I went up to the organ
loft of Trinité, and listened to the master's marvelous improvisations
upon the organ. Guilmant's facility and perfection in this obsolescent
art is one of the musical wonders of the day. The choir and antiphonal
organ across the spaces of the church would give the stanzas of a
hymn—perhaps the Spanish Hymn;[3] and between each stanza Guilmant would improvise upon the theme, treating it each time in a

---

[1] From *MA* 9 (13 March 1909): 14.   [2] Farwell's remark that his winter of study in Paris was
"uneventful," along with several items of communication from Guilmant in AF Collection,
raise questions regarding how much time Farwell actually spent with his instructor of counterpoint. Three letters to Farwell from Guilmant dated 29 January, 13 February, and 9 March
1899 (in AF Collection), indicate that lessons were weekly, not twice-weekly as Farwell
states; a bill from Guilmant (dated 18 March 1899) for three lessons also indicates weekly
sessions. In the letter of 13 February, Guilmant offers to make up a missed lesson of the
previous week, and in the third letter we learn that Farwell has suspended lessons for reasons
of health. There is no indication as to whether or not the lessons resumed. If Farwell did
continue his studies, it would have been for only a few weeks, since he left Paris for London
before setting sail for home the last week of April, arriving in New York on the steamer
Menominee around 2 May (according to the diary of Farwell's mother, Sara Farwell [AF
Collection]). It is doubtful that Farwell began his study with Guilmant before December. He
appears to have been in England at least until late November 1897 (a letter from Hedwig
Humperdinck was sent to him there at that time; see p. 61, n. 6). That Farwell was in Paris by
the following month is indicated by a calling card from Guilmant dated "Dec. 1898" admitting
"Monsieur Farwell et sa famille" to the organ loft at Trinité. Possibly this was Farwell's initial
meeting with Guilmant, since he does not seem to be aware that Farwell is not with members
of his family. It would seem that Farwell had no more than ten weeks of study with Guilmant.
[3] Farwell is perhaps referring to the tune known as "Spanish Hymn" (or, sometimes,

different manner. First he would treat it in a lyrical, and again in a dramatic way; then he would modernize it, weaving into it the tints of the modern French school. But most remarkable of all were his contra-puntal improvisations. It is no great feat to let one chord fall into another, with occasional passing notes to heighten the musical interest. But to invent and carry forward simultaneously a number of involved contra-puntal parts, to lead them safely through the troubled waters of modu-lation and dissonance into the calm harbor of consonant harmony, all the while keeping close to the theme—this is a different matter. To watch Guilmant do this, and do it with a composure and sang-froid that was absolute, is a musical experience to remember.

Readers of that delightful book, *Trilby*, are likely to infer that the "good old days" of the Latin Quarter are past and gone.[4] For those for whom they are gone, they are undoubtedly gone. But while one gen-eration is concerning itself with retrospective joys, another, and a younger, is immersed in the flooding joy of very present youthful days, "good old days" as they may at some future time seem. Who cares about the particular past delights of his grandfather, when life holds enough for him at the moment to brim his own cup! Bohemia is ever young.

I fell in with a group of young Australian painters, who had quarters on and about the Boulevard Raspail. The Australian is a particularly desirable breed of Englishman. He has the culture and the manners of an English gentleman, but his rearing in the land of the "bush" has freed him from the insular conventionalities and peculiarities of that culture. In particular, I frequented the studio of Edwin C. Officer, for the truly poetic quality of whose landscapes I had much admiration.[5]

The days were filled with work, and we planned no amusement or

---

"Madrid") found in Protestant hymnals in America. The British composer Benjamin Carr (1769–1831), who emigrated to America in 1831, published a set of piano variations on the tune in 1825, referring to it as "an ancient Spanish melody." As a hymn tune it appeared in M. Burgoyne's *A Collection of Metrical Versions* (London, 1827). See William J. Reynolds, *A Survey of Christian Hymnody* (New York: Holt, Rinehart, & Winston, 1963), 254.   [4]*Trilby*, a novel by the English writer and illustrator George du Maurier (1834–96), was highly successful in the United States, being first serialized in *Harper's Magazine* during 1893. The novel's central character was a young artist's model in Paris and, as an early symbol of women's liberation, made an imprint on American popular culture as the name for such items as a restaurant, woman's shoe, bathing suit, and cigarette (Thomas Beer, *The Mauve Decade: American Life at the End of the Nineteenth Century* [New York: Alfred A. Knopf, 1926]: 48f.).
[5]The Australian-born landscape painter Edward Cairns Officer (1871–1921) studied at the

relaxation until the evening, although an afternoon concert by Saint-Saëns, Weingartner,[6] or other notable, would take us across the river. All the painters are fond of music. Evenings we would meet for a more jolly than substantial dinner at the American Club, or the "Hole in the Wall," or more frequently at the "Rougerie," which latter place our group eventually monopolized. There we often saw Tanner, the famous painter of negro origin, whose religious paintings burn with a deep sincerity. At that time one was already hung on the walls of the Luxembourg gallery.[7]

Dinner over, we drifted on the tide of the first inspiration which came to any of our number. Mere coffee and billiards it might be, if imagination ran low. Or, better, a cake raid—not an infrequent occurrence in this city of marvelous cakes—which consisted in seeking out one of those wonderful little Parisian cake shops, rushing in maenadic frenzy and devouring all the *savarins, religeuses, babas* and other deadly concoctions which we could seize from the window and the shelves. The reckoning for these devastations was sometimes a complicated matter. Ayton, a sculptor from St. Louis, carried off the honors for a cake appetite.[8] If after such a Gargantuan dessert we were still in marching order we would go swinging arm in arm down the dark crooked little streeets singing at the top of our voices, "O——h, how I love my A——da, Ada with the gol——den hair," until from under a dingy gaslight a gendarme, true to the traditions of French politeness, would call out, "*est-ce que vous avez fini* [Are you finished]?" The goal of such a rejuvenating evening would probably be the Café Pantheon,

Academie Julian while in Paris and exhibited at the Paris Salon. See Grant M. Waters, *Dictionary of British Artists Working 1900–1950*, 2 vols. (Eastbourne, England: Eastbourne Fine Art Publications, 1975–76), 1:40.   [6]Farwell appears to be referring to the Austrian conductor Felix Weingartner (1863–1942) who had recently taken a position at Munich, though he made innumerable visits as guest conductor elsewhere in Europe as well as in the United States.   [7]Henry Ossawa Tanner (1859–1937) had expatriated to France in 1891 after growing up in Philadelphia and studying with Thomas Eakins at the Pennsylvania Academy of the Fine Arts. Farwell would have seen Tanner just as the painter's star was rising and right after he had turned from themes portraying African American life to biblical subjects. Farwell refers to Tanner's *The Resurrection of Lazarus* that was purchased in 1897 by the French government for its Luxembourg Gallery, an honor that had gone only to a select few Americans, including James Abbott McNeil Whistler and John Singer Sargent (Sharon Kay Skeel, "A Black American in the Paris Salon," *American Heritage* 42 [February-March 1991]: 81).   [8]Charles William Ayton studied in Paris as well as with St. Gaudens in the United States. His works are exhibited in the St. Louis Art Museum. See *Who Was Who in American Art: Biographies of American Artists Active from 1898–1947*, ed. Peter H. Falk (Madison, CT: Sound View Press, 1985).

where, like the ghosts of the kings before Macbeth, there passed in panorama before us the types of the Quarter.

More Olympian were the evenings spent quietly, except for the occasional violence of our discussions, in Officer's friendly studio. On such occasions we ranged, not Paris streets, but the limitless fields of the imagination, and the broaching of whatsoever topic, be it Camembert cheese or the Bal Bullier, would inevitably lead us, through hours of absorbing discourse, to the consideration of some such subject as the origin of pre-Mosaic law or the constitution of the interplanetary ether.

Officer played the violin after a fashion, as did I, and another painter friend, Pshotta, from the United States, played viola.[9] Pshotta had one of the largest studios in the Quarter, the acoustics of which, for string music, were magnificent. We accordingly organized a string quartet, having got into communication with a 'cellist. We set Thursday afternoons for our meetings, which were a sort of combination of rehearsal and social gathering. The first one finished the 'cellist, who was proud, and could not consent to lower his dignity by rehearsing again with such amateurs as we. We filled his place with a young Englishman, less austere and unapproachable than his predecessor, and thereby inaugurated one of the pleasantest institutions of our Paris days.

Toward the end of the Winter—this was in 1899—I received word of the opportunity to give a musical lecture at the close of the current term at Cornell University. This was to have for its object a possible course of lectures to follow. Accordingly I chose for a subject Richard Wagner, especially since, in my association with James Grun in Berlin I had gone so deeply into his life, his art-methods and his theories. The thought of giving such a lecture was frightening in the extreme, in those days of profound ignorance of platform usage. I took therefore the most over-scrupulous care in its preparation. To accustom myself to the expression of Wagnerian principles, I brought up the subject *ad nauseam* upon every occasion, and when my friends finally rebelled and tabooed the topic I gave the lecture every afternoon at four o'clock to the ducks in the Luxembourg garden.

I had spent two years in Europe—two very rich years—meeting many interesting persons, seeing many beautiful sights, and learning

---

[9]Perhaps Farwell writes of a Charles Psotta, who studied in Paris with Laurens and Constant according to *Who Was Who in American Art*.

not only the technical matters which I went there to study, but much more which does not find its way into any text-book, and which comes only from contact with persons of fine nature and of deeper and wider experience than one's self. As to the advisability of studying abroad? Well, I am glad that I did not go earlier, or stay longer; I am glad that I did not go through one of the prolonged pedantic courses of the European schools, and that my studies, earnest as they were, were but a fraction of the best and most profitable of all my European experience.

And now I was to say good-bye to life in Europe; and despite the rapture of it all, I did not regret it. I longed for familiar faces, a familiar tongue, familiar dishes. I could smell baked beans across the Atlantic. But first the Channel must be braved. Some one told me that the real thing to do, to withstand properly this ever-terrifying experience, is to drink a quart of champagne and eat a hearty dinner just before embarking, which I accordingly did. The plan is not to be recommended. They will tell you that the passage from Dieppe to New Haven is longer than the other crossings, but that it is smoother. It is not so.

I spent several days in London, and the last English sight I remember is the figure of James Grun waving me a farewell from the wharf.

CHAPTER 9

1899–1900
Discovery of Indian Music[1]

Not in a dream, as Diana to Endymion, did the Goddess of Liberty first truly reveal herself to me, but in her proper person upon her pedestal in New York harbor, one bright Spring morning in 1899. The first glimpse of America after a first absence abroad, and that a prolonged one, is a sort of second birth. We knew America before, that is plain; but now we know her why and wherefore, and the knowledge comes like a draught of the elixir of life. We know now the burden of old-world traditions which the mind and soul of humankind have thrown off that we may breathe the air of a freer, if newer and cruder land. One realizes instinctively that an American must be a different kind of being from all others, and that he needs his own institutions, his own ideas, his own arts.

A singer friend of mine was recently advancing some ideas on the voice. A listener objected with the charge that the doctrine was revolutionary.

"Well," replied my friend, "it was a revolution that made the United States."

The tolerant reader who has thus far companioned me on these Wanderjahre will have perceived in their experiences thus far a certain aimlessness, a desultoriness, an absence of any goal other than the general study of music and the technic of musical composition. It was all intake during this period, all observation of things as they were, without thought of action toward adding any dubious iota to the universal complexity. If the tolerant reader persists and accompanies me upon the last part of this journey, "for which the first was made," he

---

[1]From *MA* 9 (20 March 1909): 26.

will become aware of the introduction of certain disturbing elements, unforeseen and unintended. If these elements rob the remainder of the narrative of some part of its inconsequentiality, they may compensate for the loss by adding some spice of adventures incident to the pursuit of an elusive and Protean idea. In spite of our most ardent longings for a care-free existence, responsibilities to persons, or to ideas, will creep in.

The Wagner lecture, which, with the aid of the Luxembourg garden ducks as auditors, I had contrived in Paris, I now delivered to more highly developed beings at Cornell University, and returned to Boston to spend the Summer in old haunts.

And now a day must be recorded, in that Summer of 1899—a day fraught with ominous and fateful significance—a day which was to throw the shadow of a far-reaching doom upon my subsequent course in life—was to drive me to distant corners of the land and involve me in endless wars and controversies. Upon the day in question, in search of American legendary lore for literary purposes, I went down to Bartlett's old Cornhill book shop, in Boston. A clerk put into my hand a little red-brown book with totem poles on the cover—*Indian Story and Song from North America*—by Alice C. Fletcher.[2] Could a beneficent stroke of apoplexy have ended my life at that moment all would have been well. But, as the "Trompeter" sings, "it was not so to be."[3]

I bought the book and looked it over carefully, as I thought. The legends impressed me much, for they took me back to the scenes of my early life in the West, and gave meaning to many vivid recollections of things seen, but little understood. The Indian, his life, customs, ro-

---

[2]That Fletcher's *Indian Story and Song from North America*—her first book—was published in 1900, calls into question Farwell's recollection of coming across it in the summer of 1899. Elsewhere, Farwell disagrees with himself, noting that he had discovered Fletcher's book in the fall of 1899 (Farwell, "The National Movement for American Music," *American Review of Reviews* 38 [1908]: 721). The ethnologist Alice Fletcher (1838–1923) had since 1883 devoted her life to the study of Native Americans of the Great Plains. In 1886 she joined the Peabody Museum of American Archaeology and Ethnology at Harvard University, being awarded the Thaw Fellowship created for her in 1891. In addition to her best known work, *Indian Story and Song from North America*, her publications include over forty monographs on Native Americans. Farwell was to befriend Fletcher sometime shortly after reading her book and remained ever respectful of her work. She in turn was encouraging to Farwell in his subsequent composing of works based on Indian melodies.   [3]Apparently a reference to *Der Trompeter von Säckingen*, an opera written in 1884 by Viktor Nessler (1841–1890), that was notably successful in Germany. It received its United States' premiere in 1886, followed by a production at the Metropolitan Opera the next year.

mance—in books or in real life—constitute a world in which every American boy revels at one time or another. I had lived in an Indian village on Lake Superior, seen the Sioux in strange sun dances, and heard the impressive speeches of the old priests. On my father's hunting expeditions we had been taken into the great woods by Indian guides; and I had seen Sitting Bull in captivity and had heard of his exploits. There was something almost uncannily impressive in it all, something unescapable. To this day I never see an Indian, especially an Indian on horseback, even in a "Wild West Show," without a tingling thrill coursing up my spine, such as I experience from the climaxes of certain music. Well—the legends in the little book brought all this back, but I could make nothing, at the time, of the music. It seemed to me unimportant, and, as the Germans say, *"nichtssagend"* [meaningless], a judgment which later I had most overwhelming reason to reverse.

The Fall took me to New York, where I spent the Winter teaching, going to Ithaca from time to time to give lectures on musical history at Cornell University, an outcome of the Spring effort in this direction.[4] The book of Indian songs lay by untouched. The one important gain which I remember from this Winter's experience is something which I learned from a painter. Certain of the remarkable canvases which I had the opportunity of seeing in the studio of Arthur B. Davies produced an effect upon me akin to much of Wagner's music.[5] I finally arrived at the fact that, *whether or not* they represented actual scenes from mythology, these particular pictures were mythic in expression—expressive of the feeling of a race, transcending mere individual thought or mood. This led to a discussion of the technic of the matter, and finally to an understanding of some hitherto baffling points in Wagner's music, and

---

[4]A newspaper clipping in AF Scrapbook, on which is noted by hand "Cornell [illegible] News, 1900," reports that Farwell will give a series of lectures on the history of music, covering music of antiquity to the Russian School, and finally, the music of America.   [5]About the time Farwell came to know Arthur Bowen Davies (1862–1928) the subject matter of this American painter, printmaker, and tapestry designer began to shift from Romantic landscapes to idyllic settings inhabited by nudes and mythological beings. Two works inspired by Davies' paintings—both for oboe and piano—were published in Farwell's Wa-Wan Press in 1903— the already mentioned *Landscape* by Farwell's friend Rudolph Gott (See p. 31, n. 6) and *To Morfydd* by Farwell (*WP* 2:59–61). Davies was one of the primary organizers of the historic Armory Show of 1913 which brought avant-garde works by Duchamp, Matisse, Picasso, and others to New York. Farwell must have seen Davies as a kindred revolutionist in trying to introduce a more progressive spirit into America's artistic life, for Farwell, who witnessed the exhibition, describes it as a revolt against the "arrogant academicism" that dominated painting in his time, and believed, with Davies, that art in New York would never again be the same (undated clipping of a letter to the editor by Farwell, *New York Sun*, AF Collection).

his means of attaining at times a super-personal—in short, a mythical expression. By this knowledge I was able to profit much in subsequent work with Indian music, which took me into mythical fields.

A more extended course of lectures on musical history for Cornell was now to be prepared for the following season. To prepare these I went, for the Summer, to visit the companion of my earlier European travels, whose Summer place lay on the wooded shores of Owasco Lake, in New York State.[6] Here I pitched a tent by the water's edge, under a clump of enormous willows, and set up a sort of rustic table at its doorway, so that I could sit and work, looking out over twelve miles of glassy or wind-rippled water. With a canoe pulled up on the beach and a few good books at hand, I felt like the monarch of a rich domain. Here I went carefully through the five volumes, in German, of Ambros's *History of Music*, that exhaustive and delightfully written work at which the writer spent a lifetime, and then got only as far as Palestrina![7] This work is no less spicy reading than the critical writings and the *Instrumentation* of Hector Berlioz.[8]

Thus with study, canoeing, swimming and music, the Summer sped past.

The Fall found me established in quarters at Ithaca. Here, in leisure hours, I picked up the book of Indian songs again. This time, however, I did not play these melodies over on the piano, with the elementary harmonies with which they had been provided.[9] Divesting them of these harmonies, I sang them, as actual songs, softly to myself, taking pains to carry out the rhythms exactly as indicated. Here was a revelation! The melodies took on a new meaning. Primitive as these songs were, each now appeared to be a distinct and concentrated musical idea, some extremely vivid in their expressiveness, and others less so. Even now, however, the full force of the rhythm, the rhythmic idea, of

---

[6]Farwell is referring once again to Thomas Mott Osborne (see p. 42, n. 15). Owasco Lake had inspired a piano suite in 1899, *Owasco Memories*, Op. 8, dedicated to Osborne and published in the Wa-Wan Press (1907; *WP* 4:167–79).   [7]Over thirty years after first reading *Geschichte der Musik* by the Austrian historian August Wilhelm Ambros (1816–1876), Farwell still considered it one of the few important works of its kind (Letter of Farwell to E. J. B. Walsh, 6 March 1936 [AF Collection]).   [8]The reference is to the *Treatise on Instrumentation and Orchestration*, published in 1844 by the French romantic composer Hector Berlioz (1803–69).   [9]The melodies in Fletcher's book had been harmonized by John Comfort Fillmore (1843–1898), who was one of the first musicians to be employed by late nineteenth-century enthnologists attempting to record Native American melodies. See James C. McNutt, "John Comfort Fillmore: A Student of Indian Music Reconsidered," *American Music* 2 (1984), 61–70.

these songs did not appear. But the material took a strong grip on me and I was impelled to develop something out of it. Had it not been for the vast background of poetic and imaginative mythical and legendary lore behind these primitive tunes, and had it not been for my early life among the scenes of these legends, this would probably not have been the case. But here was congenial poetic material, the substance of art, in inexhaustive quantity, and the spur of melodies twin-born with it, to set it moving in a musical direction. Nothing was more natural than to take advantage of the situation. In fact the combination of circumstances fairly called out for action of some kind.

As an experimental beginning in the use of this material I gave some of these melodies from *Indian Story and Song* the harmonic setting which their legendary or mythical significance seemed to demand.[10] The intention was to produce, in a small experimental way, sketches for piano which should be, in the first place, expressive of the legendary and mythical subject, and, in the second place, to employ in doing so, the native Indian melodies.

---

[10]Fillmore's approach to harmonizing Indian melodies used in Fletcher's book was far too much in the European tradition to suit Farwell, even though it appears that he looked into the fairly elaborate theory developed by Fillmore in this regard—a copy of Fillmore's *The Harmonic Structure of Indian Music* (New York: G. P. Putnam's Sons, 1899) is among Farwell's papers (AF Collection). Apparently, even Fletcher was not completely in agreement with Fillmore's ideas on harmonization, making it clear in her book that the songs were "harmonized by John C. Fillmore for interpretation on the piano" (Joan Mark, *A Stranger in Her Native Land: Alice Fletcher and the American Indians* [Lincoln: University of Nebraska Press, 1988], 385, n. 23). On the other hand, Fletcher wrote Farwell's mother that she was impressed by the depth of expression of Arthur's Indianist pieces (Alice Fletcher to Sara Farwell, 13 September 1903, AF Collection). In the introduction to the issue of the Wa-Wan Press which featured Farwell's first essays with Indian melodies, he said that he had tried to go beyond what was suggested by the melodic structure, consulting "the poetic nature of the particular legend or incident of which each song was the outcome" and focusing on the song's "specific religious significance" (*WP* 1:24).

1901
A Publishing Project in New York[1]

These early experiments with Indian melodies during the Ithaca sojourn were made merely for the pleasure of making them. No ulterior
thought intruded itself; no foreshadowing, even, of the interminable
discussion of "American folksongs" and their relation to American
music, which was to arise later. I had no other aim than to produce
something beautiful to the modern musical sense; even the thought of
doing something new and different never entered my head. I knew
vaguely of Dvořák's references to Indian songs, and I had heard Mac-
Dowell's *Indian Suite* years before. For the latter work, as music, I have
always had the greatest admiration, but have never regarded it as
particularly expressive of the Indian.[2]

At length a number of these simple sketches were finished, "The
Old Man's Love Song," "The Mother's Vow," "The Song of the
Deathless Voice," and others, after the melodies and legends in Miss
Fletcher's book.[3] I was naturally desirous of trying the effect of them
upon others. I therefore introduced two into one of my morning
lectures at Cornell, as a result of which I was asked to play them the

---

[1]From *MA* 9 (27 March 1909): 19.   [2]Farwell's statement regarding his first experiments with
Indian melodies is interesting in light of his later comments, both public and private, that he
was one of the first to heed Dvořák's advice that American composers look to Native and
African American music as sources for a truly national music. Antonín Dvořák (1841–1904)
had come to the United States to direct the National Conservatory in New York (1892–95).
While here, he encouraged American composers to look to their country's folk music as a
source of inspiration, a theme he takes up in his article "Music in America," published in
Harper's New Monthly Magazine (1895; reprinted in *Dvořák* in America: 1892-1895, ed. John
C. Tibbett [Portland, OR: Amadeus Press, 1993], 370-80).   [3]In all, ten of Farwell's sketches
were published as *American Indian Melodies*, Op. 11, in the first volume of instrumental music
of the Wa-Wan Press (see *WP* 1:21–51).

same afternoon at the house of one of the professors, for Mme. Modjeska, who was playing in Ithaca.[4]

My auditors thus far not only not rebelling at these tentative musical expressions, but seeming to find them both enjoyable and novel, I determined to put them to the test of a broader hearing. To this end I invited an audience up to Barnes Hall, on the campus, one evening, to hear all that I had made, together with an explanatory talk on the subject, touching upon some interesting phases of Indian mythology. This crude but successful affair was the basis of a more complete lecture-recital which I developed two years later, and by means of which I was able to travel to far corners of the land and meet many interesting people, gaining thus experiences most delightful and profitable. All of which goes to show that if a man minds his own business all goes well, critics or no critics.

Cornell University being apparently hopelessly remote from the establishment of a thoroughgoing modern university course in music, and the faculty having refused to grant a petition for expansion along these lines, I left there in the Spring of 1901 and went to Newton Center, Massachusetts, one of Boston's pleasant suburbs, the home of my parents since their removal, a year earlier, from Minnesota.

Not relishing a state of idleness, I engaged a small hall in Boston, started in to give a course of lectures on the "Relation of Art to the People," and got a few—a very few—of them out to hear me. I had a fine stock of ultra-idealistic ideas of which to unburden myself, and except for a young art student, I am certain that none of my auditors had any notion of what I was talking about.

Being commissioned to write a part-song for a prospective book for school choruses, I abandoned world-converting (though I am still convinced that my ideas were good). The new occupation took me to New York to meet Frederick Manley, who was literary editor of the new book, and who was engaged in looking up and sizing up composers, and assigning to them the poems most nearly fitted to their talents.[5]

---

[4]The Polish-born actress Helena Modjeska (1840–1909), emigrating to California in the 1870s, was greatly regarded in the United States for her Shakespearean roles, but also for contemporary dramas; her production of A Doll's House in 1883 was the first Ibsen play to be performed in this country.   [5]The "prospective book" that Farwell refers to is The Laurel Song Book: For Advanced Classes in Schools, Academies, Choral Societies, etc., ed. W. L. Tomlins (Boston: C. C. Birchard, 1901). The collection's Introduction must have been encouraging to Farwell, as it reflected nationalistic ideas just beginning to germinate for him: "the

Frederick Manley proved to be an Irish whirlwind. I called to see him at the St. Denis Hotel at nine in the morning. He told me that he had to see Edgar Stillman Kelley, and asked me to go with him. Kelley's address was at this time "the end of Flatbush avenue, Brooklyn," a far Cathay to which he had retired in order to compose the now famous Quintet.[6] First Manley had to smoke a cigar. Then he proposed walking down to the Brooklyn Bridge, as the morning was fine. On the way he casually stepped into a hat store, bought a silk hat and a gold-headed cane and ordered them sent back to the hotel. At the bridge he decided that it would be a bad plan to drop in on Kelley at lunch time, so we hunted up Old Tom's, a famous old down-town English chop house, since torn down, and had a leisurely lunch. Manley then had to buy a pipe, and almost came to blows with the touchy seller of pipes, who would not listen to Manley's praise of another make than his own. Then we started on what promised to be an infinite journey to the "end of Flatbush avenue." Jules Verne's *Trip to the Moon* was nothing to it. Let all composers seeking perfect seclusion dwell at the "end of Flatbush avenue."

We arrived there in the course of the day, dragged the composer from his retreat, transacted the necessary business and induced him

---

time is at hand for the fullest recognition of the writers [i. e., composers] of our own country, for a change of attitude in regard to the artists of America, and also for the realization of . . . a National Art." Perhaps Farwell, acknowledged for his "valuable advice" along with others, may have influenced this position, as well as the publisher's stated aim to empha- size works by contemporary American composers. The book pioneered the use of "art music" rather than folk songs which had heretofore predominated in school song books (Christine M. Ayars, *Contributions to the Art of Music in America by the Music Industries of Boston: 1640 to 1936* [New York: H. W. Wilson, 1937], 45). Farwell's specific contributions include three works. Two are adaptations of pieces in *American Indian Melodies*: "Song of Greeting" (entitled "The Old Man's Love Song" in the piano version) and "Song of the Ghost Dance." "Build Thee More Stately Mansions" is a work for four-part mixed voices on a text by Oliver Wendell Holmes. Farwell contributed a supplementary volume to the *Laurel Song Book*, published also by Birchard, in 1902, entitled *Songs and Music of To-Day with Special Reference to The Laurel Song Book*. Directed to educators, the book is primarily a discussion of the American composers who contributed to the 1901 anthology. Working on these publishing projects was clearly important to Farwell and may have been an impetus for the establishment of his own Wa-Wan Press, which came about in the fall of 1901.   [6]Farwell was to gain particularly high regard for Edgar Stillman Kelley (1857– 1944), believing that he was "the first composer to use the post-Wagnerian harmonic vocabulary without the result sounding like Wagner" (*AM*, 370). Kelly's strong nationalis- tic beliefs regarding music that were expressed in a number of his published articles would also have gained Farwell's respect. The Quintet alluded to is Kelley's Op. 20, completed in 1901 and revised in 1907.

Edgar
Stillman Kelley

to play some of the Quintet. He played the second movement for us, with its far-away dream-bells and still, moonlit waters. I have since learned to know the work on its proper instruments, strings and piano, and do not wonder at the success which it has made in Germany.

Marching by short stages, bivouacking along the way—with puffs at the new pipe—and taking remote trolleys, Manley and I finally reached civilization again on the same night. By this time we had become good friends, and instead of the two days which I had expected to spend in New York I remained there two months.[7]

---

[7]Manley provided texts for seven musical settings in the *Laurel Song Book*, including Farwell's two Indianist songs. In addition to Manley's contribution to the song collection, he produced

These were memorable months. First, because we led an ideal life, where work in our chosen arts was providing our living; and, second, because I was meeting all the composers within a reasonable radius of Manhattan. Besides Kelley, there were Henry Hadley, Harvey Worthington Loomis, Maurice Arnold, Horatio Parker, Victor Louis Saar, David Stanley Smith, Henry Holden Huss and others, with some of whom we were in constant contact during this period.[8] There was work for us all. These were Elysian days. We lived in the cafés, a congenial group of us, and lived well. Manley's poetic fervor stimulated us all to work. He himself wrote many of the poems which he dealt out to us, and we wrote the songs, in cafés, hotel corridors—anywhere, with the occasional help of any friendly piano which we could press into the service. It was a joyous, creative life of companionship, artistic effort and emulation and freedom from care—a veritable little Renaissance. It was nothing less than a revelation to see how greatly our

---

several other works also published by Birchard, including *A Monkey's Tail, and Other Poems of Childhood* (1915) and, with Harvey Worthington Loomis, an English language edition of Gounod's *Faust* (c. 1921). Little further information has been uncovered on this colorful figure who was highly valued by Farwell for his inspiration in directing this publishing venture. Manley seems to have been a part of Farwell's circle of acqaintances in Boston during the first decade, for he was one of the founding members of the American Music Society there, for which Farwell was music director (this is noted on a printed prospectus of the Society in AF Collection). For more on Farwell's relation to the organization, see p. 128f.   [8]Henry Hadley (1871–1937), like Farwell, was a strong advocate for American music, and he, too, had studied with Chadwick in Boston. At the time, he was teaching at St. Paul's School, Garden City, New York. After study with Dvořák at the National Conservatory in New York, Harvey Worthington Loomis (1865–1930) devoted himself to composition. Loomis was also interested in Native American music and had published with the Wa-Wan Press his two-part collection *Lyrics of the Red-Man*, Op. 76 (WP 2:245–57). Altogether, ten of Loomis's works were published by the Press between 1902 and 1907. Maurice Arnold (1865–1937) was hired by Dvořák in 1894 to teach composition at the National Conservatory. Dvořák had earlier in the year heard a performance of Arnold's *American Plantation Dances* and was interested in the potential the work showed for making use of African American melodies (*Baker's Biographical Dictionary of Musicians*, fourth ed., s. v., "Arnold, Maurice"). One of the distinguished members of the so-called "Second New England School" of composers, Horatio Parker (1863–1919) had been Dean of the School of Music at Yale University since 1894. The Dutch American teacher and composer Louis Victor Saar (1868–1937)—as his name appears in most references—was hired as an accompanist at the Metropolitan Opera in 1894; in these early New York years, he also taught at the National Conservatory and the College of Music. The youngest member of the group cited by Farwell, David Stanley Smith (1877–1949), had recently completed a degree at Yale, working under Parker. He was soon to embark for a year of study in Germany before taking a post at his alma mater where he would eventually succeed Parker as Dean in 1920. Henry Holden Huss (1862–1953), who settled in New York after returning from study abroad in 1885, gained equal acclaim as a pianist and composer.

productiveness increased under these ideal conditions. Spirit was wooed from its customary depths to the surface, and creation became an immediate and unstrained act. One does not wonder that great art works have been produced by epochs when such conditions have prevailed for years throughout whole cities and nations. As the demand rises and persists, the spirit rises to meet it.

The heat of Summer finally dispersed our little group, but not before we had had the satisfaction of realizing in some measure an ideal circumstance, or before I had seen, in a flash, that the creative musical impulse was awake and ready in America.

1901

"An Ideal Enterprise"[1]

New York City presents a gay and cheerful aspect in the Spring. A bit of green appears here and there even in the most unpromising places; femininity decks itself out in Spring attire, and happy children throng the parks. The city seemed a good place to stay in, and not foreseeing the deadly heat wave that was to devastate it in that Summer of 1901, I decided to stay in New York. Everybody I knew would be going away, and at least there would be quiet for uninterrupted work.

During the period in which I had been thrown into association with the composers, in the preparation of the book of school songs, I had spent much time with them going over their other compositions. These were for the most part the men of the younger generation, whose work was not yet broadly known. I was determined to know exactly where we had got to in musical composition in the United States, to know what influences were at work and what tendencies were show-ing themselves.

The results of this cruise of discovery were to me profoundly interesting. My first sensation was astonishment at the great amount of original, imaginative, characteristic work by American composers, in manuscript, and wholly unknown. My astonishment was increased when I learned that the publishers would have none of this music. Practically without exception, the composers, one and all, told me that the publishers would take their insignificant and lighter works, but had no use for the music in which they had suc-ceeded in expressing their individuality, or into which they had put their best work and thought.

---

[1]From *MA* 9 (3 April 1909): 19.

The Summer now came on, and the disappearance of my friends one by one gave me time to think. And certainly all of my recent experiences had given me food for thought—an abundant meal of it. I had met many composers; I had seen the creative impulse alive and at work, and I had seen many interesting, original, and neglected compositions in the obscurity of manuscript. The nature of these compositions was such as to make me feel that we were, nationally, on the eve of a signal extension of the musical imagination, into the broadest possible sense, and—excepting a number of strong individual creators whom the country had already produced—that the epoch of national assimilation was about to close and the epoch of output, of original creation, was to begin.

The necessity now arose of making plans for the Fall, of engaging in some definite work. In the long hours that I had to myself in that torrid and death-dealing Summer in New York City, I thought the matter over from every possible point of view.[2] The life of teaching usually entered upon by the young musicians returning from European study appeared, on investigation, anything but attractive to me. It seeemed only in the rarest instances to lead out to any broad fulfillment or goal of life. As a player, either of the violin or the piano, I never had any serious ambition. What, then, was the alternative? Evidently there must be a revolution from the usual courses.

There was still just one thing that seemed to me the reason, the goal, the core, the very grail of life—and that was musical composition. Whether mine or anybody's else, it mattered not, so long as it was beautiful. Nothing seemed worth undertaking that did not aim straight for that, for its accomplishment, its advancement. The problem was to find an occupation which, practical in itself, would lead to this ideal end.

The ends for which William Morris aimed, and the ideals presented by him, had always very strongly attracted me.[3] To have an art, and

[2]It should be noted that it was Farwell's good fortune to acquire in this period, as he had acquired before going to Europe, the financial support of a benefactor. In a letter to the composer Arne Oldberg from about a decade later, Farwell speaks of being "staked" in his early years in New York by a Mr. Olbrig, "a rich holder of Standard Oil stock and great supporter of arts" (Farwell to Arne Oldberg, 3 January 1910, AO Collection).   [3]The ideals of the English artist, poet, and socialist William Morris (1834–96) were frequently lauded by Farwell in his writings (see, for example, "Considerations," [WP 4:30] and "Society and American Music," p. 191 of the present collection). Morris's Kelmscott Press established at his estate in 1891 was an impetus not only for Farwell's Wa-Wan Press, but also for the latter's private printing of his compositions through lithograhic process in the 1930s.

side by side with it a practical occupation, whether closely related to it, as in Morris's own case or that of William Blake, or remote, as in the case of the shoemaker-poet, Sachs,[4] or the lensmaker-philosopher, Spinoza—this seemed a desirable arrangement of the compromise necessary to those whose desires and visions make them feel like strangers in this world. I had been a printer long before the beginning of these Wanderjahre.[5] There was a thought! I followed it up as rapidly as my wits would allow, and it led to this: I would print the compositions which I had seen; I would take precisely the opposite view from that of the publishers, and select music which was the best art that the composers could produce, regardless of all other considerations; and I would include the printing of my developments of Indian music, which, upon repeated trial, were giving evidence of an increasingly favorable reception. This plan seemed practicable, however ideal in intent. At least it aimed straight in the direction in which I wished to go. Here again, in leaving the beaten path, I was innocent of the tribulations which I was inviting upon myself, and here again a cruel Providence refrained from granting me a timely end.

In the Fall I went over to discuss the matter with Edgar Stillman Kelley, who was occupying the chair of music at Yale during Dr. Parker's sabbatical year. I obtained from him the manuscripts of his two great songs, "Israfel" and "Eldorado," upon the poems by Poe. These songs had been in existence for ten years. The first five years, Mr. Kelley told me, he could not get the publishers to take them, and the second five years he would not let them have them. Mr. Kelley was much interested in my plan, and I decided to make a start with those two songs and a number of the little sketches on Indian themes which I had made while in Ithaca.[6]

---

[4]See p. 37, n. 7.   [5]As a boy, Farwell, with the help of a friend, built a workable printing press (Evelyn Davis Culbertson, *He Heard America Singing: Arthur Farwell: Composer and Crusading Music Educator* [Metuchen, NJ: Scarecrow Press, 1992], 10).   [6]Kelley's "Israfel" and "Eldorado" were published in the premiere volume of the Wa-Wan Press offerings in 1901 (see *WP* 1:1–19). Farwell was grateful to have the advice and support from Kelley, who, fifteen years older and more experienced, was the only composer of those published by the Wa-Wan Press who enjoyed some status—he had been elected in 1898 to the National Institute of Arts and Letters. Kelley was, however, apparently wary about the "cryptic name" chosen for the press, though Farwell was not to be dissuaded, feeling that "the moment demanded a striking and curiosity-provoking title" (Farwell, "Pioneering for American Music," *Modern Music* 12 [1935]: 118). In any case, Kelley felt indebted to Farwell, writing in 1941 to Edward Waters: "The Wa-Wan Press exerted a great influence on my career and I am most happy to record my appreciation of Arthur Farwell's rare helpfulness to myself and other American composers" (Edward N. Waters, "The Wa-Wan Press: An Adventure in Musical Idealism," *A Birthday Offering to Carl Engel*, ed. Gustave Reese [New York: G. Schirmer, 1943]: 231).

LYRICS·OF·THE·RED·MAN
BY·HARVEY·WORTHINGTON·LOOMIS

THE·WA-WAN
SERIES·OF·AMER
ICAN·COMPOSITION·
VOLUME·2·NUMB
ER·2·STRING·QV
ARTER·INSTRUME
NTAL·PART·THE·WA-
WAN·PRESS·NEWT
N·CENTER·MASS·1903

From Harvey Worthington Loomis's *Lyrics of the Red Man*, issued by the
Wa-Wan Press, 1903; cover design by American architect Frank Chouteau
Brown (1876-1947) after an original drawing by Ohetowit, a Kiowa chief

Newton Center, Mass., seemed the logical place to begin this
work, for wherever my wanderings might take me, I should have a
permanent home there with my parents, as a center to work out from
and to return to. Besides, it was a part of my plan that my father should
actively engage in this work with me. I accordingly went over to Boston and busied myself studying up the matter of music lithography,
consulting with the proprietor of lithographic presses in Boston. The
shop of John Temperley, printer, of Newton Center, became the central
point of our activities.

What to call the youngster thus launched now became the question. I was so filled with enthusiasm over the Indian music at that time
(and still am, though not so greatly to the exclusion of other things) that

nothing but an Indian name would do. Had I foreseen at that time that such name would mislead people as to the broadly American aims of my undertaking, I would probably have chosen otherwise. Many of the Indian melodies which I had been studying and developing were a part of the great Wa-Wan ceremony of the Omahas. The name Wa-Wan may be translated "to sing to some one." In the ceremony the emblematic pipes of peace were presented by a man of one tribe or gens to a man of another, an important relationship being thus established between them. The ceremony, in which the whole village shared to greater or less extent, lasted five days. Its object was the bringing about of cordial and peaceful relations, and its entire significance was expressed through song. Nothing seemed more appropriate to my intentions than this, and I accordingly christened my child "The Wa-Wan Press."

It was a busy Winter, spent between Newton Center and New York, in which latter place I had taken a little studio up near the sky. There was an infinite amount of preparing and mailing announcements. It was my plan to appeal at first only to those persons whom there would be reason to suppose would be truly interested. At that time compositions were brought out in the form of a quarterly series, in a chaste severity of style contrasting with the usual styles of the time.

At this time of need the movement was to find a strong ally in the person of Henry Gilbert. I first met this man of militant musical originality in the early months of 1902. At that time he existed in an obscurity out of which he was later brought by his setting of Stevenson's "Pirate Song," "Fifteen Men on a Dead Man's Chest," so delectably sung by David Bispham to the delight of many audiences throughout the United States.[7]

---

[7]Gilbert's "Pirate Song" was published by the Wa-Wan Press (*WP* 1:138–41) along with fourteen other of his works between 1902 and 1910. The Philadelphia-born baritone David Bispham (1857–1921) sang at the Metropolitan Opera from 1896 to 1903, as well as in European houses. He was successful also as a recitalist, committed to programs of works solely in English and a great promoter of songs by American composers.

CHAPTER 12

1902—1903
Henry F. Gilbert[1]

My meeting with Henry Gilbert took place shortly after an episode in his life which was characteristic of the man, and at the same time worth recording for itself. For years Gilbert had inhabited that mid-world which lies between the composing of music on the one hand and the earning of one's living on the other. His plan, and it has elements to recommend it, was periodically to utterly forget music long enough to earn sufficient money, no matter how, to enable him to utterly forget business. Having succeeded in this, he would retire, Thoreau-like, to some Walden of his choice, and there await the visitations of the goddess. A certain acquaintance of Gilbert, a man of music, eminently practical and successful, once said of him: "Henry is a queer fellow; he no sooner gets a good job somewhere, and you think he's getting established finely, than he goes and throws it up."

One of these periods of material industry, however, lasted for a period of four years. Gilbert had a notion that he wanted to go to Paris and hear one or two of the important works of the modern French school, especially Charpentier's opera *Louise*, which could not be heard in this country. Accordingly, he held his place in a music lithographing establishment until he was in command of the necessary funds. Paris was visited for two weeks, *Louise* was heard, and Gilbert returned. This spurred him to work, and he sought seclusion in a barn in Quincy, Mass. In this he acquired the privilege of living by taking care of a horse and a cow, its only other occupants. With a piano moved into an unused stall, a soap-box for a piano stool and an apple barrel with a board across it for a table, he was established in the finest imaginable

[1] From *MA* 9 (10 April 1909): 21.

Henry F. Gilbert

circumstances for composition. As he had experienced difficulty in pleasing others with his music, he now determined to take the other tack, and compose something which should at least please himself, regardless of what others would think of it. The product of this effort was a scene for soprano upon a text chosen by Gilbert from Flaubert's *Salammbô*—the scene where the princess invokes the moon-goddess Tänith.

About this time the cow died (presumably not as a consequence of this composition), and the horse was sent off to pasture. It now became almost too lonesome in the barn even for one in search of seclusion. Before this exodus, when he woke up in the night and heard some strange sound, Gilbert said, it was attributable to his fellow lodgers; but after their departure, when he heard such sounds in the night, Heaven knew from what awful thing they might proceed.

Gilbert was living in his native town, Somerville, Mass., some months after this episode, when he brought me the manuscript of *Salammbô's Invocation*. He played it through in his characteristic unapologetic manner, before several of us who were critically inclined. All were agreed upon the high and unique order of imagination which the work showed, and together with a *Negro Episode* on slave-song rhythms, it was the first work by Gilbert to appear in the Wa-Wan Press.[2]

The appearance of Gilbert at this juncture was very fortuitous. He felt strongly the need of the movement which I had undertaken, and had the time and will to work for it. Without his presence on the scene of action, I should not have been able to make the long trips to the Far West which occupied a large portion of the following few years. And as a revolutionist Gilbert fairly outdid me. He opposed on principle nearly everything in the existing order of civilization.[3]

We were busy as beavers through the Summer of 1902[4] and the following Winter. In the Fall we organized a *Stammtisch*, the members of which met Saturday evening in a café in Boston. These gatherings are among the pleasantest recollections of these years. Among the musicians who thus foregathered were John Marshall, now occupying the chair of music at Boston University; Alfred de Voto; Felix Fox; Arthur Hadley, 'cellist, and brother of Henry Hadley, the composer;

---

[2]*Salammbô's Invocation to Tänith* and *Negro Episode* are reprinted in *WP* 1:100–05 and 114–16, respectively. In all, sixteen works of Gilbert were to be published by Wa-Wan between 1902 and 1909.   [3]Henry Gilbert (1868–1928) and Farwell shared several passions. They both had a great interest in folk music as a source of creating a national style. Gilbert's interest in Native American music resulted in, among other things, transcribing Indian melodies from recordings for volumes VI-VIII of Edward S. Curtis's the *North American Indian* which were published in 1911. In the same year Gilbert provided orchestral music to accompany a lecture-presentation of Curtis's Indian photographs at Carnegie Hall, entitled "The Story of a Vanishing Race." Farwell saw Gilbert as one of the first composers to vitalize American art music through his "identification . . . with the spirit of the American Folk" ("The Struggle Toward a National Music," *North American Review* 186 [1907]: 569). Gilbert and Farwell had a mutual love for Wagner, but it was Gilbert who introduced Farwell to the music of recent French and Russian composers, thus "broadening . . . my own musical vision and experience" (Farwell to Helen Gilbert, 3 June 1928, Henry F. B. Gilbert Papers: MSS 35, Beinecke Rare Book and Manuscript Library, Yale University). Farwell claimed that Gilbert was the first American composer to "reveal a genuine and significant influence from the new French school in America" (Letter of Farwell to Miss Burdick, 6 February 1934, AF Collection). Farwell's lengthiest assessment of Gilbert appears in two issues of the *Wa-Wan Press Monthly* (*WP* 4:119–21 and 143–44). For another personal view of Gilbert, this one by Olin Downes, a mutual friend of Gilbert and Farwell, see "Henry Gilbert: Nonconformist," *A Birthday Offering to Carl Engel*, ed. Gustave Reese (New York: G. Schirmer, 1943): 88–94.   [4]In the original text "1892" is given erroneously.

Alvah G. Salmon, alias "Uncle Rimsky," because of his Russian affili-
ations; Percy Atherton, composer of many songs and larger works;
and, of course, Henry Gilbert, with the corncob pipe which levied as
many claims on his attention and affection as did the ass of Sancho
Panza upon its master. Architecture, romance languages, and other
professions were represented. Thus we relaxed weekly, compared
notes, and exchanged views, which gave us all fresh inspiration to
battle with the problems of the week to come.[5]

With the Spring came a consuming *Wanderlust*. This was
prompted by several things. First of all, I had long had an ardent desire
to pass the Minnesota boundaries of my early life, and to see California,
the Pacific Coast, and the Far West generally. Second, I wanted to
know the musical conditions of the whole country at first hand, to
know whither we were trending, and what the future might seem to
promise of national musical development. And last, I had now completed, among other things, a number of compositions based upon the
Indian melodies and legends, and wanted to give them a broad trial
before all kinds of audiences. Also, I wanted to get out into the Indian
country, and hear the Indians sing. And, beyond all this, I now first had
the means of making the journey. And this means was, curiously
enough, the very thing disparaged by such critics as had noticed it, and
from continuance in which some of my conservative friends and ac-
quaintances were already laboring to dissuade me, namely—the Indian
music. It was like laboring to dissuade a starving man from eating bread
because it wasn't cake. I had discovered that recitals of the Indians
compositions, accompanied by some account of their relation to Indian
myth and legend, were a salable commodity. The thought that, as a
minstrel, I could travel where I pleased was exhilarating. As Wieland
the Smith, lamed by the tyrant, forged himself wings to fly away, so I

---

[5]See p. 36, n. 6, regarding John Marshall. Alfred DeVoto (d. 1933) taught at the New England
Conservatory and was for several years official pianist of the Boston Symphony Orchestra.
The German-born Felix Fox (1876-1947) settled in Boston in 1897 as a piano teacher,
establishing with Carlo Buonamaici a piano school in 1898 that gained considerable reputation. Arthur Hadley was a cellist with the same orchestra from 1904 to 1912. Alvah Glover
Salmon (1868–1917) was a pianist who introduced many new Russian works to American
audiences. Salmon, who studied with Alexander Glazunov in St. Petersburg, lectured and
wrote on Slavonic music, and had collected an extensive library of Russian music, both
published scores (some 3,000 volumes!) and autograph manuscripts (*Baker's Biographical
Dictionary of Musicians*, fourth ed., s. v., "Salmon, Alvah"). Percy Lee Atherton (1871–1944)
graduated from Harvard the same year Farwell finished at MIT. Following this was extensive
study in Europe, from which he returned not too long before joining Farwell's group.

realized that in the making of this Indian music I had forged the wings by which I could fly out of my Eastern prison.

At this time I was making an active propaganda for the "American folksong idea," the idea touched upon earlier by certain American composers, notably George W. Chadwick and Edward MacDowell, and broadly proposed by Antonín Dvořák. This mass of characteristic and poetic folksong peculiar to the soil of America—Indian, negro, cowboy, Spanish-Californian and other varieties—appeared to me to be a vast mine of valuable musical ore, to be wrought into music of new types and colors. In view of the Teutonic domination in America, it presented what, it seemed to me, might be called the "margin of the unGerman."[6] My enthusiasm for this new material and new opportunity, however, did not diminish my belief in a spontaneous "American music" arising directly as a free and American development of the music of Europe. I supported this belief by printing and by composing much music having no relation to American folksongs. But the element of novelty and sensation in the "Indian music" outweighed all else that I could do. I had "nailed myself to the cross," as a certain eminent publisher put it to me, and in sheer despair I have long since ceased to bother much about explaining myself to those persons who insist on having me the proclaimer of the idea that "Indian songs are the basis of American music."

A photograph of the Grand Canyon of Arizona, which I chanced to see, now acutely whetted my appetite for the West, and early in the Summer of 1903 I began active preparations for an extended tour of minstrelsy out into "God's country."

---

[6]Farwell treats the matter of developing a uniquely American music and first uses his phrase "the margin of the unGerman" in an extensive introduction to the September 1903 issue of the Wa-Wan Press (*WP* 2:64–67).

1903
The First Trip West[1]

To lay the foundations of the projected tour, I spent the Summer of 1903 in bombarding the West with letters announcing a lecture-recital, "Music and Myth of the American Indians." A number of experiences with audiences had enabled me to get the material to be presented into the best form.[2] This labor of correspondence was interrupted only by a short visit to the home of John Beach, at Gloversville, N. Y., and a flying trip to the Adirondacks. I had first met Beach and seen his compositions—then all in manuscript—during the previous Summer, and had found him a welcome addition to the ranks of workers in the good cause.[3]

The response to my correspondence was prompt and vigorous, and by Fall I had arranged a series of engagements from Boston to

[1]From *MA* 9 (17 April 1909): 21, 31.   [2]Information pertaining to Farwell's lectures on Indian music made before his western tours is provided by several items in AF Scrapbook. A program from a meeting of the International Congress of Americanists held at the American Museum of Natural History, New York, 20–25 October 1902, lists Farwell's talk "American Indian Music; Ethnic and Artistic Significance"; an article from the *New York Herald* of 24 October indicates the success of the presentation and that "the German members [of the the Congress] took particular interest in Mr. Farwell's views and suggestions." The *Boston Transcript*, 27 April 1901, notes that Farwell's paper for the American Folklore Society was "one of the most remarkable" of its kind. H. E. Krehbiel, in an article in the *New York Tribune*, 31 August 1902, cites additional lectures of Farwell, including "Dr. Leipziger's courses for the people, New York City; Harvard Musical Association, Boston; Social Service League (Dr. Everett Hale's Church), Boston; Greenacre, Me.; . . . Cambridge Folk Lore Society; 20th-Century Club, Brooklyn; New York State Music Teachers Association, Newburgh on the Hudson; [and] Chromatic Club, Boston."   [3]John Parsons Beach (1877–1953) was teaching piano at Northwestern Conservatory in Minneapolis at the time Farwell first knew him, though later in the decade he taught in Boston. Beach and Henry Gilbert were among Farwell's staunch supporters in these early Wa-Wan years. In a typical burst of optimism while on his first western tour, Farwell wrote Beach of what the three of them could accomplish for American music if they were to work together: "Two ideas, concerning you,

San Francisco. Starting in September, and making a number of stops along the way, I arrived at my old home in Minnesota in all the golden glory of an Indian Summer in the Middle West.[4] I took the first possible moment to revisit old haunts, Fort Snelling on the high bluff, standing guard at the junction of the Minnesota and the Mississippi rivers; Minnehaha Falls, and the Indian Mounds, whose builders, from what is now Dayton's Bluff, overlooked so splendid a stretch of old Mississippi's waters.

How vastly these great scenes exceed in space and grandeur anything which may be witnessed upon the Rhine! I had never realized this before this return to them. Painters say that the last thing which observers remember of a picture is its size, and this may be true in some degree of natural scenes as well. I remember that in Switzerland I could never remember just how big the Jungfrau was without looking again at her towering snowy crest. But these great Western spaces of river and bluff, wood and plain, spread out to far horizons under the Indian Summer's golden haze, and painted with the deep red dyes of the Autumn oaks, the yellow of stubble and stacked straw, and the gentle brown of fields and distant forest edges—what scenes these are to make one breathe deep—to invite the soul to expand and rejoice! What great unwritten music lingers about these dreaming lands!

In Chicago I fell in with the composer Louis Campbell-Tipton, and made the acquaintance of his manuscript of his *Sonata Heroic*, which I lost no time in sending back to my press in the East. Campbell-Tipton is a tone painter in gorgeous and modern, if not in ultra-modern, colors; and his works, interpreted by some of the best artists of the time, are finding ever a wider hearing.[5]

---

seem to stay with me—that we should be more closely associated,—and that your work should be more widely known. Long live the American renaissance! If only Gilbert and you and I could live near together for a year so that more things would develop through friction—we could move the United States several inches along the map" (Farwell to John Parsons Beach, 30 January [1904], John Parsons Beach Collection, New York Public Library at Lincoln Center). Altogether, thirteen works of Beach were published by Wa-Wan, mainly songs and piano selections.

[4]Newspaper clippings, programs, and other items in Farwell's scrapbook fill in details of the itinerary that are omitted from his account. He reached the Minneapolis area in late October, with a lecture in that city on the twenty-ninth and one in St. Paul on 4 November. One of his first talks on the tour appears to have taken place in Auburn, New York, the home of his friend Thomas Mott Osborne, probably on 17 October. As he moved West, there followed talks in Rochester (20 October) and in Erie, Pennsylvania (23 October).   [5]Louis Campbell-Tipton (1877–1921) taught theory and composition at Chicago Musical College, 1901–04, before

Louis
Campbell-Tipton

Another American composer, Ernest R. Kroeger, made my stay in St. Louis a pleasant one. In the midst of a blizzard which, even as a Minnesotan, I shall not easily forget, he took me out to the Exposition grounds, where the great buildings were in process of construction for the following year. It was at this exposition that Mr. Kroeger distinguished himself as Master of Programs, showing great judgment in his selection and arrangements of works presented. Mr. Kroeger's compositions, both orchestral and in the smaller forms, have been broadly heard, and the History of Music in America will write him down as one who has done an incalculable amount of good work in

moving to Paris where he stayed for the remainder of his life. His *Sonata Heroic* (*WP* 2:123–145) is commended by William T. Upton ("Our Musical Expatriates," *Musical Quarterly* 14 [1928]: 148), while one reviewer "in many respects" prefers Campbell-Tipton's later impressionistic works to those of Debussy (see Louis C. Elson, "American Composers Since 1900" in Rupert Hughes, *American Composers* [New York: Page, 1914], 539). In addition to the sonata, Campbell-Tipton's *Four Sea Lyrics* were published by Wa-Wan.

raising and maintaining the standards of music throughout a very large part of the country.[6] Once leaving the hospitable homes and the immigrant-packed station of Kansas City, and striking out across the plains, I felt that I was really beginning to get westward. A stop among delightful people in the little town of Kinsley[7] will be long remembered. It was there that a stray cowpuncher, in search of a lively time, read the legend "American Indians" on a placard in the village street announcing my lecture-recital, and determined to take it in. He paid his quarter without asking any questions, like a good sport, and went into the little church where the event was about to begin. Leaning over the back of a pew, he timidly touched a man in the audience on the shoulder and said, "Say, is dis a show?" Being assured that it was, he took a seat and attended carefully; but after waiting vainly for half an hour for the scalping, or at least a little shooting to begin, he slid quietly out into the night in search of more thrilling adventures.

After the breadth of Kansas plains came the clear heights of Colorado, and after several delightful days in Denver I set out with eager expectancy, for the Grand Canyon of Arizona.[8] An incident of this departure gave me my first real gripping sensation of the enormous extent of the western part of our land. Shortly before eight o'clock in the evening, the time of my departure from Denver, I stepped up to the window to buy my ticket over the Santa Fe to the Canyon. I knew vaguely that the Canyon was somewhere between Denver and the Pacific, and that I should arrive there in the evening. Denver I had always regarded as being well across the continent. But it took me a

---

[6] According to newspaper clippings in the scrapbook, before reaching St. Louis, Farwell's tour took him eastward from Chicago for engagements in Fort Wayne, Indiana (7 November), Cincinnati (29 November), Columbus (30 November), and Cleveland (3 December). Farwell is referring to the Louisiana Purchase Exposition held in St. Louis from 30 April to 1 December 1904, that marked the centenary of the historic event. Ernest Richard Kroeger (1862–1934) received his musical education in St. Louis and became a key figure in the musical life of the city as a teacher, organist, and composer. Elsewhere, Farwell credits Kroeger with playing an important part in building the musical life of the Midwest (see *AM*, 380). The Wa-Wan Press published Kroeger's song cycle *Memory* Op. 66.   [7] Farwell spoke in Kinsley ("Kingsley" was given in the original text), Kansas on 17 December. A clipping from a Topeka, Kansas, paper dated 20 September 1903 (in AF Scrapbook), in addition to stating that Farwell would tour Kansas in December of that year, tells that he was offered the chairmanship of the Fine Arts Department at the University of Kansas, but that Farwell declined because he wished to "carry on his work of composition."   [8] Farwell was in Denver on 22 December 1903, according to a local paper which reported an "informal lecture" given at the home of one of the city's residents (AF Scrapbook).

Ernest R. Kroeger

few moments to collect my scattered wits when I learned that I should not arrive at the Canyon until the evening of the *second* day. Nothing was surprising in regard to distances after this, and I was prepared to believe anything.

Going over the Great Divide, and into New Mexico for the first time, it is hard to believe that these strange infinite stretches of opaline desert, mesa-girt and mysterious, are part of the same old United States that we have always known. A dweller of the East, the Mississippi Valley, or the Northwest suddenly dropped into this extraordinary region would certainly think himself nowhere except in Eygpt, or possibly on Mars. And the strange beings that came crowding up to the train at the stopping places—no one familiar with the Sioux or any of the Middle Western tribes would take this unfamiliar race at the first glance for Indians.[9] But such they were and populated the curious

---

[9] I have removed from this sentence a dash which seems to have been placed unintentionally after the word "tribes" in the original version.

pueblos that seemed as much a natural part of the landscape as the very mesas themselves. At the pueblo of Isleta, near Albuquerque, I first had the opportunity of seeing these strange and picturesque desert dwellers in the midst of their native surroundings, and of casually hearing a few of their songs.

Thus I journeyed, wide-eyed and attentive, through New Mexico and Arizona, accumulating an incalculable store of new experiences and impressions, and soon knew myself eligible for the increasing ranks of the desert-lovers. And at the end of the second day after leaving Denver this perpetual crescendo of interest reached its climax when I arrived at the edge of the world.

I had often wondered what it would be like to die and wake up on the other side, or to be Beethoven, or Wagner, or Dante. But such slight experiences are engulfed in the great one of that first glimpse into the incredible other-world of the Grand Canyon of Arizona. One cannot write about this place. There is no word, no phrase, no description that does not belittle it, unless we go to the Apocalypse. Enumeration, however poetically presented, of dimension and distance, color and form, sensation and experiences, goes for naught in the face of the indescribable—the ineffable! On Christmas morning, with snow covering the ground above, and warm Summer in the gulf below, I took my station at a remote spot on the rim, building a fire to melt the snow and keep me warm. All day long, until nightfall, I sat there watching the lights and shadows play and change over the strange distances and depths of this wonderworld, and heard the unwritten symphonies of the ages past and the ages to come.

Nothing short of the anticipation of California could have reconciled me to the ending of the week which I spent at the Canyon, on horseback along the rim, or on muleback or afoot threading into its Dantesque depths. The time of shaking myself out of this dream, and pursuing my way, arrived. And it was a wonderful early January experience to leave to cold, clear airs of an Arizona Winter one night, and to awake the next morning to a paradise of sunlight flooding down upon the deep green and gleaming gold of miles of orange trees, and on the dim blue mountain ranges in the distance.

Thus to traverse in a brief space of time the gentle farm lands of the East, the broader rolling landscapes of the Mississippi Valley, the limitless plains of Kansas, the highlands of Colorado, the immensity of vast deserts, and the flowery paradise of California, forces upon one a mighty impression of the ampleness of the land we live in, in manifold variety of scene and climate, as well as in sheer extent. And greater than this is the thought that comes to one of the race of men and women inhabiting and increasing in this land, and weaving out a racial and national destiny—to what end who knows! Pioneers have conquered the soil and captains of industry have established a material civilization. It is unthinkable that upon this magnificent foundation there should not arise from these inspiring scenes and these active, inventive, curious throngs a development of the arts, of painting, music, literature, drama representative of the realities of American life and the ideals of our nation as they take shape.

It is leaders that we need—persons of initiative, who see that this vast national material, people and art-media alike is plastic, mouldable—persons who have the vision, the will and the courage to create new and definite shapes, whether in the forms and methods of our civilization or the forms and methods of our art. We need the spirit which impels us to act, and to act at once, and should be forever discontented with a spirit which waits for others to act. And now the train rolled past the ostrich farm, and the *arroyo seco* which was to be my home the following year, and into Los Angeles.

1904
Charles F. Lummis[1]

Los Angeles is an Eastern city with the possibilities of a Western. It is populated by a vast throng of people who have gone from the East and Middle West over the mountains to settle down in this wonderful and alluring Occidental Italy. In artistic development the city has not the same obstacles to contend with as those pioneer cities whose population has not been subsequently made up of an influx of persons already somewhat advanced in the knowledge of art. Every circumstance of climate and population favors an extraordinary art growth in this most prosperous of Southwestern cities. Its vast total of intelligence and energy, by no means as yet reduced to concerted and systematic action for artistic accomplishment, affords such an opportunity for leadership as is rarely to be found. In 1904 those conditions were plain to read, which have recently made it possible for Los Angeles to place itself second to New York in the magnitude of its accomplishment in the American music movement.

In early January, with many flowers in full bloom and palms everywhere lending a tropical aspect to the scene, I gave my recital of Indian music developments, accompanied by a talk on the subject, before one of the clubs. Now, there is a man in Los Angeles who keeps a sort of fatherly eye on all the Indians of the Southwest, Californian, Arizonian and New Mexican. If there is anything to be known about these Indians, he knows it. This interest extends equally to the Spanish population of this region. Moreover, he also keeps an eye on the artistic and intellectual development of Los Angeles, and edits a magazine, *Out West*, containing a "Lions' Den" department, in which the lion, who is

[1]From *MA* 9 (24 April 1909): 11–12.

the man in question, eats up all intruders, and has a special relish for Easterners.[2]

The authorities in the club in question thought that it would be well if, before the event of the lecture-recital, I would call upon, if not actually beard, this lion in his den and propitiate him a bit. They did not want to have their own visiting would-be lion chewed up by a local lion. It would have looked badly. As a matter of fact, I bore with me from the East an introduction to this dread monster, but had not the opportunity to present it until after my recital.[3] My confidence rested somewhat upon the knowledge that he was compelled to acknowledge the environs of Boston as his birthplace, while I would point to the Mississippi Valley as mine. This man, who was no other than Charles F. Lummis, honored me with his presence at my affair, and the fact that we became good friends is the best proof that he did not regard my efforts as misdirected. In fact, he invited me to his extraordinary house of elastic hospitality, where I spent some days and nights. This house is worthy of more than passing remark. When Mr. Lummis decided to remove West he walked from Chillicothe, Ohio, to Los Angeles, and then wrote a book about it called *A Tramp Across the Continent*, which is good reading.[4] After archaeologizing in Peru for a year or so, he returned to Los Angeles. Here he chose a location out in the *arroyo* between Los Angeles and Pasadena, and started to build a house *with his own hands*, without other help. This house was to be on the old Spanish plan,

---

[2]The as yet unnamed individual is Charles Fletcher Lummis (1859–1928), editor of *Land of Sunshine* from 1895 to 1901, when the magazine's name was changed to *Out West*, and continuing in that position to 1903, though affiliated with the publication until 1909 (see Edwin R. Bingham, *Charles F. Lummis: Editor of the Southwest* [San Marino, CA: The Huntington Library, 1955]: 51). Lummis solicited an article from Farwell which would tell of the latter's work and aims, but it turned out instead to be an urgent plea to composers to look to American musical resources in order to create a national art (entitled "Toward American Music," it is included in this collection, p. 185; a manuscript of the article in Farwell's hand is in the archives of Braun Research Library, Southwest Museum, Los Angeles. Written in the wake of Farwell's successful first trip West, the tone of the piece seems to reflect some of Lummis's feistiness towards the East.   [3]Farwell's letter of introduction to Lummis may have been provided by Alice Fletcher who had come to have high regard both for Farwell's Indianist compositions and for his mission in general (Alice Fletcher to Sara Farwell, 13 September 1903, AF Collection). Fletcher and Lummis were comrades in arms, struggling together to get the Archeological Institute of America to recognize the importance of American studies at a time when Greek classicism received almost the sole support of the society (Joan Mark, *Four Anthropologists: An American Science in its Early Years* [New York: Science History Publications, 1980], 62). Farwell's lecture-recital where he met Lummis probably took place at the Ebell Club on 11 January 1904, an event reported in the *Los Angeles Times* (12 January 1904; newspaper clipping in AF Scrapbook).   [4]Farwell leaves out an interesting detail of the

having four wings joining at right angles, and thus surrounding a square court yard or *patio*. The materials for the house were boulders rolled up from the surrounding land. These were for the outer walls and towers. Bricks and plaster were used for the inner walls. This was not to be any amateur makeshift house, but a good sized and indestructible castle. Round logs were used for rafters, a reddish cement for floors and a similar color of plaster for the walls. Mr. Lummis had been at work on the house some seven or eight years when I first saw it, and it had then assumed very considerable proportions. There was not a planed surface in the house, and, I believe, not a nail. All flat surfaces the builder hewed with the adze, and all joints were mortised. Inside, the house was a veritable museum of interest, containing Navajo rugs, Zuni earthenware and many other Indian objects of the greatest value and beauty. An old mission bell was hung in one of the towers, and massive locks from old Spanish prisons lent a romantic picturesqueness to some of the great doors. In the center of the *patio* rose a great four-trunked spreading sycamore tree, and beneath this was a large circular well with a fountain jet, the home of a number of gold fish.[5] A more charming hostess than Mrs. Lummis for such a domain is not to be imagined, and the children, especially when wildly chasing a large family of cats about the *patio*, added animation to the scene. If anything could complete this picturesque ensemble it was the two Indian boys, Ramon and Procopio, who were living there in the capacity of friends, servants, and general helpers. Their dark, lustrous eyes, dark complexion and black hair gave them something of the appearance of Orientals.

It was to such a mansion and household that I was invited to a Sunday Spanish dinner, an almost weekly institution of Mr. Lummis. As early as Saturday morning the family began the preparation of enchiladas, chile relyenos, and other hot and wonderful things. On Sunday afternoon various Spanish folk from the neighborhood of Los Angeles congregated at the house, some of them bringing their guitars. The coolness of the night air made it necessary to set the long table in one of the spacious rooms. At the head of the table sat Mr. Lummis, in full

---

story. Before Lummis left on his trek West, he was offered a position at the *Los Angeles Times*, contingent on his completing the trip and on his sending weekly accounts en route. After a walk taking 112 days, on 2 February 1885—only a day after his arrival at his western destination—Lummis took over as city editor for the Los Angeles daily (Bingham: 8).   [5]Lummis's unusual home, named "El Alisal" after the sycamore grove in which it was set, is presently the headquarters for the Historical Society of California, located at 200 East Avenue 43, in the Highland Park area of Los Angeles.

Charles F. Lummis with his children.
Courtesy of Southwest Museum, Los Angeles; Photo No. 24536

Ramon Zuñi,
Native American
singer whom Farwell
met at Lummis's
home

Mexican regimentals—drawn-work shirt, short brown jacket and trousers of a similar color, fitting close at knees and ankles.

The singing of Spanish folksongs became the order of the hour toward the close of the dinner. The guitars rang out with magic which can be imparted only by Spanish fingers, and song after song, in inexhaustible array, floated or danced upon the air. The charm, the spontaneity, the grace of these songs were indescribable. There was nothing in the nature of exhibition in this singing. The singers were singing because this was an occasion for song, because these were their own songs—and they threw themselves into their enjoyment of them with Latin ardor. Little by little all the romance of the old Spanish life seemed to be reborn and to throb again in the very air about us. One was carried out of one's self and into a world untouched and unmarred as yet by any encroachment of our modern civilization—a world of romantic adventure, of dances and serenades, of Dons, toreadors and flashing-eyed señoritas. The lights shone out through the windows and mingled with the moonlight, which lit up the great sycamore and walls and colonnade of the *patio*. The entire circumstance took on a color, a mood of its own, thrilling with picturesqueness and beauty. The very heart of the Spanish life of the old Southwest seemed to stand revealed.[6]

At length all adjourned to the great assembly room of the house. Here Mr. Lummis induced the Indian boys to sing for us, which required some persuasion. Procopio had newly come into these surroundings from his home in Isleta. A difficulty beyond the matter of mere shyness was that these songs were mostly religious, and except in very particular circumstances were not to be sung outside the actual observance of the ceremonial of which they formed a part. Ramon, however, finally took the lead, and, taking up an Indian drum, began in low tones a very insistent rhythm. To this the youths began, also in low tones, a song of very striking character, with very distinctly marked accents. From time to time would come rhythmic irregularities and complexities of the most extraordinary nature, alterations and counter-rhythms in the drum beat and the song, which I believe would baffle for some time any musician on earth. Each time one in particular of these episodes returned I made strenuous efforts to catch the rhythmic rationale of it, for it was plain to hear that it had a definite system of its own, if one could but fathom its subtleties. It was not until the following year, when I had the opportunity to repeat this melody ad infinitum upon the phonograph, that I fully grasped its rhythm structure.

This phonographic record, which with many others I afterward studied, was made upon the spot. It required coaxing and a prolonged council of war between Ramon and Procopio. Procopio at this time had never had experience with the phonograph. Finally, standing before the bell of the machine, the two boys repeated the song. Mr. Lummis, substituting the reproducing for the recording needle, then made the machine repeat the song. Procopio's face darkened, and, muttering "No good!" he hastily retreated to a far corner of the room from which no coaxing served to draw him for the remainder of the evening. Mr.

---

[6]Lummis's home became a center for creative artists who sought out his advice. As a gathering place for many distinguished guests visiting Los Angeles, including the naturalist and essayist John Burroughs, the opera star Mary Garden, the Polish American actress Helena Modjeska, and the poet Edwin Markham, El Alisal was a sort of American version of the European salon (Bingham: 21, 135).

Lummis then ran off for our benefit a number of records of Indian songs which he had made, all of intensest interest and of the most varied character. He also ran a remarkable record of "La Paloma," the dramatic and spirited manner of the singing of which by the Spaniards shows our usual feeble and sentimental interpretation of this song in a strange light.[7]

Our host, in true old Spanish style, went part of the way with the departing guests. I remained, and a cot was fixed for me in the large room, the house being full, and I went to sleep to thoughts stranger than dreams.

The next morning at breakfast I tried to get Ramon, who was serving us, to sing over the song of the evening before for me, so I could catch that elusive rhythm. Perfect blankness of expression was his only response. He disclaimed all knowledge of such a song. I began it for him, to refresh his memory, but he was still the personification of blankness. Five minutes later I heard him singing it softly in the kitchen in a quiet conversation with Procopio. Commend me to the Indian for perfect concealment of knowledge in blank and wondering innocence. Poor, stunningly handsome "Copio" was destined to be shot and killed in this same house of wonders some years later by an old Spaniard whose life he was seeking.

But, as Mr. Kipling says, that is another story.

---

[7]Lummis had at this time just begun an extensive project to record Indian and Spanish American songs of the Southwest on behalf of the Southwest Society, a chapter of the Archaeological Institute of America that he had helped to form in 1903. During the time of the recording project, 1904–05, Lummis, like Farwell, was lecturing throughout the country on Native Americans. The two Indian singers staying with Lummis, Procopio Montoya (1882–1907) and Ramon Zuñi—both from Isleta Pueblo, New Mexico—recorded the largest number of Native American songs in Lummis's collection of cylinder recordings. Lummis recorded well over 500 cylinders, including multiple takes of the same song; individually, about 300 Spanish and 160 Indian songs can be accounted for in the archives of Southwest Museum in Los Angeles, which Lummis was instrumental in founding. A complete inventory of Lummis's Indian and Spanish songs appears in John Koegel, "The Lummis Collection of Cylinder Recordings as a Source for Hispanic Music in Southern California in the Nineteenth Century" (Ph.D. diss., Claremont Graduate School, 1994). Information in this note is taken from Koegel's unpublished article, "Hispanic Music in Nineteenth-Century California: The Lummis Collection of Cylinder Recordings at Southwest Museum," which the author kindly let me read.

1904
Composers in San Francisco[1]

*A*t Mr. Lummis's house these first Los Angeles days, in January, 1904, were spent in a little world of Spanish-Californians and Indians. I not only heard many of their songs, I swam in the musical atmosphere of them—the suave or vivacious songs of the Spanish settlers and the weird, sombre, and mysterious songs of the dwellers of the desert. When I went on my journey I took with me very vivid impressions indeed of this folk music of the Southwest, so intensely characteristic and colorful. Before leaving Los Angeles I met the singer, Harry Barnhart, who has since proven himself so doughty a pioneer in the singing of these songs of the West, and which fall at first strangely upon Eastern ears.[2]

Stopping a few days in the remote and beautiful Ojai Valley, I went on to San Francisco, in both of which places I found a welcome for my minstrelsy.[3] At the famous Bohemian Club in San Francisco I increased my acquaintance with composers by meeting with William J. McCoy, H. J. Stewart, Edward Schneider, and Joseph Redding,[4] all of whom have contributed their talents in no unstinted measure to the upbuilding of the great midsummer High Jinks, or Forest Festival, at the club's

---

[1]From *MA* 9 (1 May 1909): 29.   [2]Harry Barnhart (1874–1948) is cited in *Musicians of Los Angeles: 1904–05* (N.p.,n.d.) as conductor of the Apollo Club and the Temple Baptist choir which boasted over 100 voices, and as a teacher of voice. The directory notes also that he had just returned three years before from vocal study in Italy and England. Barnhart and Farwell, in the years after 1910 when Farwell's interests turned to civic music, worked closely together in promoting the community chorus (see my article "'The New Gospel of Music': Arthur Farwell's Vision of Democratic Music in America." *American Music* 9 [1991]: 194f.). The two were to become lifelong friends; Barnhart was best man at Farwell's marriage to Gertrude Brice in 1918.
[3]Before leaving southern California, Farwell lectured in Redlands on 15 January, according to a news clipping in AF Scrapbook.   [4]Stewart's initials are incorrectly given as "H. G." in the original text. For more on these San Francisco composers see n. 6 below.

grove of giant redwoods on the Russian River. McCoy invited me cordially to be present at the Jinks, of which he was the composer and Will Irwin the poet,[5] and which was to take place in August of the same year.[6]

One of the most interesting experiences of this first visit to San Francisco was meeting with still another composer, Carlos Troyer. Professor Troyer was not of American birth, but had early gone from Europe to South America, where he conducted an opera company *en tour*, in what might be called the early days. Of the perils of such an expedition he told me an amusing anecdote. On one occasion he was being entertained at dinner by several Spanish gentlemen in one of the Spanish-American cities of South America. One of them asked him to tell them about his duels.

"Duels!" he exclaimed. "Why, I never fought any!"

"What!" exclaimed his host, "in the company of caballeros, and

---

[5]Will Irwin (1873–1948) is probably best known as a journalist who during his time in San Francisco was on the staff of the *Wave* and the *Chronicle*. He left San Francisco the year after Farwell met him to join the New York *Sun*.   [6]The all-male Bohemian Club of San Francisco was founded in 1872 and over the years became known for its annual outdoor performances, at first called "Midsummer High Jinks," but later also the "Forest Festival" or "Grove Plays." The latter names refer to the Bohemian Grove where the productions took place, an 800–acre tract of redwood forest northwest of the city on the Russian River. Music played a large part in the Grove Plays, at times verging on opera. The American baritone David Bispham, who had the title role for the 1910 production, *The Cave Man*, noted that the plays "have grown so famous and have developed so steadily in high purpose that I was highly complimented at being asked to play the prinicipal part in the one forthcoming." Bispham speaks of the fine symphony orchestra hidden from view, the superb acoustics in the forest, and "a combination of stagecraft and music [as remarkable] as I have ever known" (*A Quaker Singer's Recollections* [New York: Macmillan, 1920]: 353–55). The productions given between 1902 and 1920 are listed in the article on the Bohemian Club in the *American Supplement* to *Grove's Dictionary of Music and Musicians*, 3rd edition (ed. Waldo Selden Pratt [New York: Macmillan, 1934). Among composers named is William J. McCoy (1848–1926), who wrote for two productions, one of which, *The Hamadryads* (1904), Farwell thought the first to raise the artistic standards of the Grove plays (*AM*, 396f.). Humphrey J. Stewart (1856–1932) wrote the music for three plays, Edward Schneider (1872–1950) who taught at Mills College (1901–36) also for two, while Joseph D. Redding (b. 1859) wrote the music for two and the text for two others (Redding is also known as the librettist for Victor Herbert's opera *Natoma* [1911]). Elsewhere, Farwell cites these and others of the "San Francisco Group" of composers who have written for the Grove productions, lamenting that San Francisco "holds a record as a city of composers that is little appreciated in the Eastern part of the U. S." (*AM*, 396–99). Farwell's earnestness in promoting these San Francisco composers is likely responsible for the brief unsigned article in *MA* (9 [30 January 1909]: 9) with a photo that includes Schneider, Stewart, Redding, McCoy, and Otto Vogt and is captioned "Members of San Francisco's Bohemian Club."

never fought any duels!" The musician at once expressed his willingness to withdraw.

"That is unnecessary," his host said, "but I will see that a duel is arranged at once."

The duel came off according to schedule, and the kindly musican had the pleasure of shooting off the finger of a caballero. Thus was the high social estate of caballeros maintained.

At a later period Professor Troyer, who is a man deeply versed in the arts and sciences, a veritable savant, became the friend of Frank Hamilton Cushing, and with him underwent certain of the initiations into the mysteries of the Zuñi tribe. The professor had already availed himself of his sojourn in South America to study the Incas and other ancient races and tribes, and to record a number of their songs. He was thus already qualified to deal with the Indians, and by this knowledge, and even more especially by his violin, he won his way at once to their favor. He astonished them by the quickness and accuracy with which he could reproduce their songs upon his instrument. They insisted that he was a reincarnated Zuñi. Thus he was able to collect a number of their most ancient and sacred songs, which he put into a form, vocal or instrumental, available for the modern singer and musician.[7]

One of these songs is particularly uplifting and inspiring in character. This is the "Sunrise Call," sung by the sun priest at sunrise from the

---

[7]The German-born Carlos Troyer (1837–1920) claimed other unusual achievements: that he had known Jenny Lind, played frequently for Liszt, taught the élite of New York, and had become, while touring South America with his opera company, the personal friend of Emperor Pedro II of Brazil. He settled in San Francisco in 1871, thereafter changing his name from "Charles" to "Carlos" (see *New Grove's Dictionary of Music and Musicians in America*, s. v. "Troyer, Carlos"). Farwell provides in a letter an unusual anecdote regarding Troyer's relationship with Frank Hamilton Cushing (1857–1900), the brilliant ethnologist who, after a four-and-a-half year stay at a Zuñi pueblo, enjoyed popular fame as "the man who lived with the Indians." Troyer apparently "prolonged" Cushing's life: "It was his medical knowledge that enabled him to help Cushing, whose stomach was perforated as the result of eating raw meat in his Zuni initiations" (Farwell to James M. Sheridan, 9 March [between1937 and 1939], AF Collection). In the same letter, Farwell acknowledges that Charles Lummis doubted the veracity of Troyer's claims regarding his experience with the Zuñis, but Farwell dismisses it as professional jealousy on the part of Lummis—"[Lummis] wanted to be the only one who knew anything about Indian music." It seems, however, that Lummis may have had grounds for doubting Troyer's claims. The reputable Indian scholar Frederick W. Hodge (1864–1956), who was director of the Southwest Museum in Los Angeles from 1932 to 1955, was unequivocal in his opinion of Troyer. Hodge appended the following note to a newspaper clipping concerning Troyer on file at the Southwest Museum: "Troyer was an old faker. He never lived among any Indians. F. W. Hodge" (article from *San Francisco Examiner*, 22 April 1917, on file in G. Wharton James Collection, Southwest Museum, Los Angeles).

rooftop of the pueblo. The Zuñis look for a redeemer, a god Montezuma, who is promised to appear in the clouds at sunrise. The song, with its stirring calls of "Rise, Arise!" is sung to call forth the people to greet the god as he appears in the splendor of the approaching dawn. Upon certain occasions this is followed by the "Coming of Montezuma," a song of acclamation, and musically of great directness and breadth.

Stranger than these is the "Ghost Dance of the Zuñis." This extraordinary ceremony, the purpose of which is to summon back the spirits of departed friends and ancestors, was witnessed by Professor Troyer. The ceremony is held on the top of the "Thunder Mountain," near Zuñi, at night, and only at a certain season. Two concentric circles of great fire piles are arranged with but a small space between each fire. The inner fire piles are first ignited and the fire dancers appear, nude, and passing in and out between the great fires in so intense a heat as to render the feat apparently incredible. Even at a little distance, where the people of the tribe stand watching the cermony, the heat is almost unbearable. As the fires burn higher and higher the excitement of the dancers and the spectators rises. The dancers chant, "*Hec, hec, hec, hecta, hec*" (come, be with us), and utter strange calls and cries of animals. As the fires and the growing excitement reach their greatest height, ghostly forms seem to appear descending and hovering over the flames. At length the fires subside, the forms disappear and the outer fire piles are ignited. The cycle of phenomena is repeated, and as the forms appear a second time the people burst forth with wild shouts of acclamation. As the forms disappear the excitement of the people is no longer controllable; they rush in, but all have disappeared, spirits and dancers alike, and only the dying fire piles remain.

The melodies and sequence of this strange ceremony Professor Troyer has reduced to a work for piano, to which a violin and a gong may be added to heighten the effect. These works and others impressed me as deeply interesting in themselves, and as containing material in which an increasing national interest will develop. My Wa-Wan Press seemed the place for them, so with compositions by two of the other San Francisco composers whom I had met, namely, McCoy and Schneider, back they went to Newton Center.[8]

A morning in the studio of William Keith, the great painter of the

---

[8]Altogether, five of Troyer's works were published by Wa-Wan, three in 1904: *Traditional Songs of the Zuñis* (*WP* 2:149–173), which is dedicated to Cushing and includes the mentioned

heights of the Sierras, was one of the pleasantest experiences of my
San Francisco visit, and in that city I also met Maynard Dixon, who has
most profitably lent his brush and pencil to scenes of Indian and cowboy life.[9] Professor Troyer accompanied me to the ferry when I left, and
I remember vividly his parting injunction to me: "Never grow old!"
And so the journey went. At Portland I saw Mr. Ladd's magnificent
collection of Barbizon paintings, and met local musicans.[10] At Seattle I
had the pleasure of meeting Mr. Curtis, who has spent his life in making
a series of photographs of the Indians of North America, which will be

"The Sunrise Call" and "The Coming of Montezuma"; *Ghost Dance of the Zuñis* for which
Troyer's introductory remarks are provided (*WP* 2:151–53; 183–189); and a second series of
Zuñi songs (*WP* 2:221–43), *Kiowa-Apache War Dance* and *Indian Fire Song*, appeared in 1907
(*WP* 4:73–83 and 89–97). *Ghost Dance* has been recently recorded by Dario Müller on
compact disc (6821, Nuova Era). Farwell admitted later that Troyer's abilities as a composer
were limited, that his settings of Indian melodies had "none of the modern acumen in getting
at the expression of the primitive [that] was in them" even though "the boldness of the
melodies caused them to carry pretty well through the somewhat thin veil of German
harmony he put to them" (Letter of Farwell to Sheridan cited in preceding note). One of the
Zuñi melodies used by Troyer was destined to receive yet another incarnation at the hands of
Giacomo Puccini, who used a melody from the second series of Troyer's Zuñi arrangements
published by Wa-Wan for *La Fanciulla del West* (1910). According to the letter just cited,
Farwell preferred Troyer's settings, for at least he was not able to "kill them [the Zuñi
melodies] completely as Puccini did by his Italianization of the 'Sunrise Call' in the first act of
the 'Girl of the Golden West' " (Farwell mispoke himself here; Puccini actually borrowed the
"Festive Sun Dance," as pointed out by Allan W. Atlas, who discusses Puccini's use of the
melody in "Belasco and Puccini: 'Old Dog Tray' and the Zuni Indians," *Musical Quarterly* 75
[1991], 362–98). Farwell published a single song of McCoy, *The Only Voice* (1904; *WP*
3:78–80). In the case of Schneider, who in these early days Farwell said was "perhaps the
most talented and poetic composer in the West," (Farwell, "Western Life," *Newton Center
Town Crier*, 17 October 1905; in AF Scrapbook), two works for violin and piano were
published: *A Midwinter Idyl* (1906; *WP* 3:178–83) and *A Romantic Fantasy* (1907; *WP* 4:51–
63).   [9]Both the Scottish-born William Keith (1838–1911) and Maynard Dixon (1875–1946)
were part of Charles Lummis's circle, and it is likely that through him Farwell made his
connections with the artists. Keith was arguably "California's best-known landscape painter"
at the turn of the century (Doris O. Dawdy, *Artists of the American West* [Chicago: Swallow
Press, 1974], 130). Dixon worked both as an illustrator and a painter, showing an intimate
knowledge of many Native American tribes in the United States, Mexico, and Canada which he
obtained over fifty years. Among his significant achievements are the murals, depicting scenes of
American Indian life, done in the 1930s for the Department of Interior building in Washington, D. C. When in the 1920s Farwell collaborated with Lummis on producing a book of
Spanish American songs, Farwell hoped that Dixon could be secured to do the cover illustration, though this never occurred (Letter of Farwell to Charles F. Lummis, 15 February 1921,
CFL Collection).   [10]Farwell likely refers to William Mead Ladd (1855–1931), a prominent
banker and art collector of Portland, who was a founding member of the Portland Art
Association that established the city's art museum during the 1890s (see William L. Brewster,
William Mead Ladd of Portland Oregon [Portland: Metropolitan Press, 1933]: 57–59, 89–90).

a monument to the greatness of an ethnological endeavor of vast proportions and incalculable significance." A very remarkable collection of Alaskan objects I remember in Tacoma. But it was everywhere the people, and not the things, which seemed so wonderful to me—all so busy building, building, a great civlization—and to what end?

After the mists and moderate airs of a North Pacific Winter came the blinding blizzards of Montana and the Bad Lands, the crystalline and marrow-congealing days of my Minnesota Winter, well known of old; and when the circuit was completed and I again found myself in quiet Newton Center, the Spring was already begging for admission at the yielding gates of Winter.[12]

The house—what with Wa-Wan Press and other activities—was too much like a beehive to admit of doing quiet, creative work; so, remembering Henry Gilbert and his barn, I rented an old shed, put in something which passed for a piano, and went to work on the revision and orchestration of *Dawn*, the first of my larger developments of Indian themes.[13]

Now came an exciting propostion, threatening to break up once more that coveted quiet which has always been the object of my search, and never the object found. Mr. Lummis wrote proposing that I go back to Los Angeles to help in completing a study of the Spanish-Californian and Indian music for the Archaelogical Institute of America. Deep in my consciousness somewhere I heard the strange chants of Ramon and Procopio echoing and echoing, and the voices and guitars in the *patio* ringing, and saw again those vast and alluring stretches of Arizonian desert, fraught with uplift and inspiration and bigness.

But just when I had made up my mind that the great Southwest was my place, came the disappointing news that the Archaeological Institute would not provide the necessary money. It was either give up

---

[11]Farwell made a presentation in Portland on 25 January, in Tacoma on the next day, and in Seattle on 2 February, according to newspaper clippings in AF Scrapbook. Edward S. Curtis (1868–1952) was the noted photographer-anthropologist who dedicated his life to preserving the memory, on film and in word, of his views of over eighty Native American tribes. With the financial aid of J. Pierpont Morgan, Curtis undertook his research which resulted in a twenty-volume work, *The North American Indian*, published between 1907 and 1930.   [12]A letter to John Beach fills in some of the details of Farwell's projected itinerary as he made his way East: on 5 February he was to be in Helena, Montana, and on 7 to 8 February, Minneapolis; from there he would proceed to Chicago, leaving on 19 February to stop in Cincinnati on 21 February (Farwell to John Beach, 30 January [1904], New York Public Library at Lincoln Center).   [13]Referring to the piano version of *Dawn* (1904), Farwell recalled years later to pianist John Kirkpatrick that he played the piece frequently with success on his early lecture tours, "but I didn't play it as you do unfortunately" (Typescript of letter from Farwell to John Kirkpatrick, 27 August 1944, AF Collection).

or enter what seemed a hopeless fight. I could not say which was wisdom.

The Indian, quite apart from his tribal and family life, prepares a spot in the wilderness for the living of such moments of his life as must be wholly his own. There he goes to pray his private prayers, think his private thoughts, work out his private plans. Now, I had such a place in a secluded wooded spot, not from any desire to imitate the Indian, but from dire need, and thither I went with my problem. As I stood thinking it over—what I should do—a peculiar stone, almost buried in the earth at my foot, attracted my attention and I stooped to pick it up. What was my astonishment to find that it was a magnificent flint arrowhead! As a student of science and a graduate of the Massachusetts Institute of Technology, I am not a superstitious person, but this little piece of flint, I must confess, sent a strange tingling up my spine to the roots of my hair. Flint is not found in this neighborhood, and one no longer expects to pick up Indian relics about Newton Center. It was a question of centuries—when the last Indian battle could have been fought upon this spot.

Perhaps that timely and eloquent arrowhead decided me—perhaps not. At least I decided, took the earliest possible train to New Haven, where I carried the point with the late Dr. Seymour, then president of the institute, and it was settled on the spot that I should go to the Southwest for the society that Summer.[14] At Dr. Seymour's house I talked with Horatio Parker, and remember his saying to me, with all the suicidal courage of the musical purist, that there has been no music written since Mozart.[15]

---

[14]Thomas Day Seymour (1848–1907), President of the Archaelogical Institute of America from 1903 to 1907, was a professor of classics at Yale University. "Dr. Seymour treated me royally in New Haven, and put the matter through at the council in N. Y.," Farwell elatedly writes Lummis, adding that the Institute had granted him $200 for three months that summer (Farwell to Lummis, 18 May [1904], CFL Collection).   [15]Seymour's colleague at Yale was Horatio Parker, then Dean of the School of Music. Although Farwell's remark indicates that Parker's conservative philosophy of music was out of step with his, Farwell nonetheless made an attempt—though it turned out to be fruitless—to acquire a work of Parker for publication in the Wa-Wan Press: the Rhapsody for Baritone and Orchestra, *Cáhal Mor of the Wine Red Hand* (Farwell to Horatio Parker, 15 May 1903, Parker Papers, MSS 32, Beinecke Rare Book and Manuscript Library, Yale University).

1904
Second Trip West[1]

*A*ction once taken has an inconvenient way of necessitating further action, until every hope of peace and quiet one has ever cherished fades to the most shadowy of dreams. The web of action draws tighter and tighter as we spin its subtle strands, until we long for that happy day when, through action, we shall be released from action, as the Sacred Books of the East[2] promise. That day had evidently not arrived for me, for now, just after completing a six-months' circuit of the United States, I was to start out across the continent again. Mr. Lummis wanted assistance in the study of Spanish-Californian songs for the American Institute of Archaeology, and through a natural sequence of events, the task fell on me.

Early in the Summer of 1904, I went to Chicago,[3] where I again augmented my knowledge of American composers by meeting Arne Oldberg, who holds a high position in the School of Music at the Northwestern University, at Evanston, Illinois, and a higher one in the sanctuary of creative musical art. At the house of Dean Lutkin, who has made this great school what it is, I heard Oldberg's Quintet in B minor, for piano and strings, played by the able string quartet organization of the school, and the composer. I was very greatly impressed by this work, as pure music of the highest type, nor have I suffered any

---

[1] From *MA* 9 (8 May 1909): 23, 31.   [2] It seems likely that Farwell is referring to a specific multi-volume publication of important texts of the major Eastern religions, *The Sacred Books of the East*, 50 vols., ed. F. Max Müller (Oxford: Clarendon Press, 1879–1910). The citation is significant in that it is one of the few places where Farwell indicates, at least in publications from before 1910, possible sources for his spiritual views.   [3] A letter written by Farwell while in Chicago indicates that he was there in early June (Farwell to Rudolph Gott, 8 June 1904, AF Collection).

Arne Oldberg

diminution of this impression upon subsequent hearings of this or any other of this composer's chamber music works. Oldberg is a melodist of the first order, with a highly acute sense of thematic development, two qualities inevitably leading to a devotion to the chamber-music forms. He was also at work at this time upon a piano concerto, part of which I was privileged to hear, and which was subsequently added to the output of the Wa-Wan Press. Orchestral compositions—a symphony, and an overture *Paolo and Francesca* which has since been performed by the Theodore Thomas Orchestra—are among this composer's works, all of which are certain to be heard as the nation progresses in its demand to hear the serious works of American composers.[4]

---

[4]Arne Oldberg (1874–1962) became a highly respected friend and confidant of Farwell. Over sixty letters from Farwell to Oldberg (AO Collection), written between 1905 and 1915, are an important source of information on Farwell in this period. Oldberg became head of the piano department at Northwestern University in 1899 after returning to the United States from

Rejoicing in the rapidity of the realization of my hopes for American composition, I went on my way to St. Louis, where the blizzard-struck frameworks of the previous December had now become the gay and magnificent scenes of the St. Louis Exposition. Here I was joined by the "Prince" of the old Boston days, whom I had rediscovered in Chicago the previous year. On July 1 we heard the first performance of *Dawn*, the score of which I had so recently finished, by the festival orchestra of the exposition, under Mr. Ernst's direction.[5]

The Prince and I now made a leisurely trip down through the wonderful desert lands again on the Santa Fe "Overland," stopping off at Albuquerque to see Mr. Switzer's treasure trove of Navajo blankets and other Indian products, and again visiting that silent and vast invoker of the ineffable, the Grand Canyon.[6]

But soon I was established down in the *arroyo* at Los Angeles, among the scenes and circumstances which had so greatly impressed me the previous Winter.[7] There was the Lummis house again—a Spanish castle—with its towers, its walls of boulders, the *patio* with its great round well and spreading sycamore, and all the treasures within. To work here seemed more like a romantic holiday than a labor. But I was soon hard at it, in a corner of the main room which had come to be called the "museum," transcribing from the phonograph the great num-

---

study with Leschetizky in Vienna and Rheinberger in Munich; he held that position until retirement in 1941. Farwell devotes considerable space to Oldberg the composer in *AM* (373–75), believing that he is "among the most earnest and advanced leaders of American musical standards." Farwell reports here that the overture *Paolo and Francesca* was played by the Theodore Thomas Orchestra (what would become the Chicago Symphony Orchestra in 1912) on 17 and 18 January 1908. Five works of Oldberg were published by Wa-Wan in 1907 and 1908, including a two-piano edition of the G-Minor Piano Concerto to which Farwell alludes, the longest work published by the Press (*WP* 5:1–75). A brief, unsigned article on Oldberg appears in *Musical Courier* 33 (5 August 1896): 22, along with his picture on the cover. Peter C. Lutkin (1858–1931) was made the first Dean of the School of Music at Northwestern University in 1895, after having undertaken the tasks involved with assimilating the American Conservatory of Music into the University.   [5]See p. 116 for an earlier reference to *Dawn*. A program of the concert in AF Scrapbook indicates that Alfred Ernst was the conductor; no further information on Ernst can be given.   [6]It seems that Farwell is referring to H. Schweizer (not "Switzer") who was an "expert in native crafts of the Southwest" and a "leading authority on Navajo blankets" (Charles A. Amsden, *Navaho Weaving: Its Technic and History* [Santa Ana, CA: The Fine Arts Press, 1939], 35, 146). Schweizer was the Head of the Indian Department of the Fred Harvey Company in Albuquerque, at the time one of the principal dealers of Navajo rugs in the country (George W. James, *Indian Blankets and Their Makers* [Chicago: A. C. McClurg, 1914], 202).   [7]In a letter to Lummis, Farwell writes that he will probably arrive in Los Angeles on 16 July (Farwell to Lummis, 9 July [1904], CFL Collection).

ber of songs already recorded, and whenever the opportunity afforded, making new records.

When I arrived, Doña Adelaida Kamp, of Ventura, was visiting at the Lummis house, and singing, with a voice no longer young, all the old Spanish songs of the region which she remembered. Among the sixty-four songs which she sang, was a serenade which had been composed and sung for her—well, one should not say just how many years before—when she was a young and undoubtedly entrancing señorita. The old Spanish manners survived in this lady. Mrs. Lummis forgetting this one morning, admired the dress in which she appeared, one which she had not hitherto worn.

"It is yours," promptly responded the wearer.

"But it is so much more becoming on you," said the hostess, not to be taken off her guard, and the incident was closed.

Miss Manuela Garcia holds the record for folksongs, however, having sung no less than one hundred and fifty different songs into the phonograph.

Don Rosendo Uruchurtu, a blind boy, and a conjurer with the guitar, contributed many songs. Altogether I transcribed from the phonograph, and from actual singing, about six or seven hundred of these songs, which will eventually appear as a report of the "Southwest Society" of the Institute, and a number of which will be given out in proper form for popular use. A good number are of high quality, and some are remarkable finds, nuggets of folksong of the greatest rarity and beauty.[8]

---

[8]The publishing of Farwell's melodic transcriptions in the Southwest Society's Bulletin never came about, though plans were announced for issuing an initial volume of Spanish songs in 1904, with a book of Indian melodies and a second collection of Spanish songs projected for the following two years ("A Brief Summary," *Southwest Society of the Archaelogical Institute of America. First Bulletin* [Los Angeles, CA, 1904]: 25). The same report notes that Farwell had already transcribed over 100 songs and that by the year's end 600 were expected to be finished. This goal seems not to have been reached, for Lummis, in a letter on behalf of the Executive Committee of the Southwest Society, thanks Farwell for fulfilling his commission in transcribing "some 300 of the old Spanish folk-songs of the Southwest, which this Society has recorded by phonograph" (Lummis to Farwell, 21 October 1905, CFL Collection). As to the present status of Farwell's transcriptions, though only a very few of the Indian melodies have been preserved, at least 350 of the Spanish songs survive (information provided in John Koegel, "The Lummis Collection of Cylinder Recordings as a Source for Hispanic Music in Southern California in the Nineteenth Century," Ph.D. diss., Claremont Graduate School, 1994), primarily at the Southwest Museum, with some in AF Collection. Koegel, who has checked Farwell's transcriptions against the Lummis recordings, finds that the "accuracy of Farwell's musical transcriptions is usually of a quite high standard . . . [which is] especially important since

The Indian songs were much more exciting to work with—the field being far less familiar, and the songs being of so surprising and extraordinary a nature. These records had been made by Mr. Lummis during his various sojourns among the desert Indians. Some of them were of such complicated rhythmic structure, and such unusual melodic nature as to require hundreds of repetitions before I could transcribe them to my own satisfaction. The weighty Krehbiel sits comfortably in his dean's chair up in New York, and pleasantly says that the Indian's songs consist of basic stock phrases which "serve them equally well for a gambling song, a war dance, a ghost dance or any other purpose." Well—I wish the comfortable dean a long and prosperous life.[9]

---

they represent the only surviving record of those cylinders which are presently broken, damaged, or lost" (John Koegel's unpublished article, "Hispanic Music in Nineteenth-Century California: The Lummis Collection of Cylinder Recordings at the Southwest Museum"). A few of the Spanish melodies were given harmonized settings by Farwell and were published over the years. "La noche està serena" appears in an article in the Southwest Society Bulletin along with photographs of the Spanish singers Farwell has mentioned—Manuela Garcia, Doña Adalaida Kamp, and Don Rosendo Uruchurtu (Charles F. Lummis, "Catching Our Archaeology Alive," Southwest Society of the Archaelogical Institute of America. Second Bulletin [Los Angeles, CA, 1905]: 3–15 [reprinted from Out West, January 1905]. Two more harmonizations of Spanish songs were published by Wa-Wan: Folk-songs of the West and South: Negro, Cowboy and Spanish-California (1905): "The Hours of Grief" ("Las horas de luto") and "The Black Face" ("La cara negra") (see WP 3:50–54). Some years later, Lummis and Farwell together produced for popular consumption Spanish Songs of Old California, Collected and Translated by Charles F. Lummis; Pianoforte Accompaniments by Arthur Farwell (first published privately by Lummis, 1923, and then later in the same year by G. Schirmer). The slim volume contains fourteen songs, only a sample of the songs the two had been working on sporadically for over fifteen years, as shown by the extensive correspondence between Lummis and Farwell between 1909 and 1926 (CFL Collection). Lummis had hopes for publishing up to seventy of such arrangements, and, indeed, a large number of these in various stages of completion are found in AF Collection. But difficulties in finding a publisher, along with Farwell's heavy schedule that did not allow the time for working on such a project, seem to have pre-empted the original plan.   [9]Henry Edward Krehbiel (1854–1923), often referred to as "the dean of American musical critics," wrote for the New York Daily Tribune from 1880 to 1923. Taking his cue from Dvořák, Krehbiel favored American composers drawing on African American melodies, but apparently did not have the same feelings about Native American music: he "kept incessantly howling, particularly against me, that Indian music was 'only ritual, and had no relation to art'" (Farwell to Arnold Schwab, 3 February 1951, AF Collection). Farwell's somewhat acid tone regarding Krehbiel's theory of "stock phrases" in Indian music doubtlessly reflects his reaction to the critic's devastating comment that had appeared only weeks before in a review of Farwell's Dawn Fantasy: "Any cool-headed student of the music of the American aborigine ought to be able to duplicate it [one of the stock phrases] fifty times in an hour" (Henry E. Krehbiel, "Music: A Concert of American Compositions," New York Daily Tribune, 19 April 1909: 7). A few years before, Krehbiel had

It was at this time that I made my first really savage composition on Indian themes, a *Navajo War Dance*. I had earlier inclined to the more pastoral songs and peace chorals, and folks reasoned naively that these could not represent the Indian, since the latter was a savage. Evidently I must reform and do something really Indian. The theme of the *Navajo War Dance* was something to make your blood curdle and your hair to stand on end.[10] I afterwards learned that the man at whose house I was ensconced with my piano, near the Lummis mansion, said to a friend at the time, "That Farwell is a queer fellow. He goes down in the *arroyo* and sits on a white rock in the moonlight, and then comes up and makes the d—dest discords you ever heard in your life." But that is pardonable, for one has Richard Strauss to compete with in these days.[11]

These were days and nights in the Land of Heart's Desire. The early sun scattering the silver mists from valley and mountain, and awakening the luminous vivid green of the spreading orange groves; the deep burnt orange of the evening sky through the tall swaying eucalyptus; the blue distance of the Sierra Madres, these were scenes from Paradise. And such romantic surroundings for the workaday life, the hospitable table spread thrice daily at the Lummises in the dining-room opening on the sycamore-sheltered *patio*, the singers and guitars at

---

shown respect for Farwell's early attempts at setting Indian melodies, claiming that he "has made the first sustained attempt to infuse them . . . with poetical significance and emotion by means of harmony . . . The result of his experiment is extremely interesting, and justifies some discussion of his method of procedure" (from clipping of *New York Tribune*, 31 August 1902, in AF Scrapbook).   [10]Farwell wrote two compositions entitled *Navajo War Dance* in this period, the one mentioned here, composed in the summer of 1904 (cited as Op. 29 in Brice Farwell, ed., *A Guide to the Music of Arthur Farwell* [Briarcliff Manor, NY: published by the editor, 1972], 9) and the other written sometime in 1905 (cited as Op. 20, no. 1 in Brice Farwell's *Guide*, 10). Farwell revised the 1904 composition a few years later, giving it a higher opus number than the the 1905 piece and calling it *Navajo War Dance No. 2*; he reportedly published it with Wa-Wan in 1908, though Brice Farwell is unable to verify the existence of such a publication. Three decades later, the pianist John Kirkpatrick produced an edition of *Navajo War Dance No. 2* (Music Press, 1947), performing the work frequently on programs that featured American composers. The *Navajo War Dance* of 1905 was published in Wa-Wan as the first piece of the suite *From Mesa and Plain* (Op. 20; *WP* 3:57–60); but apparently Farwell was dissatisfied with it, for he wrote "obsolete" on the manuscript, publishing another version of the piece with G. Schirmer in 1912 (*Guide*, 10).   [11]These were the years when Strauss produced his operas *Salome* (1905) and *Elektra* (1909), both controversial for their violence and dissonant harmonies. Farwell respected Strauss's work at a technical level, but found the German master's compositions at odds with his view of the spiritual function of music. He saw Strauss's music, as well as that of Brahms and Debussy, as "purely artistic invention . . . a Godless, a soul-less world of art" (Farwell, "The Coming Composer," *MA* 21 [10 April 1915]: 28).

Spanish American singers who performed at Lummis's home

dinner, the *chuchupate* to drink, the dark Indian boys to serve us, all contributed to make life seem a dream.[12]

Then to pass from dream to deeper dream, in August, at the full of the moon, I went up to accept McCoy's invitation to the High Jinks of the Bohemian Club of San Francisco.[13] Everyone now knows something of this great annual event held up at the club's grove of giant redwoods on the Russian River.

---

[12]*Land of Heart's Desire* is the title of a brief play by William Butler Yeats (1865–1939) first produced in 1894. This "Land" is described as a place "where beauty has no ebb, decay no flood, / But joy is wisdom, Time an endless song," and appears as a symbol for that state of mind in which all ideals are within the realm of possibility. Farwell's time in California in these years must have given great hope that his dreams for American music could be realized. He was fond of Yeats's works and clearly in tune with the Irish writer's mystical thought as well as his efforts for a national literary revival in his homeland. Interestingly, it was in California, some fifteen years later when Farwell took up residence there, that he had the opportunity to meet with Yeats who had come on a lecture tour (Evelyn Davis Culbertson, *He Heard America Singing: Arthur Farwell: Composer and Crusading Music Educator* [Metuchen, NJ: Scarecrow Press, 1992], 340).   [13]The production Farwell witnessed was *The Hamadryads*,

At the Club, in San Francisco, I was told to drop all my luggage. The High Jinks celebrates the slaying and burial of Care. A trip of several hours brought a number of us to the grove, at which accomodations are provided for two weeks for the Bohemians and their guests, at this season. The engine poked its nose among the very trees at the edge of the tract which is the grove. Free handed we walked into the joyous—the joyously-solemn depths of this temple of the Ancient of Days, where impudent man seems like an intruder unless he conducts himself like a god. We passed under a great banner with the device of an owl, the patron bird of the Bohemians, and were conducted to our tents, where we found our luggage all in place, it having gone on before us.

The freedom of the forest—freedom from Care! that is the spirit of the Forest Festival. Artists of the club were already at work in the grove making signs, cartoons, droll and humorous, for the direction and edification of the Bohemians and their guests. Day by day a company of some seven hundred men was gathering, to see Meledon, the spirit of care, slain by Apollo, coming in the glory of the dawn, and to rejoice at his funeral pyre. And such men as these were who gathered, who created and attended this event! They seemed indeed gods, playing with heroic toys, their voices ringing through the vast towering forest-silence which overhung all these deeds and revels as the mute immensity of night domes over the music which penetrates and shakes it.

On the nights preceding the chief ceremony there were gatherings at the great circle in the heart of the grove. A huge fire sent up its flames into the darkness, which was spotted here and there with the light of numerous high-hung lantern-clusters. The circle was broken at one point by a low platform containing a grand piano. The various talents of the gathering were put in requisition, and mirth, admiration, and wonder ran high.

But to hear a great orchestra in this forest! The afternoon before the day of the jinks there is a full rehearsal of the drama. It is a point of honor for all those not particpating in any capacity to leave the grove during the rehearsal. As I walked away alone, the sombre and wild notes of the Prelude arose. Never shall I forget the first magic of those tones of the 'cellos and the horns and the oboes as they blended and rose and spread through the mighty hush and expectancy of the glade.

---

with music by McCoy and text by Will Irwin. Farwell gave one of his lectures on Indian music while at the Bohemian Grove and was made an honorary member of the Club, a membership he was proud to retain for the rest of his life. See Farwell to W. C. Bacon, 1 June 1937, AF Collection.

It was like a dream come true—the dream of dreams. It was as if one had passed the gates of Heaven and heard a voice saying, "Thy sins are forgiven thee." I stood still and wept—there was no help for it.

But in this festive company such a mood could not hold one long. We walked and talked and swam and delighted ourselves as we pleased until Saturday night. After the great banquet at tables in concentric circles, the eager throng assembled at the stage, framed by giant trees and backed by the rising hill. The orchestra is sunken, as at Bayreuth. There we watched and hearkened, while the gentle Hamadryads issued from the trees into the pale moonlight, while Meledon came and gloated over them vaunting his power to keep them tree-prisoners, and while in a burst of light rivaling the very dawn, and to the choral acclaim of the Hamadryads, Apollo came, and from high above slew the god of Care with his fiery dart.

It was a triumph of art, for McCoy, the musician, and Will Irwin, the poet.[14]

---

[14]Farwell's high regard for the Grove Plays would be expressed in numerous articles of the following years (see, for example p. 223. in this collection), though most fully in two pieces for *MA*: "How the 'Midsummer High Jinks' Came into Existence," 10 (17 July 1909): 2–3 and "The Bohemian Club High Jinks of 1909," 10 (16 Octocber 1909): 3–8. The important influence these productions were to have on Farwell's work with community music is discussed in my article " 'The New Gospel of Music': Arthur Farwell's Vision of Democratic Music in America," *American Music* 9 [1991]: 199f.

1904–1905
Boston's American Music Society[1]

After the full moon of August, 1904, passed, taking the *Hamadryads* "Jinks" with it into the domain of history, there were four months more of work in Los Angeles transcribing the Indian and Spanish songs from the phonograph.[2] Christmas Day, as on the previous year, found me at the Canyon. A lunch with Carl Busch in Kansas City[3] and a dinner with Ernest Kroeger in St. Louis, and I was back in Chicago, where for several months I was engaged in musical work still unripe for mention in this record of completed experiences.[4]

Returning to Newton Center and Boston, it chanced that I was asked early in April to give a talk for the Twentieth Century Club on my

---

[1]From *MA* 10 (15 May 1909): 11, 31. Beginning with this installment of the "Wanderjahre" articles, Farwell opens each of the remaining chapters in the series with this brief explanatory statement: "These articles cover a series of experiences from years of European study, through the writer's pursuit of the American Idea in music from East to West, up to the present time. They picture in a narrative way America's musical pathfinding as contrasted with European traditions." [2]Items in AF Scrapbook indicate that Farwell was also involved with lectures and recitals both in the Los Angeles area and, during December, in San Francisco. An article from the *Newton Center Town Crier* of 3 February 1905 reports that while in California, Farwell gave twenty concerts of works representing the Wa-Wan Press. A program from one of these, given on 15 December at Lyric Hall in San Francisco, featured Carlos Troyer and Farwell playing their own Indianist works.   [3]The Danish-born Carl Reinholdt Busch (1862–1943) came to Kansas City in 1887. He founded the Kansas City Symphony Orchestra in 1911 and was its conductor until 1918. In addition to guest conducting duties which took him over the United States and Europe, Busch was a composer, who (perhaps through Farwell's encouragement) studied with Humperdinck. *MA* reported his study with Farwell's old teacher and notes also that Busch "has finished a number of new compositions based on Indian lore" ("From Beyond the Seas," *MA* 3 [17 February 1906]: 10).
[4]Evidence in AF Scrapbook conflicts with Farwell's claim that he was in Chicago "for several months" in early 1905. First of all, the news clipping referred to in n. 2 above states that Farwell had just returned home from his trip West. After having spent Christmas at the

experiences and observations in the West.[5] In this talk I went at some
length into an account of the composers I had met on my Western
wanderings—Campbell-Tipton, Arne Oldberg, Ernest Kroeger, Carl
Busch, William J. McCoy, Edward F. Schneider, Gena Branscombe,[6]
and others, some little known and some wholly unknown in Boston and
the East generally. Also I gave a description of the Midsummer High
Jinks of the San Francisco Bohemian Club, and of my work, as well as
that of others, with the Southwestern and other "American" folksongs.
Members of the club asked me if there were any regular way of hearing
these Western musical expressions in Boston. Learning that there was
not, it was proposed that a society be formed for the purpose.

    Accordingly a meeting was called, and on April 20, 1905, the
American Music Society came into being. The plan of the society was
essentially democratic. American music was for the people, not for a
few musicians. The society made a modest beginning (such matters
must be conducted with propriety in Boston), but was broad in the

---

Grand Canyon, most of January was taken up traveling eastward with known stops in Kansas
City, St. Louis (a talk was given there on 5 January), and in Detroit (a lecture on 10 January).
There was barely time for him to have spent more than several *days* in Chicago. No further
information has been uncovered that would provide the nature of Farwell's "musical work still
unripe for mention" in 1909.   [5]Founded in 1894, the Twentieth Century Club attempted to
provide a forum for airing a broad range of timely issues, from municipal reform to arts and
education. Music became a more active concern of the Club in 1904 when a Committee on
Dance and Music was formed. Farwell had in that year given one of his Indian talks for the
Club, while other lecture-recitals included Henry Gilbert's on Celtic music and Henry
Worthington Loomis's on Negro music. (Information provided by *A Survey of 20 Years: 1894–1914*
[Boston: The Twentieth Century Club, 1914], as well as the following privately printed publica-
tions of The Twentieth Century Club at Widener Memorial Library, Harvard University: *Bulletin
of the Twentieth Century Club* (1904–05), and the *Fourth Annual List: Lecture and Pamphlet
Service: 1904–05.*   [6]Farwell had met the Canadian-born Gena Branscombe (1881–1977) when
she was teaching at the Chicago Musical College (1900–07). In *AM* (438f.), Farwell says that
Branscombe is "one of the very few women composers of America who have established for
themselves a genuine creative musical individuality." Farwell appears to diminish Branscombe's
achievement, however, in asserting that her compositions typify those of other women composers in showing no interest in "structural ideas." But in Farwell's mind, this was in Branscombe's
case not a weakness at all, in view of her "startling character of intuition." Intuition for Farwell
was key to the creative act and of a higher order than that of technique, which included the issue
of form. Between 1905 and 1906, three of Branscombe's songs were published by Wa-Wan.
Whether through Farwell's influence or not, it is interesting that Branscombe studied with
Humperdinck between 1909 and 1910. It seems significant to note that besides Branscombe,
eight other women composers were published by the Press—in all, one-fourth of the thirty-
six composers represented in Farwell's publishing venture: Natalie Curtis Burlin (1875–1921),
Julia Damon, Eleanor Everest Freer (1864–1942), Alice Getty, Katherine Ruth Heyman
(1877–1944), Virginia Roper, Caroline Holme Walker, and Louise Drake Wright.

inclusiveness of its council, which contained Harvard, Boston University and Wellesley professors, not in all cases from the musical departments of these institutions, a leading man in settlement work, members of the literary profession and composers. There were thirty-two founders. Mr. William I. Cole, of the South End House, one of the gentlemen of the Twentieth Century Club who first spoke to me of the matter, was made president. John P. Marshall, Henry T. Gilbert, Walter R. Spalding, Clarence Birchard, Miss Helen A. Clarke and Miss Sophie Hart were upon the council.[7] I served the infant society as musical director. We held monthly meetings at the rooms of the Twentieth Century Club, and in the Spring of 1906 ventured a tentative concert in which Arne Oldberg's Quintet in B Minor received its first Eastern hearing, the composer being present and taking the piano part.[8]

In the four years from April, 1905, to April, 1909, the American Music Society has grown from this small beginning to the establishment of "centers" in about a dozen of the chief cities of the United States. It comprises among its officers many of the leading musical thinkers and workers of the country, and is giving chamber music

---

[7]*The Musical Courier* (50 [31 May 1905]: 13) reported that the Society had its first meeting on 23 May. Of those council members who are not identified elsewhere in these notes, William I. Cole (d. 1935) was a distinguished sociologist and writer, in residency at Boston's South End [Settlement] House from 1894 to 1913 (see Obituary, *Boston Evening Transcript*, 27 September 1935). Walter R. Spalding [appears as "Spaulding" in the original text] (1865–1962) had been teaching at Harvard University since 1895 and was selected in 1903 to head the music division there, succeeding John Knowles Paine. In addition to three music theory texts, Spalding wrote a history of music at Harvard, published in 1935. Clarence C. Birchard (1866–1946) established a publishing house in Boston in 1901 that specialized in educational books for public schools. The firm's first publication was *The Laurel Song Book* to which Farwell made contributions (see p. 82, n. 5). Helen A. Clarke (d. 1926) was a poet, student of philosophy, translator, and literary critic, as well as one of the founders and editors of *Poet Lore*, a quarterly established in Boston during the 1890s which first introduced English readers to works of Maeterlinck, Strindberg, Gorky and others (see Obituary, *Boston Evening Transcript*, 9 February 1926). No information on Sophie Hart could be found.   [8]The very first concert of the American Music Society which included Oldberg's Quintet in B Minor for Piano and Strings occurred on 15 November 1905 (printed program in Twentieth Century Club file at Harvard University). Farwell was outraged by the critical response to Oldberg's work: "The critics—the only two who took any notice whatsoever of the concert—were scurrilous. [Henry Taylor] Parker of the [Boston] Transcript—a beast—said that 'such work was turned out by the ream in Germany—where it was the wholesome discipline of young students.' Such outright viciousness makes one rage—or incline to—but let the dead bury their dead" (Farwell to Oldberg, 18 December 1905, AO Collection). A concert given by the Society on 27 April 1906, to which Farwell apparently refers here, included another quintet by Oldberg, this one for woodwinds and piano in E-flat (not B Minor, as Farwell inadvertently

concerts in Mendelssohn Hall, and has just given, on April 18, 1909, its first orchestral concert, in Carnegie Hall, New York City.[9]

The time was plainly ripe for the birth and growth of this idea. If the idea had not embodied itself in the American Music Society it would have done so in something which would have been the equivalent of it. The idea was there, like a seed; the soil and the season were ready. It was inevitable that the seed should sprout. An instant's glance at the conditions which existed will make this plain.

Here was a mighty land, a new land, which was just bringing to completion and self-understanding its material establishment from East to West. Artistic development had progressed so far that our leading men in literature and painting—arts which invaribly precede music— had gained world-wide fame. The country had established a vast musical machinery—the means of musical production and performance throughout its length and breadth. It had imported the entire musical product of the Old World and swallowed it whole. Not only had it devoured the classic masterpieces, but was beginning to devour the works of the European decadence as well. But all this while the country was doing something else. It was, and had been for years, sending from every corner of the land almost the entire mass of the best of its musically gifted youth to the schools of Europe to learn how to sing, how to play, and last, but not least, how to compose. It was not to be conceived that this could go on forever without a visible result—a flowering of these talents at last upon our own soil. This army of young people, returning from study abroad, scattered again. It was a new factor in the country's musical development that a great number of these students were now from the West. Most of them went back to their home, and, although they were continuing to develop—as the result of their broadening European experience—and were being constantly reinforced, still, it was a disconnected, a disunited development. A few composers of distinction had already arisen in the Eastern cities, but they had an advantage not shared by the younger men of the central and western part of the country, for they stood directly in the

notes). Farwell was again disillusioned by the critical response, writing Oldberg: "It will be a long time before the clear atmosphere of your work can be breathed by the critics, who, for the most part, live the mental and spiritual lives of swine" (Farwell to Oldberg, 29 April 1906, AO Collection). This latter of Oldberg's quintets had been dedicated to Farwell, who was honored, praising it as "the greatest American work that I know, and greater than any analogous European works of the moderns." (Farwell to Oldberg, 31 August 1906, AO Collection).   [9]Farwell discusses these concerts in Chapter 24.

musical current flowing in from Europe through Boston and New York, and distributing itself over the land. Their names and their works were carried far and wide. The man of Indiana or Missouri or Colorado was at best in a mere circling eddy. His work might become known in a narrow local circle, but he had no means of artistic representation before his countrymen North, East, South and West. He had tried the publishers again and again, and they, for very practical reasons, refused him first and last except in the case of little works which were without meaning for his larger artistic growth. Great artists, conductors, singers, he could not easily get at, and when he could reach them, could accomplish little or nothing. Composers East or West who, by dint of persistence, of patient waiting upon opportunity, of stratagem and tact, had toilsomely brought it about that Madame So-and-So, of the Metropolitan Opera House, was singing one of their little songs in some of the Western concerts on one of her tours—composers so happy as this would talk about it for months. This was a stride indeed! And, everything considered, it was a stride. But these same composers had on their shelves the completed manuscripts of sonatas, trios, quartets, quintets, of choruses and orchestral works, indeed of symphonies and operas. From Maine to Vancouver, from Hatteras to Catalina, it was everywhere the same—a piling up of the manuscripts of completed works on one hand, a perfected national machinery of musical performance on the other, and an impassable gulf between—the total lack of a general national acceptance of the new idea "American composer."

A deadlock had been reached. Musical composition, whatever the ultimate worth or worthlessness of the works already in existence, had grown to a point where something in its hampering environment had to snap. If ever there was a time when something was to be *done*, this was the time. And so the American Music Society came into being, quickly and quietly, evoked by a living Need and spurred by a great Idea. And when, three weeks ago—April 18, 1909—the straps were taken off, and I saw our composers, ready and waiting, one after the other step forth and take the baton to conduct their own works on the stage of Carnegie Hall; when I saw this and saw the mass of people—they, too, ready and waiting—back them up and cheer them on, my heart leaped high. Vision led me on, and I saw the same scene coming to pass in city after city, until America and its tone-poets shall have been bound in indissoluble bonds of affection.

Thus I have been compelled to halt my narrative in order to paint a picture, and I must ask the kind reader's indulgence. Some things that must be said lend themselves better to picture than to story. To find our way back into the course of events, then, after this little truancy, we must go to Newton Center, Mass., in that Spring of 1905. Unheard of composers have a way of turning up there from time to time, and this time it was Arthur Shepherd, of Salt Lake City, who thus had a glimpse of the New England town that was to become his future home. Shepherd first became widely known by his capture of the Paderewski prize for orchestral compositions, although it must be averred that he has not become widely known by the work itself, a circumstance not illuminating in the study of American conditions. He had earlier studied at the New England Conservatory of Music, and subsequently returned to Salt Lake City, where he conducted the Symphony Orchestra and established himself as a teacher.[10] On the occasion of our meeting he was making a flying trip East to look up the possibility of the publication of some of his compositions, and fate, in the form of Lawrence Gilman, of New York, directed his footsteps to the Wa-Wan Press.[11]

---

[10]Arthur Shepherd (1880–1958) became a lifelong friend of Farwell, and, in view of the thirty-nine extant letters of Farwell to Shepherd (AS Papers), also a confidant. Farwell gained respect for Shepherd's compositions soon after their meeting and had one of his songs performed at the first meeting of the American Music Society (Letter of Farwell to Arthur Shepherd, 7 June 1905, AS Papers). Later, in AM (417–19), Farwell speaks of Shepherd's use of harmony as "one of the most daring and original in the employment of ultra-modern resource." Five of Shepherd's works were published by Wa-Wan between 1905 and 1909. Shepherd had won the Paderewski Prize in 1905 for his Overture Joyeuse. For more on the relationship between Farwell and Shepherd, see Richard Loucks, Arthur Shepherd: American Composer (Provo, UT: Brigham Young University Press, 1980), especially 7–11.   [11]The music critic Lawrence Gilman (1878–1939) was a staunch supporter of the Wa-Wan Press, writing in 1903 that it was "probably the most determined, courageous, and enlightened endeavor to assist the cause of American music that has yet been made" ("Some American Music" Harper's Weekly 47 [7 March 1903]: 394); though the editorial is unsigned there seems little doubt that it was written by Gilman, who was the music editor at Harper's at this time. When the Wa-Wan Society—an adjunct organization to the Press—was formed in 1907, Gilman was chosen to serve on its executive board; he contributed one article to the society's organ, the Wa-Wan Press Monthly ("The Programme-Musician and the Public"; see WP 4:65–66). Gilman was a self-taught musician who was not without talent as a composer; three of his pieces were published by Wa-Wan in 1903 and 1904 (for an appreciation of them as well as Gilman's musical insights in general, see Carl Engel, "Views and Reviews" Musical Quarterly 26 [January 1940]: 113–21). Even in later years, when the paths of Farwell and Gilman rarely crossed, their mutuality continued, as when in an exchange of letters written in the 1930s they regretfully opine that they are among the few remaining Wagnerites (Letter from Farwell to Gilman, 21 April 1935, and from Gilman to Farwell, 2 May 1935, AF Collection).

1905–1906
Third Trip West[1]

The Spring of 1905 thus saw the founding of the American Music Society, in Boston, and first brought Arthur Shepherd upon the scene. The Summer added still another to my circle of composer friends, in the person of Noble Kreider. He came from his home in Goshen, Indiana, bearing the inevitable portfolio of manuscripts— that wondrous and mysterious portfolio, which it may be will contain shining records of the most dazzling sun-flights of the imagination, and it may be, will not. This was one of the pleasant surprises, however, and in Kreider's compositions there were numerous evidences of the truly poetic nature, and of the unmistakable touch of the artist. These compositions were all for piano, and showed a far better handling of pianoforte technic and a far greater sympathy with the pianoforte style than is customary with American composers. Kreider had drunk deep at the fountain of Chopin, and if the draught had somewhat qualified the nature of his own imagination, this was no more than happens to most successful composers whose earlier works are apt to disclose the sources of their first inspirations. But Kreider's music revealed also an imaginative quality of its own, which asserted itself with increasing strength in his more recently composed works, and indicated that here was a personality which was bound to find its way to individual expression.[2]

---

[1] From *MA* 10 (22 May 1909): 19, 27.   [2] Very little additional information on Noble Kreider (1874–1959) from this period can be cited. A lifelong resident of Goshen, Indiana, he taught piano and theory there (Obituary in *Goshen News*, 21 December 1959). Over sixty letters of Kreider to Farwell, all only partially dated but apparently from the 1930s, are in AF Collection; from these we learn that Kreider made weekly commutes to Chicago to teach harmony classes and piano. Kreider and Farwell remained close even in later years. It appears, however,

During the Summer I was experimenting with some of the material which I had gathered in the Southwest, and with other Southern and Southwestern themes which I had come upon in different ways in the course of my wanderings. One melody which interested me particularly, an Omaha Indian song, was so complex and difficult in its rhythm as to render it virtually impossible as a song to be sung by any known singer except an Indian, and suggested treatment as an instrumental work. This was "Pawnee Horses," and was originally sung by an Omaha who had evidently taken so many of the horses of his enemies, the Pawnees, that he was quite superiorly indifferent to any further conquests of the kind. Seeing a number of horses galloping in the distance he sang, "There go the Pawnee Horses; I do not want them. I have taken enough." The melody carries the rhythm of the gallop and the spirit of the scene as only an Indian would have conceived it.

Among the melodies less remote from ordinary vocal possibility was one of the many versions of the refrain of the "Dying Cowboy."

> Bury me not on the lone prairie
> Where the wild coyote will howl o'er me,
> In a narrow grave, just six by three,
> O bury me not on the lone prairie.

With the accompaniment of this song I had a vast deal of difficulty, providing for the necessary rhythmic license of the melody, the free and easy way of singing it which alone could preserve the effect of the song as heard on the plains; to do this without interrupting an accompanying effect which should suggest the continuity, the unbroken loneliness of the plains, was a knotty problem. It was finally solved,

---

that they met a year later than what Farwell has recalled above; in letters to Arthur Shepherd and Arne Oldberg written within days of each other in the summer of 1906, Farwell states that a new musician, Noble Kreider, has just recently come to Newton Center (Farwell to Shepherd, 20 August [1906], AS Papers; Farwell to Oldberg, 31 August 1906, AO Collection). Farwell's respect for Kreider's abilities never diminished. In a letter to John Tasker Howard, whose recently published *Our American Music* had been sent to Farwell from the author, Farwell praises the book but notes the omission of Kreider's name, adding that "he is one of the rarest souls that has composed in America, and his music is among the most beautiful that we have. But not much of his has been published, and that is mostly his earlier work. The war set him back—almost ended him—but he is now producing work of the rarest and most exquisite order, almost all for piano, being like Chopin in this respect" (Farwell to John Tasker Howard, 19 April 1931, AF Collection). Six of Kreider's works, all for piano, were published by Wa-Wan between 1906 and 1910.

after throwing away entirely several accompaniments over which I had labored long and hard, by a species of compound tremolo which alone could represent the constant limitless plain, while the melody should go its own characteristic way. The results of this experimenting in the Summer of 1905 resulted in two small volumes, one of vocal works called "Folk Songs of the South and West," and one of instrumental, "From Mesa and Plain."[3]

The one who lends himself sympathetically to these fresh Western inspirations will certainly be driven to new modes of expression in his endeavor to give them musical form. They give a fillip to the imagination which shakes it out of old ruts, and leads to styles of tone painting previously unheard, and which, if developed with sufficient art—which will take time and application—will bring about worthy music of a new order, characteristic of some highly poetic and picturesque aspects of our own land. Nor is it needful that such music should be cramped, or restricted to the point where it is incapable of becoming "world-music," by reason of its relations to the locality of its original impulse. It need "leave no more aftertaste of the soil from which it is grown" than a good apple does. It all depends upon the expansiveness of the soul through which it finds expression. The impulses and the dreams engendered by the great West are big enough for anyone in mortal shape, and it requires only the combination of the large point of view and the requisite musical gift to rear out of it symphonies that shall make a world appeal.

In July I went out into the western land for the third time, taking with me my mother upon this occasion. After sojourning for a few days with the glories of the Canyon in Arizona, we went on to Los Angeles, where I continued the work of transcribing Indian and Spanish-Californian songs for the Institute of Archaeology.[4] It was during this visit that the little

---

[3]Farwell's statement that the pieces in these volumes were written during the summer of 1905 is contradicted by their publication date, as they appear in Wa-Wan's Spring Quarter issue of 1905, which is prefaced by Farwell's prose introduction dated "April, 1905." "Pawnee Horses" was published in *From Mesa and Plain* (*WP* 3:57–67); the song Farwell refers to here as "Dying Cowboy" appeared with the title "The Lone Prairee" in *Folk Songs of the West and South* (*WP* 3:39–55).   [4]Farwell received word from Lummis shortly after returning from his second trip West that the Archaeological Institute of America had granted $500 to continue the transcription project and that Farwell should "lay . . . plans to spend another five or six months with us" (Lummis to Farwell, 3 February 1905, CFL Collection). Having heard no word on Farwell's plans for coming to California that summer, Lummis wrote in early May to remind his friend of the Institute's financial committment to the transcription project (Lummis to Farwell, 5 May 1905, CFL Collection). Lummis was likely

center of the American Music Society in Los Angeles was formed, which was dissolved by a fate which subsequently took most of its leading spirits far and wide of that region.[5] But the ground was then broken, which recently, through the Herculean efforts of Eugene Nowland,[6] has been cultivated to such splendid purpose in the establishment of a strong Los Angeles Center of the Society. The impulse of the earlier Center, too, has borne fruit in various parts of the country through its dispersed members, Mrs. Kelly Campbell having afterwards done pioneer work in San Diego, California, and Lawrence, Kansas,[7] and Harry Barnhart in many places. October of 1905 found us back among Massachusetts scenes.

What with activities at the Wa-Wan Press and the affairs of the infant American Music Society in Boston, the Winter passed quickly. Suddenly, one day in the Spring of 1906, a telegram bore down upon me from New York, urgently requesting my presence in that city on a matter of importance connected with American music. I went over

anxious to hear from Farwell since it was at his behest that Farwell had received the grant as well as an honorary membership in the Institute (a certificate indicating Farwell's membership in the Institute is in AF Collection). Farwell responded to Lummis's concern a month later, assuring his friend that he was planning to come to California to continue the work he had begun, but that an understudy was needed to take care of the routine details of transcribing (Farwell to Lummis, 1 June 1905, CFL Collection). It is clear from this letter, and another written shortly after, that responsibilities of his work along with health problems had begun to take their toll on Farwell. In addition to a continuing schedule of lectures, there were the ongoing duties of the Wa-Wan Press and the new committment of being music director of the American Music Society. On top of this was the strain of managing the financial indebtedness of the Press, which seemed to be a continual plague. Then, just days before leaving for California, he writes Lummis that he has "been knocked out nervously" and is under a doctor's care, but "sleep, and the trip will fix me up alright" (Farwell to Lummis, 19 June 1905, CFL Collection). After spending nearly four months in California, Farwell returned to Newton Center in mid-October, where he received official thanks from Lummis on behalf of the Executive Committee of the Southwest Society for his "highly efficient discharge of his difficult commission in transcribing some 300 of the old Spanish folk-songs of the Southwest" (Lummis to Farwell, 21 October 1905, CFL Collection). Lummis had secured funds in August for Farwell to hire Harvey Worthington Loomis to help with the work (Lummis to Farwell, 24 August 1905, CFL Collection). Also engaged by Lummis to continue the transcription project upon Farwell's departure was Henry Edmond Earle, who notes that Farwell "with the help of Harvey W. Loomis, wrote down about two hundred melodies and would have continued the work if he [Farwell] had not been called back to the East." (Henry Edmond Earle, "An Old Time Collector: Reminiscences of Charles F. Lummis," *California Folklore Quarterly* I [1942]: 180). [5]A printed program from a recital of this society (in AF Scrapbook) indicates that it was officially organized several months after Farwell left California, on 25 January 1906. [6]See p. 177, n. 16. [7]The only information I have found on Kelly Campbell appears in Oscar Hatch

and found myself, at the old Arts Club, in a very enthusiastic meeting of young men who wished to organize a series of orchestral concerts of American compositions. In a cause which had little or nothing to lose I was as ready as the others to see something launched, knowing that in pioneer developments many starts usually have to be made before one carries through to success. It is necessary to persist in the education of public spirit before it becomes the soul of a successful planting. The American revolution was but the final fruitage of innumerable apparently futile revolutions on both sides of the water against the old-world order.

Thus the "New Music Society of America" was formed and got so far as to give two orchestral concerts during the following season, by means of a kind of cooperation with the Russian Symphony Society, of which Modest Altschuler is the conductor. At the first of these concerts there came to light in proper orchestral guise for the first time Henry Gilbert's Aria *Salammbô's Invocation to Tänith*, composed years before in the barn in Quincy, Massachusetts, already made familiar to the followers of these wanderings.[8] Also Arthur Shepherd's prize *Overture Joyeuse* had on this occasion its first hearing, and one of the only two hearings which it has ever had, the other being in Salt Lake City under the bâton of Walter Damrosch. MacDowell's *Indian Suite* and his concerto in D minor, together with the works mentioned, made up this first New York program.

The fundamental and fatal weakness of the New Music Society of America appears to be that it was based not upon unconquerable and unceasing determination and effort, which alone could have brought it through, but upon the rather vague hopes of assistance from certain wealthy persons, which animated one of its founders. The wealthy persons, inspired by a too great proximity to the conduct of Metropolitan affairs, and by a lack of the deeper knowledge of American musical needs, regarded the importation of an expensive foreign conductor as a first requisite. They did not, be it understood, promise to import one. This proposition, unquestionably a *faux pas* in an enterprise distinctly American, led to the resignation of the founder in question, and to the death of even those vague

Hawley, "National Federation of Musical Clubs: the Sixth Biennial Meeting at Grand Rapids," *Musical Courier* 58 (2 June 1909): 43–45, where, along with her photo, she is cited as "Mrs. David Campbell of Kansas City, first vice president" of the National Federation of Musical Clubs. [8]See p. 93f.

hopes of assistance which had been cherished. Thus the New Music Society of America passed into history.[9]

The Summer of 1906 afforded me the opportunity to do something which I had long wished to do; namely, to give modern musical expression to the spirit and the event of the Wa-Wan, or "Pipe Dance" ceremony of the Omaha, from which I had borrowed the name of the Wa-Wan Press. This effort resulted in a suite of piano-forte sketches which push the Indian atmosphere and idiom about as far as it will go in

---

[9]Despite Farwell's philosophical posture at the failure of the New Music Society, he must have been greatly disappointed, for he had worked hard for the organization's success. His efforts on its behalf began earlier and were far more time-consuming than what he indicates here. In early November 1905, he writes Arne Oldberg that he had been called to New York "on an important mission"; a month later he tells that the new society has just been formed and in February that he is making numerous trips to New York, presumably regarding business of the Society (Farwell to Oldberg, 10 November 1905, 18 December 1905, and 12 February 1906, AO Collection). *MA* reported in late December that the organization had been incorporated at the Secretary of State's office in Albany, New York, and that Farwell was appointed one its directors along with Louis A. von Gaertner, Samuel Swift, Jacob Altschuler, Modest Altschuler, Lawrence Gilman, and Rupert Hughes ("New Music Society Incorporated," *MA* 3 [30 December 1905]: 1). According to Farwell, Louis von Gaertner (1866–1937), a Philadelphia composer, called together the first meeting; the other directors, except for Farwell, were all New Yorkers: the critics Lawrence Gilman of *Harper's Weekly* and Samuel Swift (1873–1914) of the New York *Evening Mail*; the conductor and cellist Modest Altschuler (1873–1963) who established the Russian Symphony Society in New York in 1903 and his brother Jacob, a violist; and the novelist and writer on music, Rupert Hughes (1872–1956), whose *Contemporary American Composers* was published in 1900. Personal remembrances of meetings of the Society are provided in Percy Atherton's "Boston Days (1909–1922): Some Engeliana," *A Birthday Offering to Carl Engel*, ed. Gustave Reese (New York: G. Schirmer, 1943), 28, and in Carl Engel's "Views and Reviews." *Musical Quarterly* 26 (1940): 117. The musicologist Carl Engel (1883–1944), who had emigrated to the United States from Germany only months before, found that Farwell and his supporters were too strident in pressing their views: " . . . everyone alike, in this brave little band of Wa-Wanites, was animated with the holy zeal of iconoclasts." According to a printed "Preliminary Announcement" of the Society (AF Collection), the organization projected three orchestral concerts for what remained of the 1905–06 season and were soliciting scores from composers to be considered by a committee consisting of Modest Altschuler, Hughes, Gilman, and N. Clifford Page (1866–1956), a composer and, at the time, editor for the music publisher Oliver Ditson of Boston. As it turned out, only two concerts were forthcoming, on 10 March and 2 April 1906, both at Carnegie Hall. Reviews in *MA* were lukewarm. Neither the Shepherd nor Gilbert works of the first concert was well received, while the pianist for the MacDowell concerto was called to task, understandably, for playing Tchaikovsky as an encore on this all-American program ("First Concert of New Music Society," *MA* 3 [17 March 1906]: 11). Of the second program, consisting of Chadwick's *Melpomene* Overture, Henry Holden Huss's Violin Concerto in D Minor, David Stanley Smith's companion pieces, *Il Penseroso* and *L'Allegro*, and Frederick Converse's *The Mystic Trumpeter*, only the works of Smith and Converse "proved to be deserving of serious consideration" ("American Composers Receive a Hearing," *MA* 3 [7 April 1906]: 6). Nevertheless, Farwell was enthusiastic about the response for the first concert, noting that while the hall was not crowded, the upper galleries were filled, with ticket

modern music, and which because of their experimental psychology I called *Impressions of the Wa-Wan Ceremony.*[10]

An August walking trip with John Beach in the White Mountains cleared the mental decks for the forthcoming season's action.[11]

---

sales amounting to $500. He was convinced that it demonstrated the "considerable drawing power of a concert of American compositions," despite the skepticism he had noted in some quarters regarding such an undertaking. He chided those critics who saw the event as unimportant, believing that what was needed more than anything at this point was a sympathetic attitude toward the effort, a recognition that aspiration has an important place in the development of art (*WP* 3:188f.). Privately, Farwell expressed disapointment that the concert was not "as strong a blow as could have been struck for the cause," and, as he suggests in the text of *Wanderjahre*, some of the blame had to be laid on the society itself, which "did not *know* all it should know, and was dominated too much by [Modest] Altschuler" (Farwell to Oldberg, 31 August 1906, AO Collection).   [10]Published by Wa-Wan Press; see *WP* 3:241-57.   [11]Even though Farwell was able to complete a piano suite in the summer of 1906, letters to his friends Arthur Shepherd and Arne Oldberg reveal that it was a most difficult period for him. He had been overwhelmed by work, spending a "wretched" six weeks in New York which left him exhausted—"about the lowest mental condition I have ever been in." His condition was doubtlessly exacerbated by critics, who he claimed had "visciously [*sic*] attacked and misrepresented" him, most likely for his beliefs regarding the importance of Indian song in creating a national music. Revived by his week in the mountains with John Beach, he decided to strike back at the critics with a new lecture, "A National American Music," that he will take on yet another western tour. In the talk, Farwell plans to "say something bigger about the situation than any of them have said, and stand up for some basic principles which I believe they do not even see." (See letters of Farwell to Arthur Shepherd, 20 August [1906], AS Papers, and to Arne Oldberg, 31 August 1906, AO Collection.) The main points of the lecture are set forth in the next chapter.

1906–1907
Fourth Trip West - A New Campaign[1]

The Fall of 1906 arrived duly on schedule, and it was now necessary, as the Germans say, "to begin something." The special work for the American Institute of Archaeology on folksongs in the Southwest was now over. On the second and third Western trips, as on the first, I had given many lecture-recitals on the Indian music, playing my own developments of Indian themes, and using the occasion to say a few timely things on American music in general.

The time seemed to have come now to do something broader. The work of various composers in the special field of folksong development had made considerable talk, a good deal of it showing evidence of an almost human intelligence. The matter of American music had been thrashed out pretty fully. Almost every ramification of the subject had been touched upon, but the records of the discussion were scattered, and consisted of controversial articles in various papers and magazines more or less inaccessible. Therefore I planned a new lecture-recital, "A National American Music," which aimed to synthesize the whole matter, to take up in turn each of the very few fundamental questions in the case, to state it, and in so far as the "growingness" of the situation allowed, to answer it. These questions were, "Is a national music desirable?" "What is American spirit?" "Are there any American folksongs?" and "Shall folksongs enter into a national musical art?" To these was added a fifth, "What shall we do?" as a spur to popular action in the cause of American music. The first I answered in the affirmative, provided the word national should be taken in a sufficiently large sense, as voicing the spirit of a new nation with something to say, and not

---

[1]From *MA* 10 (29 May 1909): 19–20.

as an excuse for merely exploiting this or that phase of local national "color." The second question admitted of scarcely any more definite answer than *freedom*, the right and the happiness of untrammeled artistic expression, the artist taking the risk of the worth or worthlessness of that which he chose to express. In answering the third question it appeared to me that only the songs of Stephen Foster, George Root and a few scattering songs, such as "Dixie,"² had the technical right to the specific name "American folksong," although the whole mass of American popular songs, ragtime, etc., might reasonably be admitted under this term. Indian, negro, Spanish-Californian songs, etc., had better retain their own special names as such. In answering the fourth question I took the ground that, in so far as the composer should choose to introduce any of these folksongs in his work, and should produce a sufficiently good work of art thereby, a work which the people of America would in the long run elect to retain and treasure—these folksongs would enter into our American musical art. I further took the ground that there was nothing inherent in the nature of musical art to prevent such a thing coming to pass, and intimated that since our composers in a number of instances were taking the matter seriously in hand, we might well expect a certain influx of this influence into our musical art. I also held that such a course was not necessary to the production of a national American music, which must first of all express the free, progressive spirit of the nation, whether it was to assimilate the folksongs or not. As to what to do, there was but one thing—to learn who our composers are, what they have composed, and to create every possible means for the hearing and study of their works. These various points were illustrated and emphasized by compositions from various sources.

Armed with the discourse, I ventured upon a fourth Western trip, this time with Salt Lake City as the objective point.³ Detroit was my

---

²Farwell refers here to popular song and song writers from primarily the second half of the nineteenth century. The songs of Stephen Collins Foster (1826–64) are generally placed in two groups, those composed for minstrel shows that include his well known *Oh! Susanna* (1848) and *Old Folks at Home* (1851), and the so-called "parlor" songs which aspired to more genteel tastes and include the perennial *Jeannie with the Light Brown Hair* (1854). Equal to the popularity of Foster's songs were those of George F. Root (1820–95), who was a music educator as well as a composer. Among his most successful pieces were those inspired by the Civil War, notably *The Battle Cry of Freedom* (1862) and *Tramp! Tramp! Tramp!* (1864). *Dixie* (1859) was written by Daniel Decatur Emmett (1815–1904), who penned the song for Bryant's Minstrels, one of the foremost troupes with whom he performed in the 1860s. ³Farwell left on his fourth western trip around 8 January 1907. After an initial stop in Detroit, he

first stop, and while there certain persons proposed that an association should be formed, based on the Wa-Wan Press idea, to carry out plans both of publication and performance of American compositions. I promised, accordingly, to return from the West with a working plan for such an association, and put it before a group of music lovers in Detroit, with a view to making a start in that city.[4] Upon this fourth Western wandering I had an object in view essentially different from that of the other trips. This was to look more closely into American conditions, particularly with regard to the publication situation, and the matter of American willingness to give a hearing to American works. The result of this quest was, if depressing, also illuminating in its effect upon action to be taken.

To begin with, these inquiries aside, I quickly learned that, broadly, the depth of ignorance of the best American music, old as well as new, was Stygian. It is true, the mass of American music, songs of an ordinary or even a rather nice sort, "teaching pieces," popular music, etc., everywhere heard throughout America was enormous. A certain amount of American music of distinguished character was also broadly known, but in no instance to so great a degree as where the composers themselves, like MacDowell, had concertized up and down the land playing their own works. The sporadic instances of the study of American music, as by clubs here and there, was superlatively inadequate and ineffectual. I found no single instance where any one had actually devoted time and energy to mastering the subject, or had gained exhaustive and positive knowledge of the American composers' work, from song to symphony. "American programs" were made up of chance American works that happened to be at hand. The idea seemed never to have occurred to any one to make up programs as the result of a study of the whole field and a final selection of only the best. Indeed, even the proper data for such a study did not exist. The labor of original

traveled on to Goshen, Indiana—the home of his friend Noble Kreider—for a lecture on 10 January, hoping to be in the Chicago area a day or two later to visit Arne Oldberg (Farwell to Oldberg, 29 December 1906, AO Collection). Two programs in AF Scrapbook indicate that there were talks in Davenport, Iowa (14 January) and Memphis, Tennessee (19 January). He had hoped to present lectures as well in Urbana, Illinois (at the University of Illinois), Kansas City, and Denver (Farwell to Arthur Shepherd, "Rainy Season" [probably, Fall 1906], AS Papers).   [4]The groundwork for the Wa-Wan Society had been laid, actually, a month earlier. In a letter to Arthur Shepherd, Farwell exclaims: "Great success in Detroit—a 'Wa-Wan Society' of which I will tell you—will be started there (Farwell to Shepherd, "Christmas Day" [1906], AS Papers). This had probably occurred when Farwell had been in Detroit to give his lecture on a National American Music on 6 December (according to a news item in AF Scrapbook).

research necessary for the preparation of such data would, moreover, have been such a Herculean task that only a person feeling himself especially destined to undertake it would be led to make the attempt. Rupert Hughes's pioneer work in producing his book, *Contemporary American Composers*, had been a noble start in a discredited cause, and thus far there has been no single work between two covers to surpass it. Hughes used to take delight in referring to the time when he "wrote that book and lost his reputation."

Pursuing my way to Colorado Springs, I there had the pleasure of meeting another American composer, one who, in the comparatively small amount of work which he has put out, has given evidence of a rare and perfect sense of beauty and of the subtler secrets of tone painting. This was Frederic Ayres, who has brought the best elements of the modern musical sense to bear upon the lyrics of Shakespeare, and who can write songs that are *songs*, as well as songs that are "tone poems." His setting of "Where the Bee Sucks" will delight generations to come, and those who have had ears to hear the message of Ludwig Wüllner in America will long treasure his "Sea Dirge," a setting of "Full Fathom Five," from *The Tempest.*[5]

In Salt Lake City I was royally entertained by Arthur Shepherd, and there I heard his big piano sonata for the first time.[6] What with

---

[5]Farwell had great admiration for Frederic Ayres (1876–1926), who like himself moved into the field of composing after being trained as an engineer. Ayres, he believed, "was the first American composer to have assimilated various European influences into his idiom while leaving that idiom genuinely his own. He was never anything but Frederick [*sic*] Ayres." (Farwell to Miss Burdick, 6 February 1934, AF Collection). In a lengthy, more personal recollection of Ayres, Farwell wrote A. Walter Kramer, President, Society for the Publication of American Music, that "I have never known a character where unobtrusiveness and an intense spiritual *presence* were so curiously combined. Without saying or doing much of anything, he was tremendously *present*. Composers are horrible pianists, and Ayres was the worst of them ever known (outside myself) . . . he never conveyed anything to me on the piano. But in composing, he operated all the more intensely in his mind" (Farwell to A. Walter Kramer, 12 May 1934). Other discussions of Ayres by Farwell were published in the *Wa-Wan Press Monthly* (*WP* 4:44–45) and *AM* (415–17). Farwell apparently supplied information on Ayres to William T. Upton for the latter's article, "Frederic Ayres," *Musical Quarterly* 18 (1932): 39–59; a note in Farwell's hand written at the top of the type-written letter to A. Walter Kramer cited above states: "This is something of an expansion of and improvement on my letter *in re* Ayers [*sic*] to W. T. Upton, Feb. 6, 1931." Six of Ayres's songs were published by Wa-Wan between 1906 and 1911, including the two Farwell cites, "Sea Dirge" and "Where the Bee Sucks" (*WP* 4:15–18 and 111–14); in addition, an article of Ayres, "Some Factors in Musical Progress," was published in the July 1907 issue of the *Wa-Wan Press Monthly* (*WP* 4:107–08). Ludwig Wüllner (1858–1938), a distinguished German singer who was known for his dramatic performances of songs, made two extensive tours of the United States between 1908 and 1910.   [6]Shepherd composed three piano sonatas in 1907. In a letter to Shepherd of 2 October 1907, Farwell discusses,

Frederic Ayres

conducting the symphony orchestra, the theater orchestra, teaching, filling a church position, and composing, Shepherd was an extraordinarily busy man. Nevertheless, he managed to get away with me for a trip through the fertile valleys of Utah to Logan, where I held forth for American music in the Mormon Tabernacle, and tried a Navajo War Dance on the elect.[7] I was interested to note the presence of both the Bible and the Book of Mormon on the reading desk in the Tabernacle. Joseph Smith, the head of the church, was on the train going up to Logan, and I had a half hour's conversation with him. He is a tall man of kindly demeanor, with a long, brown beard and eyes of lustre and

presumably, the one mentioned above, which Richard Loucks suggests may be Shepherd's Sonata Op. 4 (see Loucks, *Arthur Shepherd: American Composer* [Provo, UT: Brigham Young University Press, 1980], 232, 235, where the letter is transcribed).   [7]Farwell planned to spend

depth. It may have been a fancy, but it seemed to me that his eyes were those of a man who holds many secrets in the depths of his nature. The aboriginal aspects of my work being pointed out to him, the conversation fell upon Indians, concerning whom he showed much knowledge and alert interest.[8] The Mormons up through the paradise of these mountain-girt valleys, farmers mostly, interested me greatly. They are simple folk, a sort of refined peasantry, happy and full of faith. I also made a short trip southward to Provo, where, thanks to a man named Lund, whose colossal magnetism draws after it the whole musical life of the place, I had the largest audience of my experience. He also had a good sized chorus on the stage of the great hall of Brigham Young Academy, where the recital was given, and extended me the courtesy of the bâton that I might conduct one of my own choruses, in which he had previously drilled the singers. And before this I had never heard of Provo.[9]

Making a quick journey eastward, I spent several days with Chester Ide, still another American composer, in Springfield, Ill.,[10] and with a plan for organization in my pocket, went back in March, 1907, to my friends in Detroit.[11]

the early part of February in Utah (Farwell to Arthur Shepherd, 9 January [1907], AS Papers). Two newspaper clippings from AF Scrapbook show that he was in Provo for a lecture on 2 February and talked to the Ladies Literary Club of Salt Lake City five days later. [8]It appears that Farwell refers to Joseph Fielding Smith (1838–1918), nephew of the founder of the Mormon church, Joseph Smith (1805–1844). [9]Anthony C. Lund (1872–1935) was director of band and choral activities at the Brigham Young University until 1916 (the institution went from the status of Academy to University during his tenure there), when he left to become the conductor of the Mormon Tabernacle Choir (see Ernest L. Wilkinson, ed., *Brigham Young University: The First One Hundred Years* [Provo, UT: Brigham Young University Press, 1975] and Michael Hicks, *Mormonism and Music: A History* [Urbana: University of Illinois Press, 1989], 157f.) [10]The Wa-Wan Press published in 1907 three works of Chester Ide (b. 1878), who taught piano and harmony in Springfield until 1916. At that point he began teaching at the Music School Settlement in New York, where Farwell was director. [11]Farwell lectured in Springfield on 19 February according to a news item in the *Illinois State Journal* of 20 February 1907, (AF Scrapbook). While in Salt Lake City, he wrote Oldberg that he would be returning through Chicago around 22 or 23 February (Farwell to Oldberg, 1 February 1907, [writing on stationery from the Knutsford Hotel in Salt Lake City, Farwell mistakenly dated the letter "January 1, 1907"; on this date he had not yet left Newton Center], AO Collection). By mid-March he was back in Massachusetts (indicated by a program for a 22 March lecture in Boston; AF Scrapbook).

CHAPTER 20

1907
The Idea of the "American Composer"[1]

Before speaking of the organization which was launched in Detroit in March, 1907, there is a word to be said about the causes leading up to it. Somewhere in the early chapters of this narrative I gave fair warning that as we went on from the aimless enthusiasms of student days toward the years of mature and purposeful endeavor, the cheerful casualness of the story must give place somewhat to more serious considerations. Every American who takes even the smallest hand in musical affairs, as professional, amateur, or merely as a listener, is going this journey—following this quest of the American Idea in music, whether he is consciously thinking of it or not. The great question is not, What is American music going to be, or sound like? but, What is America going to do with the Musical Idea, the art of music as a factor in life and civilization? Is she merely trivially or luxuriously going to amuse herself with the work of the craftsmen of other lands, as a spoiled daughter of wealth might toy with some rare scarab of the Nile or Etruscan bracelet? Or is she coming to realize that a people cannot truly grow in musical art and culture, except that people be a creator of musical art? Will she bestir herself and hew and forge out music of her own? And if so, will she help to make a place for her workers, co-operate in making a place in her artistic and economic plan for those who sing her songs and chant her symphonies? These are the questions we must ask—the living questions in American musical life to-day, which our activities, our enterprises and undertakings of the next few years must answer.

It was in 1907, after the cessation of my specific work with the

---

[1]From *MA* 10 (5 June 1909): 22.

Southwestern folksongs, and with the turning of my attention wholly to the national situation, that I began to see with understanding eyes the real nature of the evolution and the problem that were working themselves out in the musical life of America.

Perhaps the chief notions that every American must get into his head to-day, if he is to see below the surface of the matter, are these: that

America set up and had in operation a great definite machinery for the performance and propagation of European music, when that was all there was to have, and before the American composer, in sufficient numbers and force to count, had come on the scene, and that

The whole American people for generations has thus been educated and trained to the idea that the only real music is European music.

To realize these things is the only way we can get away from the sentimental cant and twaddle about the neglect of the American composer. For all the talk about the American composer for a number of years, for all the good work done by some of our composers for decades, the idea "American composer," taking it in the broadest sense and in relation to the history of music, is a new idea in the world. A place must be made for this new idea. To make this place something must be displaced a little, moved to one side or readjusted. But even a very slight readjustment of so massive a machine as the national musical life—a readjustment which must be made, too, while the machine is running—is a pretty serious and difficult affair. It throws out of gear the calculations of many people. Everyone has the trouble of beginning a new set of computations. The orchestral conductor has to think, "Can I risk this new work by an unknown man with my audience? Will it be a sufficient popular success to warrant the support of those who maintain the orchestra, and who require that the orchestra shall show a profit or at least a minimum deficit?" He has also to bestir his musical judgment and ask: "Is this really a good work?" For new works by native composers cannot be taken on faith. There is no glamour of European reputation behind them.

Singers and players have to think nearly the same thought, though they are less beholden to backers. Glamour, reputation, money, they think, can come only by placing on programs the latest European novelty or sensation, or true fame by sticking to the classics—the poor classics, which had such an agonizing time transforming themselves from revolutionary works by dishonored native prophets into world-classics! Artists are slow to realize that an immediate money reward is not the most substantial form of reward. They are slow to see that in a land where pioneering is a prime and inevitable necessity, they fail to strike firm roots into the soil which must nourish them, when they appeal to a passing taste for exotics. Even when an artist appreciates the value of a new American work, he must stop to think, "Will my audience accept this, pay me in the end for doing such things? It takes time to prepare new works—time which might be spent upon something certain to bring me support." This is by no means a wholly mercenary thought; it is a most necessary consideration, and we may be assured that even the most courageous artistic pioneer cannot escape taking it into account in his calculations. A noted songstress was heard praising in the highest terms some new American songs.

"Why don't you sing them?" she was asked.

"Oh, it would hurt my reputation," was her quick reply.

Men like David Bispham and Harry Barnhart are far sighted, when they determine to blaze the paths of American progress, whatever the rough work it entails. They will have the vast satisfaction of having helped to build the foundations of the musical life of America, and they will have the increasing and enduring support of the people.

Again the great managerial and publishing organizations of the East are planted firmly as the rock of Gibraltar in the immense industry of selling America its European music. The very ground under the rock shifts when the creative idea in American music springs into being and America begins to look to herself for her music. Even these great organizations must begin, not without great inconvenience, to undergo readjustments.

And so all down the line the American composer trying to get a hearing sings, with the witches in *Macbeth*,

Double, double
Toil and trouble.

Neglected? Not a bit. He has not been in the game long enough to be neglected. He is a new kind of man, these ten, twenty, fifty years past, fighting for standing-room in a place where no provision has been made for him. If he is not fighting cheerfully, joyously, something is wrong with him. MacDowell's untimely end, a great hero in the fight fallen, has stirred the country to its depths.[2] With that fall a new era has begun.

---

[2]MacDowell had resigned in 1904 as the first chair of Columbia University's music department over disagreements with the school's administration. Shortly thereafter mental illness over-

These conclusions, and many others, were the result of investigation, inquiry, observation, during my four years of wandering up and down the land. I found hampering conditions surrounding the performance of American compositions and surrounding the publication of them. Artistically and commercially, there was pathmaking to be done. The influence of society, taking the term broadly, must be brought to bear on gaining adequate performance of American works. Artists must be encouraged from the audience's side to give important American works. Support must be gained for the publication of the highest quality of American music. It was at this time, and to set forth these points, that I wrote an article, "Society and American Music," for the *Atlantic Monthly*, which so greatly aroused the ire of Arthur Symons, in the London *Saturday Review*. He assumed it to be my thought that such organization would directly affect the creative act of the composer. As a matter of fact, it does so only vaguely and indirectly. The cultivation of the creative musical art of America by the American people is a different matter.[3]

As a tangible outcome of the situation, the first center of the "Wa-Wan Society" was organized in Detroit, in March, 1907. This was based upon the Wa-Wan Press idea and work, and provided for subscribing memberships to a monthly series of American music publications, and meetings and concerts for the performance of the best American music in general.[4] The music of the series was to be only an

---

took him, plaguing him for the rest of his life. He died on 23 January 1908, only a year and a half before Farwell wrote this.   [3]Farwell's article is included in this collection, p. 191. Arthur Symon's response appears under "Music and Social Flurry," *Saturday Review* [London], 21 March 1908. Symons (1865–1945), a noted British critic and poet, was particularly known for his translation and study of Baudelaire, Verlaine, and French symbolist poetry; *The Symbolist Movement in Literature* (1899) is considered his most important work. He contributed biweekly music reviews to *Saturday Review*, which he joined in 1897.   [4]Beginning in March 1907, Farwell issued Wa-Wan publications monthly—rather than quarterly as previously— along with a brief organ of the Wa-Wan Society, the *Wa-Wan Press Monthly*. In the first issue of the *Monthly*, Farwell is named as president, with an executive board comprised of an impressive roster from the musical world: George W. Chadwick, Arthur Foote, Charles M. Loeffler, Frank Damrosch, Ernest Kroeger, and Lawrence Gilman. As with the introductions to quarterly publications of the Wa-Wan Press, these monthlies of the new society contained Farwell's opinion pieces along with brief comments on new works published by the Press that month. In addition, there were reports from various newly-formed centers, news items of interest to the society, and, usually, a column entitled "American Music Study," providing lists of "characteristic" works of American composers for study at centers. Farwell hoped that the monthly would provide a forum for airing concerns about American music, reminding members in the December 1907 issue that in such a democratic organization their opinions were

incidental factor in this performance. A number of leading citizens took a hand in the organization, among them Mr. Lobenstine, Miss Edna Wallace, Miss Clara Dyar, Mr. N. J. Corey, Mr. Larned, Mrs. S. Olin Johnson and Mrs. Charles Hammond.[5] Thus a widely distributed national organization was begun which eventually, after radical changes and developments, became the present American Music Society.[6]

---

vital to its life. As it turned out, the Wa-Wan Society was dissolved only a year after its inception and a new organization, the American Music Society, was formed through the merger of the Wa-Wan Society with Boston's American Music Society. With that, after twelve issues, the *Monthly* ceased to be published. (All issues of the monthly are reprinted in *WP* 4 and 5.)   [5]The March 1907 issue of the *Wa-Wan Press Monthly* (*WP* 4:29–32) lists each of these individuals, in addition to several others, and the offices they held in the Detroit organization. Here also are identified more fully Horace Lobenstine and C. P. Larned. According to the Detroit Public Library files, Lobenstine was also known as Horace G. Preston (d. 1948), a local business man. The same source establishes that Charles Pierpont Larned (b. 1863) was a native of Detroit; that Newton J. Corey (1861–1922) was a noted organist and music teacher in the city, as well as an editor for the *Etude* and the *Detroit Saturday Night* and manager of the Detroit Orchestral Association; and that Juliet K. Hammond was the wife of millionaire packer, Charles F. Hammond (d. 1928). Edna Kingsley Wallace was to collaborate with Farwell some forty years later as the librettist for *Cartoon*, a three-act "operatic fantasy" finished by Farwell in 1948. No information can be cited for Clara Dyar or Mrs. S. Olin Johnson. The June 1907 *Wa-Wan Press Monthly* (*WP* 4:85–88) provides the Detroit Center's initial program presented on 16 May, citing along with it a list of members, which had grown to forty-four.   [6]A printed program of the "First Meeting of the Wa-Wan Society of America/Detroit Center," 16 May 1907, appears in AF Scrapbook. Mrs. S. Olin Johnson is noted as "Leader." The program included Farwell's lecture "Toward a National Music" and a recital of several composers published by Wa-Wan (the program is provided also in *WP* 4:88, though Farwell's talk is not cited there).

1907
"A Strenuous Pastime"[1]

*A*fter the establishment of the first center of the Wa-Wan Society in Detroit in March, 1907, the next event pertinent to these records was the fifth Biennial of the National Federation of Musical Clubs in Memphis, Tenn., in May. Thither I repaired from a sojourn in the mountains of New Hampshire—those friendly and eternal hills for which I have ever retained an undying affection since the days when, among them, I first became aware of the divine place of music in human life.[2]

At Memphis a step was to be taken which would concentrate the heretofore somewhat scattered forces of this great body, the National Federation of Musical Clubs, upon the American Musical situation, and give the Federation a place of new national importance and meaning. For a number of years the Federation had been gaining numbers and perfecting its organization, until in 1907 it numbered about ninety clubs, in all parts of the United States.[3] But it was felt that now the time had come to introduce some element into this widespread organization which would knit the clubs together in a common interest and for the accomplishment of a common end.

Mrs. Jason Walker, of Memphis, had for some time been interested in the American music movement, and on the occasion of an earlier visit of mine to this city of steamboats and cotton bales we had talked

[1]From *MA* 10 (12 June 1909): 19.   [2]In a letter to Arne Oldberg dated 11 April [1907] (AO Collection) Farwell notes that he is staying with J. F. Manson of Center Ossipee, New Hampshire.   [3]The National Federation of Music Clubs, founded in 1898, had as one of its goals to bring together both musician and music lover. Its first biennial convention was held in 1899 and its official organ, *The Musical Monitor*, was first issued in 1912, to be superceded eventually by the *Music Clubs Magazine*.

the matter over in a general way.[4] Before the Biennial in May, Mrs. Walker had conceived the idea of having the Federation offer prizes for works by American composers. This she put in the form of a motion, which, after some modifcation and discussion, was enthusiastically carried. This motion provided for the offering of $2,000 in prizes, to include a prize for an orchestral work, the successful compositions to be performed at the next Biennial, which was to be held at Grand Rapids, Mich. A committee was then appointed, consisting of Mrs. Walker, chairman; Mrs. David A. Campbell, of Kansas City, Mo.,[5] and myself. My own connection with the Federation was established through the Detroit center of the Wa-Wan Society, which joined the Federation at this time.

The motion as carried placed a considerable responsibility upon Grand Rapids—the weighty one of providing a symphony orchestra. Next to opera, with its zenith prices for stars, the modern symphony orchestra is one of the most expensive of luxuries—a taste not easy to indulge. But the American capacity to rise to emergencies is well known, and in electing to the presidency Mrs. Charles B. Kelsey, of Grand Rapids, the Federation found itself with a chief officer fully equal to the occasion, as subsequent developments have so brilliantly shown.[6]

Prizes were offered as follows: Class I, orchestral work, $1,000; Class II, song $500; Class III, instrumental work (piano solo), $500. It was thought that the prizes should be sufficiently large to attract national attention and be an inducement to the foremost American composers. The judges chosen for Class I were H. E. Krehbiel, Walter Damrosch and Charles Martin Loeffler; for Class II, David Bispham, George Hamlin and Carl Busch, and for Class III, Heinrich Gebhard,

---

[4]Farwell had been in Memphis for a lecture in January, on his way to Salt Lake City (see p. 141, n. 3). Little information was found on Mrs. Walker; an article about the 1911 Biennial Convention of the National Federation of Music Clubs provides her photo and states that she is the chair of the committee on American music for the Federation (Emma L. Trapper, "National Federation of Clubs," *Musical Courier* 62 [5 April 1911]: 29)   [5]See p. 136, n. 7. [6]Mary Atwater Kelsey (1860–1915), a native of Grand Rapids, was known for her efforts to enhance musical life both in her home town and nationally. An unidentified newspaper clipping in the obituary file of Grand Rapids Public Library notes that Kelsey "was largely instrumental in bringing here some of the country's greatest composers and musical artists." She was twice elected President of the National Federation of Musical Clubs, in 1907 and 1909. The obituary cites the praise that the American composer Charles Wakefield Cadman (1881–1946) had for Mrs. Kelsey: "more than any other woman in the United States [she] had labored to the best advantage in the interest of American music and musicians." She was the wife of Charles B. Kelsey (b. 1863) whose wealth came through banking and utilities. (See also Trapper, cited above in note 4, which includes a photo of Mrs. Kelsey.)

William Sherwood and Glenn Dillard Gunn.[7] It was desired in each class to secure as nearly as possible a balance between the theoretical and the practical points of view in judgment, and also to have different sections of the country represented. With the planning of this work of the competition, the Memphis meeting broke up and all went to their homes filled with enthusiasm for the carrying out of the idea.

We can know what this competition meant historically, and in relation to American ideals, only when we realize that the prize fund was raised by thousands of persons scattered over the length and breadth of the United States. History must regard this competition as the first nationally widespread democratic recognition of a creative musical art in America. The American Music Society in 1905, it is true, pointed out the necessity of such democratic recognition, and pro-phetically began its organization upon that basis; but in 1907 it was still far too young and localized an organization to undertake that which was possible to the National Federation of Musical Clubs.[8]

---

[7]Of the individuals mentioned who are not already identified in these pages, the European-born Charles Martin Loeffler (1861–1935), after settling in the United States—which he found "quick to reward genuine musical merit and to reward it far more generously than Europe"—was a violinist with the Boston Symphony Orchestra, but more importantly, one of the most respected composers of his generation. Loeffler lent strong support to musical activities in America, including the work of its composers (see *The New Grove Dictionary of American Music*, s. v. "Loeffler, Charles Martin"). The tenor George Hamlin (1868–1923) had been an active recitalist since 1895, presenting the first all-Strauss song recital in America in Chicago (1898); he was featured also in the premiere of Victor Herbert's *Natoma*, staged by the Chicago-Philadephia Opera Company in 1911. One of Boston's celebrated pianists, the German-born Heinrich Gebhard (1878–1963), taught and concertized in the city to which he had emigrated, and since 1899 was frequently featured as a soloist with the Boston Symphony Orchestra; Gebhard performed in concerts of Boston's American Music Society, including works of Farwell. Louis Elson refers to William Sherwood (1854–1911) as "the first American piano virtuoso of the beginning of the century" (*The History of American Music*, rev. ed. [New York: Macmillan,1915], 285). Notable for featuring works by Americans on his recitals, he is known also for establishing in Chicago the Sherwood School of Music (1897). Glenn Dillard Gunn (1874–1963) was a pianist, conductor, and music critic active in Chicago; he taught at the Chicago Musical College and conducted the American Symphony Orches-tra, an organization he founded to perform American works and engage American soloists. Farwell confides to Oldberg that the committee had hoped to get primarily reputable critics to adjudicate, but of those solicited, only Krehbiel accepted, "and he very grudgingly." He states further, "I am by no means satisfied with the final results—but believe the matter will be sincerely handled, and think that more actual thought will be put into it than if [William J.] Henderson, [James G.] Huneker, [W. L.] Hubbard etc. had accepted" [the first two were based at the time in New York, while Hubbard was in Chicago]. In all, 24 orchestral works were entered in the competition, along with 59 vocal pieces and 28 in the piano category (Farwell to Oldberg, 2 August 1908, and 18 October 1908, AO Collection).   [8]Farwell does

Since for the moment we are on this train of retrospective thought, if we would go further toward discovering the earliest practical democratic action in the recognition of an American musical art, it will be necessary to go back four years more, to the founding of the Wa-Wan Press in 1901. Even before this the idea was in the air; it had probably had a thousand expressions of one kind or another. A crystallization of some sort was no longer to be escaped. After the starting of the Wa-Wan Press half a dozen men or more told me that they had had for years the idea of doing such a thing.

From the Memphis Biennial I went to St. Louis, where, with the help of Ernest R. Kroeger and other friends of the movement, a center of the Wa-Wan Society was formed. At the same time, Arthur Shepherd effected the formation of a center in Salt Lake City. Both these men became musical directors of their respective centers. Frederic Ayres also organized a center in Colorado Springs, of which he was made president.[9]

The Summer of 1907 brought with it physical discouragements not easy to overcome, but a restful sojourn at the home of a friend in Saratoga toward the end of the Summer gave me fresh heart. This friend gave me invaluable help in planning out a Fall campaign for the extension of the Wa-Wan Society in New York State, and by the time the leaves were falling I was making my headquarters alternately in Rochester, Buffalo, Geneva, Syracuse and Auburn. In the three first named cities centers of the Wa-Wan Society were formed.[10]

---

not mention here that he addressed the Memphis convention on a "Democracy of Music." In addition to being appointed to help oversee the Club's competition, he was asked to prepare for the organization a listing of American composers and representative works, along with a pertinent bibliography (see "The National Federation of Musical Clubs," *Wa-Wan Press Monthly* [May 1907], *WP* 4:68).   [9]Information on the size of the various centers is provided by the *Wa-Wan Press Monthly*. The Detroit center had grown to forty-four members in the three months since it was established. The Colorado Springs and St. Louis centers, both formed in May 1907, had twelve and seventeen members, respectively, while a center initiated at Salt Lake City in October had fifteen members (see *WP* 4:87f. and 183f.).   [10]The burden of work brought on by the increase of Wa-Wan publications and the establishing of centers of the new society began to weigh heavy on Farwell. Letters reveal that the summer and fall of 1907 were far more discouraging than he was able to speak of here. Privately he refers to his "pretty bad illness—a breakdown," which has caused him to postpone yet another western trip, this one to promote Wa-Wan Society centers (Farwell to Shepherd, 18 July [1907], AS Papers). Farwell's father wrote Henry Gilbert at this time that Arthur is "not at all well and we're keeping him in bed" (George L. Farwell to Henry Gilbert, 17 June 1907, Henry F. B. Gilbert Papers, Beinecke Rare Book and Manuscript Library, Yale University, New Haven, CT). To Oldberg, Farwell lamented that the summer's illness had prevented his arranging for a fall lecture series. This lack of income was especially discouraging in face of debts accrued by the Wa-Wan Press—he owed engravers $500—in addition to unspecified

Organization is a strenuous pastime. Let him who contemplates it consider long and well before engaging in this phase of human endeavor. Once embarked, he must eat trouble as a fireman entering a burning house "eats smoke." He must even cultivate a relish for it.

To be responsible to one's self is hard, but to be responsible to an organization of other selves, which one's self has launched, is another thing beginning with the same letter. For this reason the organizer should be a zealot, a prophet, a crusader. His eye should be ever upon the great end to be gained. The most complex and discouraging obstacles, difficulties, intrigues, should be to him nothing more than momentary annoying details, undergrowth to brush aside as he goes his determined way. It should be to him so absorbing and life-giving a joy to be approaching, however gradually, the goal of his dreams, that no accident or unbeautiful circumstance can prevail against it. He who would lead must lose his self in his purpose. Taunts, insults, slurs, must pass through the eternal etheric purposefulness of his nature as storm winds pass through the yielding and elastic network of tree tops. He must not care where he lives, nor how, so long as he can serve the cause to which he has given loyalty and life.

The New York State campaign made headway, and the time came at last when a start in New York City must be contemplated. At the end of the year, accordingly, I went down there, and was hospitably sheltered by the "Prince" of the old Boston days, whose fortunes had brought him eastward since I had last seen him in Chicago."

"greater responsibilities for family" (Farwell to Oldberg, 1 November 1907, AO Collection). Feeling somewhat revived, Farwell threw his energies into establishing Wa-Wan Society centers in the East, apparently hoping to put the Press in better financial order before mounting a western campaign. In the letter to Shepherd cited above he writes: "I'm bound to win—and make this thing a big success—and lift this work above the stinking financial struggle in which it has thus far been involved. And this year is the time to do it—*with the organization of the soc*[iet]*y.*" As well as those mentioned by Farwell in this chapter, a new center was formed in Springfield, Illinois, by the close of 1907, as reported in issues of the *Wa-Wan Press Monthly;* (see *WP* 4:197–198 and 5:80). "Farwell gives further reasons for going to New York in a letter to Arthur Shepherd: "to form literary connections with the big magazines to earn money writing, and to gain publicity for the movement" (Farwell to Shepherd, 21 December 1907, AS Papers). Farwell had already published between 1902 and 1907 over a dozen articles on various musical issues in several magazines. His apparent desire to promote his cause through periodicals of wider coverage resulted in three articles of 1908, the already-referred-to "Society and American Music" in *Atlantic Monthly;* "The National Movement for American Music," *American Review of Reviews* 38 (1908): 721–24; and "What Teachers and Pupils Could Do for American Music," *Etude* (December 1908): 770. But a more important opportunity in this regard was his position with *MA* that began in November 1908; this resulted in Farwell's move early in 1909 from Newton Center to New York and would lead his crusade for American music into a new phase.

1907–1908
A New National Organization
for American Music[1]

The New York undertaking at the beginning of the year 1908 was delayed by a short trip westward, when I joined Noble Kreider in Goshen, Ind. We made a short recital trip together—a pair of vagabond minstrels—going first to Evanston, Ill. Here we were hospitably entertained by Arne Oldberg, of the school of music at the Northwestern University. We reached Evanston, in fact, just before the close of the year 1907, and had the good fortune to be present at the annual New Year's Eve celebration at the house of Mrs. Ella Dahl Rich, the pianist.[2] As regularly as this festival comes around, Bruno Steindel, the cellist, appears and gives an informal recital for the eager and appreciative guests, with the brilliant co-operation of the hostess.[3] The serious business of art over, merrymaking begins, and lasts into the small hours. When Oldberg, Kreider and I left, sometime between the dead of night and dawn, the good spirits of the company had the appearance of being wound up for still a few hours more. Merely to see the new year in is no longer a sufficient tribute to its majesty; it is an outworn, Puritanical

---

[1]From *MA* 10 (19 June 1909): 19. [2]The only information uncovered regarding Ella Dahl Rich is that she was the wife of Herbert Givens Rich (b. 1872), an executive of the publishing firm of H. S. Rich (*The Book of Chicagoans: A Biographical Dictionary of Leading Living Men of the City of Chicago*, ed. Albert N. Marquis (Chicago: A. N. Marquis & Co., 1911). [3]German-born Bruno Steindel (appears as "Steindl" in the original publication) was first-chair cellist with the Chicago Symphony Orchestra, 1892–1918 (*Grove's Dictionary*, 3rd ed.: *American Supplement*, ed. Waldo Selden Pratt, s. v. "Steindel, Bruno" gives 1866 as his birthdate, while 1869 is cited in *The Book of Chicagoans*).

institution. Nowadays one must watch to see the Apollonian light of its first day burst upon the renewed world.

Our musical forces being strongly augmented by Arne Oldberg, we gave in Evanston a concert *a tré*, offering our own compositions in friendly competition for the favor of the audience.[4] Before Kreider and I parted we visited Kansas City and St. Joseph, where we fell into friendly hands.[5]

Back in New York, I made immediate preparations for the establishment of a center of the Wa-Wan Society.[6] It must be understood that at this time the American Music Society preserved an independent and isolated existence in Boston, and was in no way concerned with the publication of music. In the Wa-Wan Society, which now had some half dozen centers about the country, the publication of a periodical series of music by American composers for members was a definite part of the plan. It was a part, too, which had given me an infinitude of trouble. In my effort to bring out works at the Wa-Wan Press of sufficient seriousness to reflect honor upon the cause of American music, or at least to awaken vigorous critical interest, I had been somewhat disregardful of the idea of technical simplicity. Not that I had avoided choosing simple works; the whole consideration was, Did a work have some claim to creative originality and artistic excellence? It might be simple as a folk-song, or as difficult as a concerto; that was a wholly secondary matter. This led to an unevenness in the monthly series that was naturally disconcerting to many of its supporters.

As I cast an analytic glance back over the music of the Wa-Wan Press thus far published, as a whole, it is plain to observe that it shuns the sentimental like poison, and cultivates its antithesis, the art-engendered quality—imagination. As most people are so unhappy and indiscreet as to be sentimental but unimaginative, this in its turn also led to difficulties—not objections, but simply the failure to understand, at least for a time.

---

[4]This concert, along with a talk by Farwell, was given for members of the Evanston Woman's Club on the afternoon of 31 December 1909 (*Evanston Index*, 4 January 1908). [5]Farwell had hoped to make a more extensive western lecture tour beginning in the summer of 1907, but because of illness he had to settle for an abbreviated one in late December and early January. It is clear that his main reason for the trip, though not stated here, is the hope of establishing additional Wa-Wan Society centers (Farwell to Oldberg, 22 May 1907 and 18 December 1907, AO Collection). It appears that he was successful in this regard in Evanston and St. Joseph (regarding the latter, see p. 177, n. 20). [6]A letter to Oldberg indicates that Farwell was back in New York by mid-January (Farwell to Oldberg, 14 January 1908, AO Collection).

Despite these growing complexities, the belief was still deeply rooted in me that the Wa-Wan Society idea was the one with which to strike the strongest blow for American music. It aimed at the betterment of both the artistic and the economic situation of the composer. To carry it, in the actual form of the society, had become a great strain; but the thought of abandoning it had never occurred to me. It would have seemed like cutting off my right hand.

With the help of friends, a concert of the Wa-Wan Society was arranged, Mr. Frank Damrosch kindly lending the hall of the Institute of Musical Art for the purpose.[7] The artists who took part constituted a more variegated assembly than often appears on a single occasion. There were local artists, pupils of the Institute, opera singers, and composers. There were, for pianists, Mary Williamson; John Beach, of Boston; Harvey Worthington Loomis and Abraham Shyman. Mlle. Gerville-Réache, of the Manhattan Opera, was rushed down in an automobile in an interval between her entrances in *Pelléas and Mélisande* to sing songs by Loeffler. Mme. Barelli and M. Crabbé of the Manhattan Opera House, also took part. Other singers were Harry Barnhart, Beatrice Fine and Parthenia Bowman. A viola pupil of the Institute named Sheasby was pressed into service.[8] I played one of my Indian compositions. Among the composers represented on the program were Arne Oldberg, Noble Kreider, Harvey Loomis, John Beach, Chester Ide, Carlos Troyer, and others, besides those already mentioned, and several Southwestern folksongs were sung.

Following closely on the heels of this concert, a musical of a more private nature was given, at which David Bispham sang a number of the

---

[7] A brief article on the concert, that took place on 28 February, appears with program in the February 1908 issue of the *Wa-Wan Press Monthly* (*WP* 5:89). Farwell notes here that the invited audience numbered over four hundred and that the program which lasted over two hours held their interest to the end. [8] Of the performers named here, Mme. Barelli is not mentioned in the program cited in the preceding note. In the accompanying article cited there, Farwell states that Williamson, Bowman and Barnhart are "resident artists," Williamson having studied with Theodor Leschetizky, and Bowman with the Welsh baritone Ffrangcon Davies. Abraham Shyman and Arcule Sheasby, he says, are both "advanced pupils at the Institute." Jeanne Gerville-Réache (1882–1915) had created the role of Geneviève in *Pelléas* in 1902 and was in seven performances of the work for the Manhattan Opera's 1907–08 season. The Belgian baritone Armand Crabbé (1884–1947) was with the Manhattan Opera Company for three seasons, from 1907 to 1910. He was to sing in the premiere of Victor Herbert's *Natoma* in 1911. No further identification can be given for Beatrice Fine.

works by American composers with which he has made a great success.[9]

These two concerts served to awaken the interest with which to go about making an organization—another center of the Wa-Wan Society, as I supposed and purposed. But now a new question arose. "We must have a proper name for this society," said New York, flatly. The *sang froid* with which New York waved aside all consideration of the previous national development of the organization under the original name, fairly took my breath away. It was felt, however, that the Indian name "Wa-Wan" would prove misleading as to the broad aims of the society.

By this time my mentality had reverted to the condition of a sort of primeval jungle. I had one society in Boston, another at large about the country of an experimental nature and involving some unsatisfactory conditions, and now there was evidently to be a third in New York. I was in sheer despair at the growing complexity. When I awoke in the mornings the thought of this horrible tangle was the first thing to come bump against my consciousness. The condition was becoming intolerable.

At last, one morning—resolving never to wake up to another day of this strain and complexity—I seated myself comfortably in one of the luxurious chairs in the apartment of the "Prince," and vowed that I would not quit it until I had straightened the matter out. By four in the afternoon I had performed the necessary feats of surgery, cut the necessary number of Gordian knots, and disentangled the strands that must be kept intact.

Facing it squarely, the situation appeared thus: The music issued monthly for the members of the Wa-Wan Society had been an extension of the series issued quarterly for independent subscribers. There had been little difficulty in appealing with progressive and somewhat revolutionary music of this nature to the two or three musical thinkers in a community who were specifically interested in modern musical advance. But when this number was increased by organization to from twenty to forty persons, a new and totally different situation was produced. While these persons would accept this same music in the

---

[9]A printed program of "Songs by American Composers" found in AF Scrapbook probably refers to this private concert. David Bispham is noted as one of the singers, along with Harry Barnhart. At the top of the program has been written in: "At Winslow Mallery's, N. Y., March 31, 1908." As noted, Mallery was Farwell's friend from his Boston days—the "Prince"—at whose New York apartment in the National Arts Club Farwell was staying.

ordinary course of things, as rendered by an artist on a concert stage, they had not, in the case of some of the music, the technical power to get its meaning from the printed page. The very growth of the movement was thus rendering the plan impracticable. This difficulty could be met by a total change of the nature of the music published, but this would have defeated the very purpose for which the Wa-Wan Press was established—the publication of works of artistic distinction by American composers, irrespective of every other consideration. As for the question of mere simplicity, a considerable number of simple works were being issued as it was. But when people ordinarily speak of simplicity in music, what they usually mean is conventionality. A simple thing of a new kind is apt to prove as baffling as a difficult thing. And as for simple American compositions of a conventional nature, the incredible superfluity of them now being published is one of the horrors of the time. To complicate matters still further, another and even more serious difficulty began to appear—the prospect that the organization in any case could not be effected at a sufficiently rapid rate to meet the increasing publishing expenses.[10]

When the whole matter thus became clear to me through a searching analytic scrutiny I decided at once what was necessary to be done. Despite my hopes for it, the Wa-Wan Society idea would have to be abandoned. The publication aspect, as an integral part of the plan at this stage of development, was clogging the growth of the organized movement. And organized movement, above all things, must go forward if the forces were to be marshalled which were to make for a hearing of American musical works on a large scale. In short, the Wa-Wan Press must be thrown out of the organization, as ballast is thrown out of a balloon struggling to rise.

This is what I determined to do: let the Wa-Wan Press go on as a wholly independent personal enterprise, preserving and even accentu-

---

[10]The issue of musical difficulty raised when Farwell was negotiating to establish a New York City center seems to have prompted a change in the Press's policy. The January 1908 *Wa-Wan Press Monthly* (WP 5:77) announced that publications "must now, for the sake of creating the needed popular movement, be of a nature to appeal to the general music lover and amateur of no great technical attainments"—though at the same time the Press said it would from time to time offer special publications of music on which no limits of difficulty had been imposed. The new policy, to all appearances a bargaining chip to gain a New York center, was in fact never adopted. As Farwell relates in this chapter, the Wa-Wan Society was to pass out of existence, while the Press was to become once again independent and thus unencumbered by the complications of making such a change.

ating its ideal artistic purpose; to organize the New York Society as a center of the American Music Society; invite the centers of the Wa-Wan Society to become centers of the American Music Society, discontinue all publication of music as far as the society was concerned, and offer a liberal selection of the existing publications of the Wa-Wan Press for the unfulfilled portions of the series to which members were entitled; go to Boston and ask the American Music Society to accept the new arrangement for a national organization under a national governing board, and itself become the Boston center of the American Music Society.

1908

Structure of

The American Music Society[1]

Everything happened as planned. As soon as the Boston Society's concurrence in the new plan was obtained I returned to New York, and the organization of the New York Center of the American Music Society was effected in May, 1908. The following board of management was elected: David Bispham, president;[2] Rudolph Schirmer, vice-president; Thomas Tryon, secretary; Spencer Trask, treasurer, and Joseph L. Lilienthal, librarian. The board of musical directors consisted of Walter Damrosch, F. X. Arens, David Bispham, Kurt Schindler and David Mannes, and the executive committee of Harry Barnhart, David Bispham, Frank Damrosch, Joseph L. Lilienthal, Samuel B. Moyle, Francis Rogers, Rudolph Schirmer, Spencer Trask and Thomas Tryon.[3]

This was followed by the formation of the new American Music

---

[1]From *MA* 10 (26 June 1909): 18; 27.   [2]Soon after being elected President of the New York center, Bispham published an opinion piece ("The American Idea in Music, and Some Other Ideas," *Craftsman* 15 [March 1909]: 671–80) on the aims of the American Music Society, particularly the support he hoped the organization would give in promoting opera in English. [3]Among the individuals listed here not already identified in these pages, Rudolph Schirmer (1859–1919) was president of the music publishing house founded in 1866 by his father Gustav Schirmer. The firm of G. Schirmer was to buy out the Wa-Wan Press in 1912. Three from the business world include Thomas Tryon (d. 1945), the stockbroker Joseph L. Lilienthal (1881–1936), and Spencer Trask (1844–1909), the financier and art patron whose summer estate at Yaddo near Saratoga Lake, New York, was to become the renowned art colony. Someone of the energy and influence of Trask, who Farwell may have met through his friend Thomas Mott Osborne (see p. 42, n. 15), was a great asset to the newly formed organization; one can only wonder whether the American Music Society, which was soon to fade away, would have

David Bispham

Society, the national organization, of which each local organization was to be known as a "center." The honor was granted me of allowing me to serve as president. Walter Damrosch was elected musical director. The presidents of the different centers became vice-presidents of the national society. Thomas Tryon was elected secretary and Joseph L. Lilienthal treasurer. The board of management consisted of the president, musical director, secretary, treasurer, three honorary members chosen for life, and the musical directors of the several centers.

The honorary members were George W. Chadwick, Charles Martin Loeffler and Frank Damrosch.

---

had a different destiny had Trask's life not been abruptly cut off in a train accident only a year after the organization was formed. Other musicians cited here include Franz Xavier Arens (1856–1932), who founded in New York the People's Symphony (1900) to provide concerts at

At the time of this reorganization the centers of the Wa-Wan
Society in the following cities came over into the new American
Music Society,—St. Louis, Colorado Springs, Salt Lake City, Rochester and San Diego.[4] Local conditions necessitated a postponement
of the Detroit reorganization. The shock of these fundamental
changes was sufficient to end the existence of four younger and less
strongly established centers, which could not face the throes of
reorganization following directly on the heels of what had been a
very difficult task of original organization. Boston and New York
were now added to the national society. There was now adopted
the following:

Constitution Of The American Music Society

ARTICLE I.

NAME.
The name of this Society shall be The American Music Society.

ARTICLE II.

OBJECT.
The object of the Society shall be to advance the interests of a
creative musical art in the United States of America by:
1. The study and performance of the works of American composers.
2. The study of all folk-music touching the development of music in
America.

---

low ticket prices; he is credited as the first orchestral conductor to program American works
in concerts in Germany and Austria (1890–92). Kurt Schindler (1882–1935) became assistant
conductor of the Metropolitan Opera (1905) and founded the Schola Cantorum (1909—
originally MacDowell Chorus). The violinist David Mannes (1866–1959) was at the time
teaching at the Music School Settlement at East Third Street; he was director there from
1910 to 1915, a responsibility that Farwell took over when Mannes left to found, with his wife
Clara, the David Mannes School of Music (1916). Another music educator, Frank Heino
Damrosch (1859–1937), was then director of the Institute of Musical Art (which eventually
became part of the new Juilliard School of Music); he also worked to bring concert music into
the lives of the working class through his formation of People's Singing Classes and the
People's Choral Union in the 1890s. Francis Rogers (1870–1951) was a well-known baritone
who later taught at Yale School of Music and the Juilliard School.   [4]A program of the
opening meeting of the San Diego center indicates its formation took place on 22 October
1909 (AF Scrapbook).

3. The publication of articles, discussions, or any significant matter relative to this development.

4. The establishment of centers of the society throughout the United States.

ARTICLE III.

MEMBERSHIP.

Section 1. The membership of the Society shall consist of men and women sympathizing with its object and paying the annual dues.

Sec. 2. Applications for membership shall be made to the national secretary upon an application blank provided by him (or by the secretary of any center) for the purpose, and the admission of the member shall then be passed upon by the Membership Committee. Such application shall be unnecessary for persons joining existing centers of the Society.

Sec. 3. Resignation of membership shall be made in writing and addressed to the secretary, and no such resignation shall be accepted until all dues to the Society from such member are paid.

ARTICLE IV.

RIGHTS OF MEMBERS.

All members are entitled to:

1. Attendance at and voice in all general meetings or conventions of the Society.

2. The Bulletin of the Society.

3. The privilege of establishing centers of the Society in accordance with the rules for such establishment, and with the consent of the Executive Committee.

4. The special assistance of the Plan of Work committee in the planning of American music study.

ARTICLE V.

DUES.

Section 1. The dues for membership shall be two dollars a year, payable on the first day of June.

Sec. 2. The dues for Life Membership shall be one hundred dollars.

ARTICLE VI.

MEETINGS.

The Board of Management shall have the power to call a National Festival Convention of the Society, in March, April, or May, at which orchestral, choral or operatic works by American composers shall be produced, in any year and place which may be determined upon.

ARTICLE VII.

OFFICERS, BOARDS, AND COMMITTEES.

Section 1. The officers of the Society shall be a President, Vice Presidents in the persons and to the numbers of the Presidents of the different centers; a Musical Director, a Secretary, a Treasurer, a Librarian, and a Board of Management consisting of the President, the Musical Director, the Secretary, the Treasurer, the Musical Directors of the different centers, and three Honorary Members chosen by the Board from prominent American musicians.

Sec. 2. The Board of Management, from its own members, shall appoint an Executive Committee of five, of whom the President shall be Chairman, to transact business and to act in emergencies.

Sec. 3. The Board of Management shall appoint a Plan of Work Committee of three, including the President and Musical Director.

Sec. 4. The Board of Management shall make by-laws for its own control and that of the Society, such by-laws to be published with the Constitution.

Sec. 5. The Board of Management shall appoint a Membership Committee of five, a Press Committee with at least one member in every center, and a Printing Committee.

Sec. 6. The Executive Committee shall elect a Committee on Nominations, composed of three members of the Society living in the same city.

ARTICLE VIII.

ELECTION OF OFFICERS.

Section 1. The President, Musical Director, Secretary, Treasurer, and Librarian shall be elected at the National Convention, on or before the first of June, by a majority vote of the Board of Management and shall serve for a term of two years. Re-election is permitted.

Sec. 2. In the absence of a convention, nominations for the above officers shall be made in writing by the members of the Board of Management and sent to the Secretary by April 15, who shall forward them to the Committee on Nominations. A ticket shall be made, taking the two names receiving the greatest number of votes for each office, and sent to the members of the Board of Management, who shall return their votes upon this ticket to the Secretary by June 1. The result of the vote shall be announced by the Committee on Nominations, and shall be declared valid by the President.

Sec. 3. The following persons are hereby selected as the Board of Management to control and manage the Society for the first two years of its existence, viz.: Walter Damrosch, New York City; George W. Chadwick, Boston; Charles M. Loeffler, Medfield, Mass.; Thomas Tryon, New York City; Frank Damrosch, New York City; F. X. Arens, New York City; N. J. Corey, Detroit, Mich; Charles G. Woolsey, Colorado Springs, Col.; Ernest R. Kroeger, St. Louis, Mo.; Spencer Clawson, Salt Lake City, Utah; Elbert Newton, Rochester, N. Y.; Agatha Pfeiffer, St. Joseph, Mo.; Mrs. Frederick Crowe, Lawrence, Kansas; John Beach, Boston, Mass.; Harley Hamilton, Los Angeles, Cal.[5]

Sec. 4. Where the Musical Directors of centers do not hold office for a period of two years, the newly elected Musical Director shall become a member of the Board of Management in place of his predecessor.

Sec. 5. The Honorary Members of the Board are elected for life.

---

[5]Of those listed here who have not already been cited in notes, I am able to identify the following individuals. Charles G. Woolsey taught music at Colorado Springs high school and Colorado College and was active as a vocalist in the city. Spencer Clawson, Jr. (1880–1917), a "well known pianist, one of the most brilliant musicians of Utah," [Obituary, *Deseret Evening News,* 7 May 1917], is perhaps the more likely reference here, though Farwell may refer to the pianist's father, Spencer Clawson, Sr., a prominent business man in Salt Lake City and son of the Mormon leader, Brigham Young. Little information has been found on Elbert Newton, who is listed as "organist" in Rochester city directories for the years 1904–05 through 1913–14. Agatha Pfeiffer is listed as "music teacher" in St. Joseph city directories covering the years 1905 to 1928 (see also Oscar Hatch Hawley, "Musical Life in St. Joseph," *Musical Courier* 60 [30 March 1910]: 39). Eugenia (Mrs. Frederick) Crowe is cited in the original text as being from San Diego, though this is contradicted in the next chapter where it is stated that she is from Lawrence, Kansas (see p. 177). This latter location is apparently correct, as Crowe is listed in the 1909 city directory for Lawrence, where she is cited as having a piano studio in her home. Harley Hamilton was a prominent violinist and teacher of Los Angeles who organized the Los Angeles Women's Orchestra (1893) and the Los Angeles Symphony (1897), both of which he conducted until 1913.

ARTICLE IX.

DUTIES OF OFFICERS AND COMMITTEES.

Section 1. The President of the Society shall preside at its meetings, shall be Chairman of the Board of Management, and shall serve as editor, or appoint such, for the Bulletin of the Society.

Sec. 2. The Musical Director shall conduct all orchestral performances given by the Society, and serve on the Plan of Work Committee.

Sec. 3. The national Vice Presidents, the Secretary, and the Librarian shall perform the usual duties attached to their respective offices.

Sec. 4. The Treasurer shall collect and hold all money belonging to the Society, and shall make an annual report to the Board of Management. He shall give a bond.

Sec. 5. The Plan of Work Committee shall formulate plans of work to be carried out as far as possible by centers, and shall submit such plans to the Board of Management for suggestion and discussion, and shall then have full power to formulate plans definitely and finally. It shall also, upon request, give special assistance in planning American music study to any member of the Society.

Sec. 6. The members of the Press Committee shall cause to be printed in their local press news and programs of their centers, as well as of the national Society, and shall send to their Chairman a copy of all notices which appear; they shall also send to the editor of the Bulletin a dated copy of all programs as soon as given. The Chairman shall provide the musical and other journals with news of the affairs and progress of the Society.

Sec. 7. The Printing Committee shall attend to the printing of all stationery, reports, etc.

ARTICLE X.

ESTABLISHMENT OF CENTERS.

Section 1. Any member of the Society, or any person upon becoming a member, may, with the consent of the Executive Committee, establish a center of the Society of not less than ten members in any city or town where no center already exists. A charter shall be given to each center.

Sec. 2. The membership fee in the centers may be any amount over two dollars. Two dollars a year of each membership fee shall be remitted to the Treasurer of the national Society, as the membership fee in the national organization, the American Music Society.

Sec. 3. Centers of the Society shall give at least one public recital, concert, or open meeting annually of the works of American composers.

ARTICLE XI.

BULLETIN.

The Society shall issue a Bulletin which shall contain articles, discussions, correspondence, news of the national Society and centers' programs, plans of work, etc., and which shall be sent to all members. The Bulletin shall be in the nature of proceedings, not of a necessity regularly periodical, and shall be issued at frequent intervals throughout the active musical season.[6]

ARTICLE XII.

AMENDMENTS.

This Constitution may be amended at any time by a three-fourths vote of the Board of Management.

With these strenuous and consuming affairs the season's activities ended, and I went back to Newton Center for quiet during the Summer months. There I was joined by Arthur Shepherd, who had determined to remove from Salt Lake City to the East.[7] What with music and outdoor exercise, the Summer passed pleasantly.

It was at this time that I discovered myself to be in somewhat the fix in which a painter friend of mine once found himself. A wealthy old lady whom he had met several days before at a dinner party was at his studio. She had just bought one of his landscapes, and it was to be delivered to her

---

[6]There were only four bulletins issued by the Society, those of June, October, and December 1908 and March 1909 (Edward N. Waters, "The Wa-Wan Press: An Adventure in Musical Idealism," in *A Birthday Offering to Carl Engel*, edited by Gustave Reese [New York: G. Schirmer, 1943], 233). [7]Shepherd had apparently written Farwell in the fall of 1907 of his wish to establish himself in the East. This came as welcome news to Farwell, who needed someone to handle the organizational work for new centers of the American Music Society. He also wanted Shepherd's help in launching a new project, a residential school of music in Newton Center where young students from all over the country could come to study during the summers. (See letters from Farwell to Shepherd, 20 November [1907]; 21 December 1907; 6 March 1908; 26 March 1908; and 26 June 1908, AS Papers). The goal of the school, as indicated in its printed prospectus (in AF Collection) and also in a published article ("In a Musical Utopia," *MA* 8 [10 October 1908]: 45), is typical of the high purpose of Farwell's ventures: to balance everyday life with the enjoyment of art.

the next day. The gracious lady, who was quite nearsighted withal, took occasion before going to admire extravagantly "those lovely reflections in the water." There was no water in the picture. The painter was horrified, and had a mental picture of her showing those "reflections" to friends who had better eyes than herself. "You should have seen me go to work painting water into that picture after the good old lady left!" my friend said to me. I had in some mysterious way, I discovered, acquired some scraps of a reputation as a composer of "Indian Songs." As I had never written an Indian song in my life except to transcribe literally and publish a little one-page "Bird Dance Song" of the Cahuillas,[8] I felt that if I was to make this shadowy reputation secure, the quicker I could write some Indian songs the better. I therefore set about making some striking modern vocal developments, boldly Indian, of some legendary and mythical material long before obtained by Miss Alice Fletcher during her sojourns with the Omahas. The only occasion on which the results, the "Song of the Deathless Voice," "Inketunga's Thunder Song," and the "Old Man's Love Song," have been put to the test before an audience reminds me of the man who said: "I can never find more than two movements in any symphony by Brahms. He makes the first movement and I make the second." For this reason I have great hopes of these songs—I had feared that they might be pleasing.[9] It may be laid down as a fundamental proposition that there must be something wrong and suspicious about any alleged Indian song which will please a New York audience on the first hearing.

---

[8]The "Bird Dance Song" was published by Wa-Wan Press as part of *Folk Songs of the West and South* (*WP* 3:55).   [9]The songs, published by G. Schirmer in 1912 as *Three Indian Songs*, were adaptations of three piano pieces from *American Indian Melodies* published by Wa-Wan in 1901 (*WP* 1:34–35; 36–37; 42–43).

1908–1909
A New Chapter[1]

By the year 1908 the immediate purposes of my seven years of wandering about the United Sates seemed to have been fulfilled. I had accomplished in a measure what I had set out for—to learn the land; to find where musical art had got to in America, both as an importation and as a native creation; to study aboriginal forms of music in the United States at their source; to meet musicians and audiences, and to urge them to direct some vital share of their attention to American composers and their music; and to engage in the active work of organization in behalf of the standing and the advancement of American musical art. It seemed to me that more could be accomplished by being a "stay-at-home" for awhile now, and taking what means presented themselves for developing the different phases of work and organization already under way. These were the American Music Society, the Wa-Wan Press, and an educational plan which Arthur Shepherd and I had developed during the Summer and had now put in operation at Newton Center.[2] Shepherd had also become a member of the faculty of the New England Conservatory of Music.

One thing only seemed lacking now—a national medium of commu-

---

[1]From *MA* 10 (3 July 1909): 19–20.   [2]To what degree the "educational plan" was "in operation" is not altogether clear. In a letter to Oldberg, Farwell refers to the "summer school idea" that "was too late to realize" in 1908, followed by correspondence a month later in which he announces that "the first pupil arrives next week" (Farwell to Oldberg, 2 August 1908 and 14 September 1908, AO Collection). Although a printed prospectus, entitled "Home Life and Music Study" (AF Collection), had been drawn up and presumably circulated, Shepherd recalled many years later that "this project never materialized" in any formal way (Arthur Shepherd to Edgar Lee Kirk, 4 May 1956, AF Collection). It is likely that Shepherd, who in 1909 began teaching at Boston's New England Conservatory, had to abandon his part in a project which never held much promise of financial support for him and his family.

nication, whereby the events and the thoughts pertaining to the American music movement could be broadly and regularly announced. The Bulletin of the American Music Society did not reach beyond the members of the society. No daily paper would answer the need, because of the localization of its circulation. A national newspaper was necessary.

I bethought me of MUSICAL AMERICA. What could be better? Its very name suggested close kinship with the cause in which I was working. Little suspecting the next step to which this was to lead, I at once in the Fall of 1908, made arrangements to send regular correspondence to the paper from Boston.

In late December came the first concert of the New York center of the American Music Society, under the direction of Francis Rogers. This gave me the opportunity to call at the office of the paper and talk matters over. And then, fizz-bang! almost before I knew what had happened to me I found myself a New Yorker. They do things swiftly in New York. The latest scientific thought places the making of decisions near the top of the list, as a means of expending energy, and in New York they think one-quarter of a second rather long for that ceremony.[3]

I did my thinking afterwards, and saw that the Wa-Wan Press could go on perfectly well in charge of my father, George L. Farwell, and the educational plan equally well in charge of Arthur Shepherd, while under the circumstances I could now accomplish more, in all ways, in New York than in Boston.

December 30, 1908, was the date of the first concert by the New York center of the American Music Society, which was held in Mendelssohn Hall. Songs by many composers were sung by Francis Rogers and Mrs.

---

[3]Farwell's reviews of Boston concerts appeared in *MA* almost weekly between 7 November 1908 and 16 January 1909. The managing editor of the paper, Paul M. Kempf, instructed Farwell regarding reviews that he was to "have a free hand in subject matter and . . . [its] treatment" but that there should be no "genuine sharp and serious criticism of musical performances" (Paul M. Kempf to Farwell, 13 November 1908, AF Scrapbook). After Farwell moved to New York, his duties at the weekly increased. Besides reviews, he began in several months writing the paper's unsigned "Mephisto's Musings" column, a task—according to Farwell's later recollection—he continued for the next three and a half years (Farwell to Arnold Schwab, 3 February 1951, AF Collection). By his own choice he curtailed his reviewing at the beginning of 1911 so that more time could be devoted to editorials and special articles reflecting his concerns for American music (Farwell to Arne Oldberg, 6 January 1911, AO Collection). Opinion pieces with Farwell's byline appear consistently from 1912 through 1915, the year he became director of the Music School Settlement in New York, though he made occasional contributions to the paper even after he gave up his regular position on its staff.

Edith Chapman-Goold.[4] Heinrich Gebhard played a group of American piano compositions, and Arne Oldberg took the piano part in his Quintet in C Sharp Minor, the string players being the quartet from the Northwestern University School of Music, at which Mr. Oldberg holds a prominent position.[5]

The second concert, also at Mendelssohn Hall, was in charge of Harry Barnhart, who sang American songs,[6] as did also Mrs. Ben Lathrop. Miss Della Thal played piano compositons by MacDowell and Walter Morse Rummel; Arthur Hadley's Concertstück for 'cello, accompanied by Arthur Depew; and Mr. and Mrs. David Mannes

---

[4]Information on Edith Chapman-Goold is supplied by an ad in *MA* (16 [12 October 1912]: 34) which notes that the soprano is available for solo and ensemble work and that she sings with the Collegiate Concert Company, the Musical Arts Quartet, and the Persian Cycle Quartet; her address is given as New York.   [5]The critics present for this and two other concerts given by the New York center during its first season were for the most part not impressed by the music they heard. Farwell, as will be noted, was undaunted, taking hope from the promise the enterprise as a whole seemed to hold for American music, something to which he believed the critics were blind. The *New York Times* reported that the audience, while "only fairly numerous," was nonetheless enthusiastic about the music. But the unnamed reviewer, apparently skeptical of a program devoted solely to American works, groused smugly that surely there were those in the audience who would have agreed they had heard better music of American composers played at concerts not so fervently committed to American music ("American Music Heard," *New York Times* , 31 December 1908: 9). The reviewer in *Musical Courier* (58 [6 January 1909]: 11) disapproved of the Indianist pieces on the program. Farwell's "Receiving the Messenger" from *Impressions of the Wa-Wan Ceremony of the Omahas* and "Navajo War Dance" from *From Mesa and Plain*, along with Harvey Worthington Loomis's "Music of the Calumet," were found to be "vain experimental efforts," demonstrating once again "the barren field his [the Indian's] music offers for serious musical exploitation."   [6]Barnhart's performance at this concert, which took place on 25 February 1909, included selections from Farwell's *Folk Songs of the West and South* and *Three Indian Songs.* For the most part, critics were not pleased with Farwell's harmonizations, nor with the concert in general. One reviewer thought that the harmonies "ruined the native beauty of the melodies," that the settings "disclose a bungling hand—a hand that would not hesitate to sprinkle the lovely scented rose with artificial perfume" ("Concert by the American Music Society," *Musical Courier* 58 [3 March 1909]: 15). Another spoke of his setting unsophisticated melodies "with the most recondite and adventurously modern style of harmony" ("American Music Heard," *New York Times*, 26 February 1909: 7), while Henry Krehbiel harrumphed that the harmonies fit the melodies "'like a fist in the eye,' as the Germans say" ("Music: Yesterday's Singular Concerts," *New York Daily Tribune*, 26 February 1909: 7). On the other hand, the critic for the *New York Evening Post* (26 February 1909: 5) allowed that "on the whole, these songs were much superior to the average 'manufactured' article." But the same reviewer raised a larger question, the value of organizations such as the American Music Society, suggesting that they often program compositions which are weak and undeserving of such attention. He argued that music which "is really good, like the works of MacDowell, [John Knowles] Paine, [and] Chadwick . . . does make its way, through other channels, and very little that is played on 'American' programmes ever gets played anywhere else."

Augusta Cottlow,
pianist performing
in concert of the
American Music
Society, Carnegie
Hall, 18 April 1909

played a portion of the Sonata in G Major, op. 6, for violin and piano, by Walter Damrosch.[7]

The third of the series by the New York center was an orchestral concert at Carnegie Hall on April 18. This concert under David Bispham's direction, was the most significant achievement of the American Music Society thus far, and gave an impulse to the organization beyond anything which had previously occurred. This concert was the first occasion of an Eastern hearing of any of the music composed for the San Francisco Bohemian Club's "High Jinks," now called the "Forest Festival." The overture to the *Hamadryads*, text by Will Irwin

---

[7] Of the musicians cited in this paragraph who are not identified elsewhere in these pages, Isabel Stevens Lathrop was, according to her obituary in the *New York Times* (28 October 1964: 45), "well known as an amateur singer as a young woman." The wife of Benjamin G. Lathrop, a partner in a London brokerage firm, she was known also for her charitable work in France during and after World War I, being made a member of the French Legion of Honor in 1919. Della Thal, a native of Milwaukee, had returned from a successful European tour in 1908; her praises are sung in "Della Thal, Gifted Pianist, Now a New Yorker," *Musical Courier* 58 (31 March 1909): 31. Compositions of Walter Morse Rummel (1887–1953) are discussed by Farwell in *AM* (448f.). Arthur Depew (d. 1940) was a rather prominent

and music by William J. McCoy, was the work chosen as the opening number of the concert. Its music deals with the brooding spirit of Meledon, God of Care, the Hamadryads in their forest revels, and the coming of Apollo in the dawn. Mr. F. X. Arens conducted the overture, and also the MacDowell Piano Concerto in D Minor, which was played by Augusta Cottlow.[8] Mr. Bispham sang four songs with viola, by Charles Martin Loeffler, Mr. Kovarik playing the obbligato[9] and Harold Smith accompanying; and later in the program George W. Chadwick's *Lochinvar,* the composer conducting. Mr. Bispham also brought his dramatic fervor to the reading of Poe's *Raven,* music by Arthur Bergh, who conducted the orchestra.[10] Harry Rowe Shelley conducted his *Creole Dances,*[11] and I, as one of the papers said next morning, waved the bâton while the orchestra played my *Dawn.*[12]

In an earlier chapter of this tale I gave my impression of this

---

organist in New York (obituary, *New York Times,* 25 September 1940: 27). Farwell considered David Mannes "the best violinist in New York," and his wife Clara (1869–1948) to be a "splendid ensemble player" (Farwell to Oldberg, 18 October 1908, AO Collection). Clara Mannes was from a distinguished musical family that included the conductor Leopold Damrosch (1832–85), her father, as well her brothers Walter and Frank Damrosch, who have been cited above.   [8]The American pianist Augusta Cottlow (1878–1954) concertized extensively in Europe and debuted with the Chicago Symphony in 1889 and in New York with Seidl's orchestra in 1891.   [9]Possibly refers to Loeffler's *Quatre Poémes,* Op. 15 (published 1904), though by this time Loeffler had written five other songs that included viola (see Ellen Knight, *Charles Martin Loeffler: A Life Apart in American Music* (Urbana IL: University of Illinois Press, 1993), 270-73. J. J. Kovarik is cited as a violist in the 1917 listing of players in James G. Huneker's *The Philarmonic Society of New York and Its Seventy-fifth Anniversary: A Retrospect (N.p., n.d.),* 37.   [10]Arthur Bergh (1882–1962) was a violinist with the New York Symphony Orchestra and the Metropolitan Opera (1903–08) and an orchestral conductor for the extensive summer program of Municipal Concerts in New York which became Farwell's charge between 1910 and 1913. Bergh's melodrama *The Raven* (vocal-piano version) was published by Wa-Wan (1910; *WP* 5:173–98) and is discussed at some length by Farwell in *AM,* (392f.). Bergh also acted as Secretary for the national organization of the American Music Society.   [11]Harry Rowe Shelley (1858–1947) was a noted organist and composer in the New York area.   [12]The *New York Times* reported a "large and appreciative audience" and that Bispham's presentation of *The Raven* was "perhaps the best received" performance of the program ("Concert of American Music," *New York Times,* 19 April 1909: 2). The critique of the *New York Evening Post* (19 April 1909: 7) said that an enthusiastic audience recalled Farwell to the stage several times after his conducting of the *Dawn* Orchestral Fantasy and noted a questionable attribute of the work: the Indian melody had been elaborated "so skilfully that even the red theme seems white." Henry Krehbiel's negative view of Farwell's use of Indian themes has already been cited (see p. 122, n. 9). Far more damaging were the remarks of the *Musical Courier* reviewer, who found the piece "dreary" and ranking "far below all the other works on the program" ("American Music Society Concert," *Musical Courier* 58 [21 April 1909]: 25). Despite the personal blows, Farwell may have been heartened at least by the cheerful response to the concert as a whole given by a reviewer of the *Evening Sun:* "this gay spring concert of American music was the first far cry in a wilderness of effete and sedentary Eastern cosmopolitanism" ("Music and Musicians," *New York Evening Sun,* 19 April 1909: 9).

concert and its meaning, a meaning not derived from a view of it through the somewhat idiosyncratic lenses of the spectacles of the critical fraternity. It was a showing of what can be accomplished, even at the outset, when the American people lend a friendly hand to their composers, in their efforts to blaze a path forward. If such events as this concert, events animated by the same artistic, national, and democratic spirit, can be followed up thick and fast, a few decades, or even less, will witness an artistic growth of Hellenic proportions and brilliancy in the creative musical life of the United States. A writer on the Pacific Coast makes a statement even bolder—"with such influences as these (the centers of the American Music Society) the cause of music will be furthered in ten years beyond the measure of a century's unaided progress." Reverting to the New York concert—even from the standpoint of the professional critic, it was really not such a bad concert after all. The enthusiasm with which the great audience greeted it is the substance out of which a greater music shall come.

Progress now became swift. Mr. Chadwick returned to Boston and aided in the giving of the largest concert yet undertaken by the Boston center, at Jordan Hall, on May 18.[13] The artists were David Bispham, Heinrich Gebhard, Alfred Gietzen, viola,[14] Harold Smith and Mrs. Genevieve Baker, accompanists, and the Women's Chorus of the New England Conservatory. Composers represented were Arthur Foote, Edward Burlingame Hill, Charles Martin Loeffler, Henry Gilbert, Clayton Johns and others.[15]

---

[13]The Boston center of the American Music Society appears to be the longest lasting of the local organizations. A program of its "40th Meeting" of 30 March 1911 is in AF Scrapbook. This number includes meetings that began in 1905, when the organization still had its independent status.   [14]Alfred Gietzen was a violist with the Boston Symphony Orchestra from 1904 to 1918. [15]The correspondent for *Musical Courier* reviewing the concert thought it was an optimistic beginning and praised the Society's effort. Bispham's recitation of *The Raven*, she thought, "was the greatest bit of dramatic conception ever offered Boston," which must have reflected the audience's enthusiam in recalling him to the stage numerous times. But the reviewer found difficult to judge Edward Burlingame Hill's *The Nuns of Perpetual Adoration*, due to the lifeless performance by the Women's Chorus of the New England Conservatory, which Chadwick conducted. Perhaps most interesting was the issue taken with program planners for allowing Bostonians to dominate the program; why were composers from the Far West not represented? she wondered (Wylna Blanche Hudson, "Boston," *Musical Courier* 58 [26 May 1909]: 38). Among those from Boston on the program, the organist, pianist, and teacher Arthur Foote (1853–1937), was of a generation older than Farwell and often associated with the so-called "Second New England School" which included Chadwick and Parker. Edward Burlingame Hill (1872–1960), a member of the music faculty at Harvard (1908–40), had a closer connection to Farwell. One of his piano pieces had been

Meanwhile Eugene Nowland, aided by musicians and music lovers, had by his enthusiastic efforts been instrumental in organizing a large center of the society in Los Angeles, next in size to that in New York, and was made its president.[16] Another center was organized in Lawrence, Kansas, with Dean Skilton,[17] of the University of Kansas, and Mrs. Frederick Crowe among its leading spirits. Following upon this was the appointment of an American Music Society Day at the Seattle-Yukon Exposition, to be held in August, 1909, and a Northern trip of Mr. Nowland,[18] which resulted in the formation of the Seattle center of the American Music Society, with a board consisting of the chief musicians and music lovers of that city.[19] Progress was also made toward a San Francisco organization, which is now on the point of consummation.[20]

---

published by Wa-Wan (1903) and a 1905 issue of the Press included in its introduction a brief statement by Hill on the need for composers to balance expression and technique in their compositions (see *WP* 3:41–42). Farwell discusses Hill's music in *AM*, 388–90. Clayton Johns (1857–1932) taught piano in Boston where he had settled in 1884 and presented almost yearly recitals of his own works, primarily songs (see Clayton Johns, *Reminiscences of a Musician* [Cambridge: Washburn and Thomas, 1929], 44).   [16]Several articles in *Pacific Coast Musical Review* provide information about the establishment of the Los Angeles Center. Eugene Nowland, a violinist of the Los Angeles area, had organized a center by mid-May 1909, with over twenty sponsors and an impressive membership of some forty-seven professionals. Its first concert was held at Simpson Auditorium in Los Angeles on 2 December 1909. See articles in *Pacific Coast Musical Review* 16 (22 May 1908): 8; and 17 (6 November 1909): 18.   [17]Charles Sanford Skilton (1868–1941) was Dean of the School of Fine Arts at the University of Kansas, Lawrence (1903–15), where he also taught organ, theory and history of music. As a composer he based several of his works on Native American themes. A program in AF Scrapbook indicates that the opening concert of the Lawrence Center took place on 6 January 1910.   [18]The original text has "Mr. Howland." [19]Farwell had taken another trip West in August 1909, both for business regarding the American Music Society and to report on the 1909 Grove Play for *MA* ("The Bohemian Club High Jinks of 1909" *MA* 10 [16 October 1909]: 3–8). He likely attended the American Music Society Day at the Seattle-Yukon Exposition (Farwell to Charles F. Lummis, 24 June 1909 and 6 September 1909, CFL Collection).   [20]A center was formed at San Francisco by August of 1909 (see *Pacific Coast Musical Review* 16 [14 August 1909]). A program from the center's opening series of concerts, 1909–10, is in AF Scrapbook. Though not mentioned in these pages by Farwell, an announcement of a center formed in Springfield, Illinois, appeared in the *Wa-Wan Press Monthly* for January 1908 (*WP* 5: 80); in addition, Farwell noted in letters that three other centers were likely to be established—in St. Joseph, Missouri and Evanston, Illinois (Farwell to Arthur Shepherd, 26 June 1908, AS Papers) and in Minneapolis (Farwell to Charles F. Lummis, 6 September 1909, CFL Collection). If the latter three centers indeed came into being, there had been established, in all, sixteen local organizations of the American Music Society.

1909
"The American Idea"[1]

*A*nd so these *Wanderjahre* come to an end. Not that the *Wanderlust* ends, not the journeying and the striving—for life itself, if we have seen what life might be, is one long wander-year. We come, we wander through time and space in search of something, we scarcely know what—ourselves, it may be, or home—and we go. One thing or another calls us on; we know only that we cannot stand still—that there is joy or the hope of joy, in the going, and shame and despair in the lagging. We burn the bridges behind us without a regret, and press on into the unknown without fear. We start continually upon quests of which we cannot see the end, and launch unnumbered ships to unguessed ports. We see a thousand tragedies by the way, and still believe that the promised land and the glory of life lie somewhere beyond, if we can but find the path. On every hand we see persons pursuing phantoms, and things that seem to us unreal. Over there is a man giving his last hope of happiness for a little measure of fame; there another who thinks that a little gold and silver is worth more to him than the truth, or the love of a friend. At every turn we meet Alberichs and Hagens and Fafners, gloating over their hoards and their vengeance, or Tannhäusers dwelling in their Venusbergs, and we go on. Perhaps we shall hear the joyous horn of a young Siegfried if we keep on, or find a glorious Brünnhilde waiting high upon some fire-encircled rock. We know that we must have something better than there is here, and we press on. Perhaps this hope, though, is but *maya*, illusion, myth. We turn again to look at the curious beings about us, so satisfied, so engrossed with their gold and silver toys, their little loves and hates, their circumscribed ambitions.

[1]From *MA* 10 (10 July 1909): 17, 27.

How do we—we who feel the urge of the eternal *Wanderlust*—how do we know that these who tarry in oases by the way have not the right of it? What is our divine justification in passing so much by—in thinking that the path we have chosen leads to a larger life than theirs? Ah, we can sympathize with them, understand them. What they have, we have within ourselves—their desires, their passions, their ambitions, their transitory loves. But beyond all these, we have something else—a spirit which surrounds these things, holds them in solution, sees them, and tells us to pass on. And they—they cannot sympathize with us. The things they crave, we forego. Sadly or joyously, we pass their prizes by. We have dreamed a dream—of things that might be, of a life that might be—that *shall* be if we are but true to our dream. They see us pass—we who wander forever—and go back to their tangible joys as we go on to the ideal ones that make us incomprehensible dreamers in their eyes. Nor do we go, however fair the distant land that beckons us on, without a measure of sadness in our joy; for there is ever that within us which is one with those who stay, and which bids us stay, too. Nor does that portion of us part from them with less pain than that with which they part from one another. But go we must, we who have dreamed our dream.

In another and lesser sense—though all-important to us at the time—we have our years of earthly wandering. They are the years when, with awakening faculties, we scour the earth to see what manner of place it is and what we should go about doing in it, and how. These are the years that carry us from enthusiastic aimlessness, or at least from vague and half-formed aims, to greater definiteness of purpose, or to the making of plans for which there is some tenable hope of realization. And it is to make a faithful record of such a period in one life—a period coinciding with the musical awakening of a nation—that these chapters have been written. They have marked the period beginning with the amazed awakening to the wonder of music—Music, an ideal beauty and order, a very heaven, to be compassed within a troublous world—a way of speaking the language of the most exalted emotions of the human soul—from this awakening to the formation of the purpose to do the uttermost that one limited soul could do toward implanting the roots of so divine an art, and the love of it—taken in its primal, its creative sense—in the foundations of the life of the nation to which that soul belongs. And so this tale, fragmentary as it is, has told of the pursuit of the American Idea in music.

And what then, at last, is the American Idea in music? Taken in the largest sense, it is many things. First of all, it must be to reverence the art of music, to hold none but the highest ideals with regard to it, to recognize in music—ideally considered—one of the highest and noblest forms of human activity, and to maintain it as such.

After this, the American Idea in music must be to regard it as a creative art, whose immeasurably great influence for national upliftment can become fullest reality only as the nation brings to birth its own music out of the travail of its own spirit. No playing with music, even the greatest, as an importation, can ever heighten the character and quality of American life as can the spiritual effort necessary to the creation of music fitted to that life's own need.

After this again, the American Idea in music is to hold a high and reverential regard for the creation of music in America as the only means by which music, the living art, can come to birth and grow to fullest power, as an integral part of the life of the people. Included in this is the national regard for the creators of music—the composers of America—through whom alone the art in its creative sense can arise and exist. The American Idea shall be to recognize the composer, while he lives, as one who would or might perform a great service for America, and to hold him responsible for the purity and dignity of his art.

The American Idea in music further means that the people of the nation are to act, and lend the composer a hand. As his art grows they are to help in building an economic and artistic circumstance in which he and his art can thrive. They are to help him in making an adequate provision for the hearing of his works—not in an isolated way here and there, but nationally, from coast to coast, in a manner to render stagnation impossible and bring motion and progress into American musical art. It is the American Idea, if this can not be accomplished through the machinery of existing organizations, to create new organizations for the purpose.

The American Idea in music means for the composer this: that in one way or another he shall draw the inspiration for his art from the life of his own land—that he shall look to making it as new and independent a spectacle in the world as his own new nation is among the nations of the world. He shall regard his gift as a trust, and use it in its highest potency in the service of the upliftment of himself and his people.

For the artist, the interpretative musician, the American Idea in music means this: that he shall lend the highest powers of his art, and some portion of his active energies, to the interpretation of the best and most serious works of his countrymen. Beyond this, it means for him that he shall trust the American people in their eventual response to the works of their own composers, and fearlessly override their initial but not deep-seated reluctance to include American works in the scheme of their musical life.

For the music-lover at large, the American Idea in music means that he shall listen and judge for himself, and accord the works of Americans the place in musical art which his own mind and feelings dictate, without subservience to fashion, reputation, or any other influence. It means that he shall not only receive serious American works hospitably and without prejudice, but that he shall trust the artist's willingness to serve him by presenting those works, and he shall require this service of the artist.

All this and much more beside, the American Idea in music means. For all, it means abiding faith and patience and ceaseless effort during this searching, formative period of American musical growth. It means the keeping of one's eyes on the large and the new for which this new land stands; of which the Grand Arizona Canyon—that mighty source of inspiration—is the type in the natural world, and such a man as Abraham Lincoln, that still mightier source—in the human world. Thus there will come to pass a major and an ascending deflection in the course of music and of humanity.

Other Essays on American Music

Arthur Farwell
during his years as critic and essayist for
Musical America, 1909–15

Toward American Music[1]

The moment we pause in our blind acceptance of things as they are, and scrutinize our vast musical life and institutions in America, we must be appalled to find that to the mass of music offered us, American influence, thought, talents and ideals contribute almost nothing. Strangest of all is this when today American composers and native resource are offering a wealth of composition and musical material of the highest order, sufficient wholly to revolutionize the present Germanic aspect of our musical life. Yet it is not strange when we recognize the vise-like grip which European musical tradition has upon the generation still in power in our musical life, a generation trained to take its nourishment from the past and the alien, and unable to adapt itself to the native regime and the new regime swiftly arising about it.

But the new generation, even of the musically untrained, is demanding a new musical diet. And the blinded devotees of decaying and expropriate faiths cry "Danger!" During a recent visit to the Pacific Coast, leaders of musical thought in more than one city said to me, "What is to be done? It is becoming more and more difficult to gain support for serious musical enterprises. All that the people seem to want is rag-time." Naturally—it is the only American music which they can get. The "serious musical enterprises" are all labeled "Made in Germany." What does a busy American with a little time and money to

[1] Appeared originally in *Out West* 20 (May 1904): 454–458. The article was solicited by the magazine's editor, Charles F. Lummis, and was written sometime after Farwell returned from his first western trip. Farwell's handwritten copy of the article can be found in CFL Collection. Perhaps Farwell presented this article as a talk while on his second trip West; a program in AF Scrapbook indicates that on 4 November 1904 he lectured to the Friday Morning Club of Los Angeles on "Toward American Music."

devote to art want with an overture or a symphony redolent in its every bar of the conventionality and conformity of European court life, or of a laborious Teutonic philosophy? What does he want with a song that reflects the essence of German sentimentality, or draws up a picture of a life he does not know, in a language he does not understand—with a song whose chief glory is an over-refinement, a Parisian delicatesse at variance with all he sees in the life about him? What does he want with an instrumental work based upon ancient rules and conventions as utterly meaningless in the light of modern life as are slavery or feudalism in the face of American civilization? Or, what does he want of even the most clever American imitations of these older wares?

It is not rag-time that the American wants so badly—he merely wants something that is his own. Or does he really want ragtime? Very well then, let him have rag-time, exalted by our American composers as Rossini exalted the common song of the Italians, as Beethoven and Wagner exalted the common song of Germany, or Gilbert and Sullivan the popular ballad of England. Let our composers look to real American needs rather than to a fancied need of copying older forms: let them expand and exalt these new and latest forces in the common music of America rather than wield the spent forces of other lands and epochs. Then it will not be so difficult to gain support for "serious musical enterprises." Why should Americans expend their forces to support European traditions on American soil? Are there no American traditions to upbuild?

It seems scarcely necessary to state that of course it would be desirable that the average American should be universal in his sympathies, and should at least be able to take keen enjoyment in a masterwork of any age or country: for such a work is human for all time. And every individual truly desiring to grow in scope and range of thought must sooner or later arrive at such a broad sympathetic appreciation. But it is useless and wasteful of effort to pretend that such a condition exists before it actually does. We must work with the material that we have in hand, if we are not to waste our time building air-castles. And the materials in hand are men craving something that is their own and crude material out of which to build that something. Now is the psychological moment to begin this work.

It is not merely in characteristic popular music that elements are found which afford that crude material. They are to be found in various forms of musical growth peculiar to America, or through proximity, having reason to influence it. Also they must be found in the work of any liberated American composer who has been able to realize that his conceptions are not necessarily original, but may be dictated by tradition, and who has therefore learned to employ his peculiarly original powers. In other words, the elements for a great and characteristic national musical art exist upon our soil, chiefly as folk-song, though in some degree as spontaneous expression of American composers.

Let it not be thought that this is but another scream of the eagle. There is not the slightest reason to boast of American creative musical achievement: it can speak convincingly enough for itself upon the rare occasions when it, at its best, is granted a hearing. Let it not be thought either that we have the slightest desire to "cover mediocrity with a cloak of patriotism."[2] It is merely desired to point out the present application of a natural law that has never yet been known to fail of operation, and to suggest that we perceive it in time and share in the power of its inevitable action, rather than oppose it and thereby doom ourselves. This law is none other than the irresistible desire of all life to expand indefinitely and to seize upon every force which may help it to that end. In art evolution it reveals itself in the inevitable seizure of every force in a new land that may contribute to art's rejuvenation and expansion. Musical art in Italy fastened upon the "plain-song" of the church, an importation from Greece, and finally upon the common music of the folk. The same art carried to Germany was forced to nourish itself on German folk-song, and again, in projecting itself to Russia, inevitably underwent a similar experience. Literature passing to Ireland found awaiting it the heretofore inadequately developed Celtic genius and myth, and we witness the Irish literary revival. Or it passes to the rough, forceful and elemental phenomena of America and we have a Whitman.

A man makes himself felt in proportion as he develops his inherent powers, and a nation—a group of men in a given land—makes itself felt as it develops its own resources, both racial and climatic: that is, its powers through racial inheritance and accretion and through territorial acquisition.

What does this imply for American music? Simply that musical art in America can not rest, nor come to its full fruition, until it has assimilated every phase of musical life, however primitive, existing

---

[2] A phrase used by the Boston music critic Philip Hale (1854–1934), according to Lawrence Gilman. In his commentary, "New American Music," *Harper's Weekly* 47 (1903): 1658, Gilman defends Farwell against such discredit, lauding the Wa-Wan Press for making accessible music that is not only American, but is "excellent art" as well.

within America's borders. If any one doubts this, let him study the history of music and a little elementary logic.

Let us then to the task. What are the undeveloped musical resources of America? First, through racial inheritance, natural genius, Anglo-Saxon, Teutonic or otherwise, acting under new circumstances and therefore productive of new results. In other words, the spontaneous work of such American composers as we consciously or unconsciously freed from slavery to alien traditions, and are still not employing American folk-song. Second, through racial accretion, the folk music of the negroes—the plantation song—which, we have long known, has nothing to do with African music, and which we are beginning to recognize as a derivative form originally from the Spanish.[3] Third, through territorial acquisition and consequent racial accretion, the various folk music of the many different tribes of American Indians. Beyond these are other American sources of musical life, as the characteristic songs of the cowboys, railroad makers, voyageurs, sailors, etc., all of which must be haled into court and tried before American musical growth will be satisfied. Also there are the folk-songs of Mexico, qualified by Spanish influence as they must be, yet which cannot but exert a powerful influence on the musical life of our Southwest. It is not a question of the mere desirability of employing these various native motives, wheresoever they may be found, but of the inevitability of assimilating them in our musical life. If we do not feed our musical life on this native diet which it craves, it will die. We can not continuously live on importations and imitations, we must have significant original productions. We must live our own lives.

The plantation song and its most obvious outgrowth, rag-time, has thus far qualified American music more than any other influence. The Indian music is now promising to be one of the most important factors. This is due to its intrinsic force and beauty, and to the intimacy of the Indian's relation to the history of all parts of these states, as well as to the powerful and suggestive mythology supporting it. In the still largely unrevealed subjective life of the Indian the ethnologist has found another world, rich in poetry, mystery, elemental philosophy, mythic lore, close to our own, yet generally unperceived by us in its true fullness and significance. Science has discovered this world: but the opportunity—

---

[3]It is unfortunate that Farwell does not indicate how he arrived at his conclusion on the origin of plantation songs, since recent studies on the topic indeed emphasize their African elements, showing the Spanish influence to be far less pervasive.

the privilege—the need—of its ideal representation in terms compre-
hensible to all, falls to art. And since the Indian has entrusted so large a
share of his own expression of his life and thought to music, the unearthing
of this music and bringing it into the open of our musical life is one of the
greatest and most obvious musical tasks before America at the present
moment. And the West is necessarily the privileged sphere of this activity.

Perhaps the greatest need of the musical world of the East today is
for her musicians to cease wasting their indisputable technical power in
futile imitative effort, and to vitalize that power through the recognition and employment of the large unharnessed native musical forces of
the West. And of the two greatest needs of the musical world of the
West, perhaps the first is for western musicians to cease complaining
because they are not East where they can hear things they do not want
to hear anyway, and to inaugurate what they want where they are, and
especially to build up a powerful and dignified musical life of their own
with the material at hand. If this is not true, what is the use of independence? There is all the talent and energy on the Pacific coast that is
needed to do this: all that lacks is cooperation, independence and
courage of leadership. The musical life of the West needs American
Leaders. There are thirty composers in San Francisco, some of whom
are still writing German "Lieder," which, however good, must remain
an absurd anatopism (the Rhine in California!), only one of whom is
developing Mexican folk-music, and none of whom, I believe, are as yet
seriously developing Indian music. If this statement is inaccurate I
should be glad to be corrected. What, too, of the splendid western
landscape—where are the instrumental and orchestral compositions to
match it? Where is William Keith[4] done over into music? The second
signal lack of the musical West is a knowledge of what American
composers, especially the innovators, have already done. The East is
also reprehensible for not inquiring in regard to the work of western
composers. The Pacific has heard of MacDowell and Nevin, and in
some places, of Chadwick and Foote. But what of Parker, Huss,
Hadley, Gilbert, Tipton, John Beach, Loomis, Kelley (one of the big-
gest and a sometime Californian), Bullard, Brockway, Hill and others?[5]

---

[4]See p. 115, no. 9.   [5]All of the composers listed here have been cited previously in notes,
except for Ethelbert Nevin (1862–1901), creator of the once perennial miniature for piano,
Narcissus, and the equally favored parlor song, *The Rosary*; Frederick Field Bullard (1864–
1904), who was a teacher of composition as well as a music critic in Boston; and Howard
Brockway (1870–1951), a pianist who, at the time Farwell wrote this, was teaching at the
Peabody Conservatory in Baltimore.

What of the orchestral works, the songs and pianoforte compositions of these and others? Is it not time for a little filtration of the knowledge of American composers throughout America?

With the splendid enterprise, initiative and talent of the West, why should there be any longer a delay in the inauguration of a satisfying American musical life there? The material is all at hand: only leaders are needed, with the courage of American ideals.

The editor has asked me to write a brief sketch of my work and its purposes. I have, however, found it simpler to sketch the circumstances which exist as conditioning factors for present needful work. My own work has been merely to promote in every possible way, by the performance of radical American works, by their publication at my headquarters—the Wa-Wan Press, Newton Center, Massachusetts—by the study of Indian music, by experimental composition, etc., the attainment of the ends advocated in the present sketch. It is recognized that the ends finally to be desired cannot be fully seen at the outset. Real issues present themselves as work proceeds. The main thing needed is not to theorize and wish, but to get something done. Progress demands action.

Society and American Music[1]

*A*merica, with the present generation, has fairly launched her native musical life. Just when the conditions have seemed most unpromising, in the midst of a commercial civilization, in the midst of so much of brutality and hurry in American life, the composer, the creator of an ideal world of tone, appears in our midst. Orpheus, in Hades, in some respects, could have found scarcely less congenial surroundings. There may be those who regard this impulse in our national life as untimely and misguided. Evolution, however, seldom produces unnecessary species, and may not the appearance of this one be providential, its purpose regenerative, and its existence to be cherished by every means in our power? Certainly, if we were to have no use for the American composer he would not have been given to us; if the time for his labor were not ripe, he would not be here. And certainly, while there are any of us left who regard art as something more than an elegant amusement imported from Europe for a wealthy few,—who see the deep need of art, the broad and simple sense used by William Morris,[2] as an inseparable beautifying element in the daily life of each of us, as maker or user,—we can ill afford to let slip the present opportunity of helping to birth in our own land an art which, if cherished, is unsurpassed in its power to lift our lives above the sordidness and routine into which so many conditions of the time would draw them.

Even the severest critic of American music—and most of the critics vie with one another for this title—cannot deny the presence of an extraordinary and ever-increasing creative impulse in American musical art. While, for reasons to be considered, no American works in

---

[1]Appeared in *Atlantic Monthly* 101 (1908): 232–36.   [2]See p. 88.   ·

large forms come to general public performance, and but few to an occasional hearing, every year witnesses a notable increase of orchestral works, chamber music, piano and vocal works, and other compositions by American composers. Of smaller piano compositions and songs, the seasons bring forth an appalling quantity, and too often, it is true, an appalling quality as well; yet in the midst of this saturnalia appear many works infinitely in advance of those usually chosen to represent American music on artists' programmes. And from time to time an American opera rises from the composer's consciousness to completion—never to performance—and sinks again into a mysterious obscurity, oblivion, or temporary neglect, we are fain to know which.

It is not the purpose of this inquiry to seek to appraise this musical output. Musical students and musicians of high standing, who make it their especial task to follow every development and apprehend every musical revelation of modern Europe, and who are familiar with every advance of American music, know that our composers have produced many works surpassing a great amount of the current European music which fills our programmes in the United States. These programmes by no means consist wholly of the works of the great epoch-makers of musical history. If they did there would be nothing to say, for scarcely any American composer, however indispensable and vital to our national musical evolution, could successfully lay claim to having produced a major deflection in the course of the world's musical history. It is very probable, however, that musical tendencies already manifest in this country will eventually produce such a deflection. Our programmes, it is plain to see, are not made up from the few great masters who have hewn out the main channel of music's progress. Society would not tolerate such a diet. They contain a vastly greater proportion of lesser works. Some of these are obvious and charming, and introduced merely as a foil to weightier works. Others are more pretentious and represent the general effort of contemporary Europe for musical advancement, an effort offering examples often no whit better than those which represent American progress, and in many cases not so good. For oftentimes mere virtuoso tricks are proffered upon the artist's programme, and it is well known that we are not without genuine thinkers among our foremost composers.

Now it is precisely this general effort toward musical advancement which is the soil that finally produces the powerful master. When it becomes easy and common to do well, there suddenly arises one who can do infinitely better, and who would never have existed except for the general culture and effort. The universal nourishment of this culture is essential to the production of masters. Of many bards, one becomes a Homer. After generations of effort, when the technical equipment was insufficient and the national spirit too unawakened artistically to admit of the development of a pre-eminent individual, our nation is at last paralleling the general status of European musical culture. The conditions for powerful individual development are no longer lacking, and in fact we now see one after another of our composers striking high above the international average.

To this question, then, does the matter at last resolve itself. Why do not the more excellent American compositions find a generous and adequate, nay, even a just, or, at the least, an appreciable representation upon American programmes? Why does not American society, in the broad sense of the term, support American music? Is it neglect on the part of the composer? But for my belief that we are about to witness a great and far-reaching revolution in this matter, the question would not have been broached. But there is at present every indication of such a revolution. The subsoil for this movement was prepared long since, when our popular music came into its own. More recently the discussion of a "national American music" and of "American" folksongs has arisen, and if no conclusions have been reached, a most important circumstance has resulted, namely, the stirring up of the rank and file of the American people to the study of the works of American composers. Individuals and clubs in all parts of the United States are taking up the study of American music, and there remains but one more step,—and that one sure to be taken,—its general acceptance by American society. Yet there still remain formidable obstacles, the nature of which must be more generally recognized before the final establishment of American music in American musical life can be brought about. We must glance at the causes of the present condition.

The time was when we had nowhere to look but to Europe for our musical art. We accepted European music as a starting-point, naturally as we accepted European civilization generally as the starting-point for ours. The love of our forefathers for the European lands of their birth but foreshadowed the depth of our love for America; and their love for the great old-world masterworks, a passion which we inherit, is the measure of the intensity of the love which we shall one day bear to our own masterworks. The eastern ports of entry, especially Boston and New York, became the authoritative centres of European music, and therefore, at that time, of all music, in the United States. There the great symphonies and operas could be heard. About this serious work for musical progress grew up a life of musical fashion, a reflex of the life of social fashion, which, while it served indeed to support the performance of the masterworks, fostered also many European developments of lesser significance. In this life the appearance of a great European artist would rival in glamour the visit of an Athenian to a Grecian province. Coming from the source of all music, his authority would be nothing less than apostolic.

Gradually, as western cities aspired to a similar culture, both of art and of fashion, a "circuit" was developed. The artist from across the water could now carry his authority to St. Louis, or even as far as San Francisco. Finally other cities, Cincinnati, Chicago, Denver, were added. The peculiar commercial and artistic conditions of the United States, reinforced by the profound European ignorance of American geography, gave rise to the necessity for able management for these visiting artists. The seat of this managerial activity could be only in New York, which had finally become the point from which each virtuoso in turn started upon his triumphal American tour. A great and profitable business thus arose, and we are to recognize that by far the greatest asset of this business became not primarily the command of artistic ability,—although this was manifestly present,—but the command of *fashion*. For one listener whose object was to learn from the artist the authoritative interpretation of the works which he performed, or for one who sought him out for sheer artistic enjoyment, twenty would go because he came from Europe and represented the summit of the musical fashion of the day, and the fashionable world could not afford to be absent.

So long as the musical fashion coincided at every point with the true development of musical art in the United States, this condition presented no disadvantage, and caused no harm. But that this fashion and art, although coincident at first, could remain so in a new land sure to rear up arts of its own, was an absolute impossibility; and at the moment when American musical art became of intrinsic worth, and the musical fashion remained fixedly European, musical fashion and musical art in America parted company. To-day the true interests of musical development in the United States have little or nothing to do with the fashionable musical life of our great cities. The facts of our creative musical development are one thing, the events of our social musical life another. Society is not aware of this. It has so long been compelled to import musical art if it wished to have any, that it cannot believe that there is any other source of this art than Europe. Society is not yet prepared to tolerate any interference with this belief, and the purveyors of its musical art are the last to initiate any such interference. Indeed, to do so would be to lose financial support; and therein lies the crux of the situation. The managers of musical enterprises care nothing for our national artistic development; their one concern is to keep secure the patronage of society.

This general condition of affairs in the eastern cities is nothing less than the model and the cue for the social musical life of the entire United States. As it is in New York, so must it be in Butte, Montana, or Pueblo, Colorado. Sane, beautiful, advanced musical art may be growing up about these western cities and towns, but it has not been the occasion of the social musical flurry of the great metropolis, and they must have *Salome*, or something of Debussy. I learned recently that more modern French music is being sold west of the Mississippi than east of it.

What is the immediate universal result of this artificial condition? It means simply that good American singers, pianists, and other artists— to say nothing of foreign—may place upon their programmes only that which is sanctioned by New York, and that is—European music. Not to do so means to incur the displeasure and lose the support of society. And these same artists, who know good and bad in music as society does not know it, are often ardent admirers of much in American music, but they must admire in private. An orchestral conductor in a secondary capacity, and for the time being in a place where he could do what he pleased, gave a number of performances of the scores of a certain American composer, with great success, and expressed himself very enthusiastically, personally, concerning them, assuring the com- poser of the pleasure he would have in conducting them in a primary capacity on a more important occasion, when the opportunity would come. The opportunity arrived, and with it the unexpected knowledge that to do as he had promised, under these circumstances, would jeopardize the social support of the orchestra. The composer received a polite note, stating that at some future time he, the composer, would probably do work more satisfactory to himself, by which he would rather become known, and that then it would be time to consider the performance of it. Such instances could be infinitely multiplied on a smaller scale, and would form a voluminous and amusing anthology of episodes of artistic and moral trepidation.

There are, on the other hand, artists of commanding powers and moral courage, who have succeeded in making some headway against the social dictum, but they are the exceptions which prove the rule. The subconscious sense of society has immediately applauded such artists and greatly exalted them, not of course, for this particular action, but for the greatness which made such impudent action safely possible.

First and last, many American compositions come to performance on American programmes. Society has always sanctioned the trivial American work as a foil to the serious European; but never the more significant American work for its own sake. Composers and their friends are able to force hearings here and there, so that the composer will not be wholly without knowledge of the effect of his work upon an audience, or for that matter, upon himself, both to a certain extent necessary things, for only in practice can art and the art-nature grow. Again, certain obvious good and appealing works, not requiring any effort of the understanding, have quickly found their way into public favor, and are safe for an artist to use. But this insistent fact remains,— that upon our concert and recital programmes generally, those works which best represent the brains and ideals of our American composers to-day are conspicuous by their absence. The army of persons whose fortune, or whose very sustenance, is assured by the maintenance of our exclusively European musical system, is kept busy explaining to society that if Americans could produce sufficiently good music, artists would place it upon their programmes. This explanation may satisfy the unthinking, but it can no longer satisfy those who see that since the artist will not be paid for performing American compositions requiring real study and work, he cannot afford to stop to master them, even if he be prompted by admiration of the compositions or friendship for the composer. If society, to-day, should turn and support liberally the production of works by our own composers, if it should, by some whimsical turn of the wheel, announce that it would not support foreign and native artists unless they would give us a good share of the works of our own composers, we would witness a zeal in the world-wide study of American music that would startle the nation. Moreover, we would be no less startled by the intense and varied interest, the high poetic worth, and the magnitude of the achievement of American composers.

If the composer have too much spirit, too great a devotion to his country's growth in musical art, to accept a pittance for his teaching and neglect for his and his brother's art, what shall he do in this situation? At first he might leave composition for a time and look deeply enough into his country's sociology and economics to learn the true nature of the conditions in the midst of which he exists. He will then learn that his own salvation depends upon the salvation of all. As a next step he might waive all endeavor to exploit his own compositions, and through a study of the works of his brother composers, learn the exact nature and strength of his country's musical art. Then, leaving the society of artists, who cannot help him, he might take his newly gained knowledge to the leaders of society,—not the hopelessly lost of the great eastern cities, but the misguided and redeemable throughout the land; and, disinterested himself, win their disinterested help for the sake of a national cause. They are more ready for him than he suspects. Whatever the depth of their regard for the masterpieces of music, their allegiance to mere musical fashions is not of the heart, and they will welcome the opportunity to withdraw their social power from an artificial situation, which can hold for them but little of real life and attainment, and devote it to the satisfying of a living national need.

National Work vs. Nationalism[1]

I read some time ago in the editorial columns of *The New Music Review* that I am "generally supposed to be the leading advocate of American music for Americans and the rest of the world,—music founded on love songs, war songs and dirges of the North American Indian, Cowboy and Greaser ditties, Congo tunes, and Creole melodies—all of them folk-songs distinctly and characteristically American—or 'Urmurrican,' as the word is generally pronounced by excited patriots." This makes one fairly grasp for breath! I had supposed that I was the happy possessor of some kind of a reputation, but it is chastening in the highest degree thus to become aware of the nature of it. Since this matter concerns national work in which many earnest persons are engaged, let us make a little inquiry into the truth and accuracy of the above presentation of the situation. Now one thing is perfectly clear, namely, that if the above statement was made by one of my disciples, it speaks exceedingly poorly for his intelligence; and if by one who is not, it speaks equally disastrously for his motive. On still another supposition, if it was the mere pleasantry of a humorist, it is a bad joke and speaks ill for his wit.

It is further said by the same writer that some one has proclaimed Mr. Charles Farwell Edson of Los Angeles the only one entitled to the above reputation, and that I have thereby been dealt a "cruel blow." Not at all. I willingly resign this reputation to Mr. Edson, without a regret. In fact, I am overjoyed to be rid of it, and hope that Mr. Edson will have much joy in assuming the mantel of Elijah. But I know Mr. Edson well enough to know that he, too, will pass it along.[2]

---

[1] Appeared in *New Music Review* 8 (1909): 432–34. [2] Charles Farwell Edson (1864–1936) was "a singer, voice teacher, and local champion of American music" (as reported in Cather-

As to my being the "leading advocate of American music for Americans and the rest of the world," I can affirm with a clear conscience that this is not my purpose or desire. I should indeed be happy to be the leading advocate of a just, hospitable, and generous recognition of American music in its place in the music of the world. And happily we are advancing rapidly toward such a recognition. The mere attitude of critics is a minor detail in this matter. The whole complex machinery of musical affairs, artistic, social, commercial, must undergo a certain readjustment to admit of such a recognition. We shall advance more rapidly toward such a goal when the composer in this country develops a sociological, as well as an artistic consciousness (Arthur Symons[3] to the contrary notwithstanding), when he ceases to be naive, to be ignorant of the real nature of his social, artistic, and commercial environment, when he sees the possibility of better things, and *acts*, as I have acted. Far from wanting to drive the music of other lands from the face of the earth with a grand charge of American music, I will say that I would rather that American music should die now, and go through the agony of beginning again, than that it should supplant the great models of the world's music to which all modern composers, American and otherwise, must turn for a vision of music's heights and possibilities.

I believe that all the world, Americans included, should hear and study the works of Bach, Beethoven, Schubert, Brahms, Tschaikowsky, César Franck, and the rest. But I also believe that these works do not say the last word for America, any more than do the British articles of constitution. There is an essential spirit in America which has not yet come to full voice in music. Therefore there is a national work to do in music. And therefore I prefer to be one of the workers rather than one of the detractors. There is greater reason for us to place the best American works on programmes side by side with European masterpieces, than to continually place mediocre European novelties there. Musical art is a thing to be cultivated, not merely to be allowed to grow wild. Germans cultivate their creative musical art; the French cultivate theirs; Europeans in general cultivate their creative musical art; but Americans *cultivate* only European musical art. The

ine P. Smith, " 'Something of Good for the Future': The People's Orchestra of Los Angeles,"*Nineteenth-Century Music* 16 [Fall 1992]: 147) and on the executive board of the Los Angeles center of the American Music Society that had been organized in May 1909 (as noted in *Pacific Coast Musical Review* 16 [22 May 1909]: 8). [3]See p. 149.

nations do a work for their art. Why should America not *cultivate* her own, however much she may be enjoying European art at the same time? It is time we became civilized enough to do this. And if the government is not ready to do it, or should not do it, we must organize. This is the need which has produced the American Music Society.

Now let us become confidential and accurate upon another point. Let me affirm and reiterate that I am not working for an obvious nationalism in music. I suppose that up to the day of my death there will be somebody who will still maintain that I am, but I put it on record now that this is not the truth. If I could box the ears of the American people while saying this, as Cellini's father did those of the young Benvenuto on showing him a salamander in the fire, so that he would never forget it, I would do so.[4] I am engaged in national work, work for the nation, in its musical development, and not in injecting "nationalism" into its music. Not that I regard myself as valuable to the nation, but I see before me like a picture the ideal musical circumstances in which I should like to live in my own country, and I shall work to the end, to create those circumstances about me. I am for *national work* in the cultivation of a creative musical art, and in the bringing about of better conditions for composers,—and not for *nationalism*.

A certain nationalism, a narrower thing than national work, we cannot avoid. It is not to be striven for in itself. It is not in itself good or bad. It is not an end, but a quality, a by-product, as a taste for cabbages, or art, in a man. A true live American cannot write a composition which shall be wholly devoid of nationalism. If he does not put an Indian song or other "American" folk-song into it, its nationalism will consist in some freedom and revolution from European methods of expression. If his composition does not show some such new invention, some creative capacity, he is merely an imitator, and unworthy of serious consideration as a composer. We cannot escape our nation. If we did not want to be Americans, we should not have allowed ourselves to be born here. What the composer should aim for, be he American or Russian, is beauty, strength, perfection of expression;—he should not bother about nationalism, to include or exclude it. In greater or less degree it is inevitable, and he had better accept it, as Margaret Fuller[5] was recommended by Carlyle to "accept the universe." And the com-

---

[4]Farwell's reference is to Benvenuto Cellini (1500–1571), the Florentine goldsmith and sculptor whose autobiography is especially valued for the view it gives of his period.   [5]Margaret Fuller (1810–50) was an American writer and first editor (1840–42) for *The Dial*, a magazine associated with the Transcendentalist movement, of which she was a founder.

poser must be allowed to engage in national work without being liable to the charge of an excited devotion to nationalism.

The writer of the editorial has trapped me. I am not to be allowed to escape without defining my attitude toward the so-called American folk-songs. The most direct way in which I can do this is to say that the implication of the editorial is the opposite of the truth. Not even in the days of my first enthusiasm upon discovering the mine of primitive material did I ever maintain that it should be, or was to be, the basis of our national American music. In my earliest writings upon this subject, any one who cares to look them up will find that I was very careful to refer to the "American" folk-songs as but one side of the subject, and to insist that we must look for new and appropriate expression equally in the new inventions of American composers without reference to folk-song. But "Indian chants the basis of American music" made a good yellow journal headline. When I gave a recital in Seattle, the paper had it that I "ran wild with the Indians when young." So the yellow journalism which a great deal of American criticism is, made the most of it. True or false, it made no difference; it was saleable copy, and easy money for journalists and critics. Even Mr. Finck,[6] most of whose writings evince an almost human intelligence, wrote not long since that I was trying to rear an edifice of American music upon a foundation of Indian melodies. It is perhaps too much to ask that these gentlemen read my writings and glance at my compositions before committing themselves in regard to my purpose, but I do not see how else they will arrive at the truth. Let me say, as plainly as I can put it, that just as I am not trying to make American music supplant all other music, so also I am not trying to base our national music on Indian or any other so-called American folk-songs. I use such folk-song motives in my own work whenever and wherever I wish, though by no means in all of them. Tschaikowsky said in one of his letters, "I would like a Russian folk-song to be heard running through each of my works." This was not because of any theory of Tschaikowsky's that music in Russia should be founded on Russian folk-song, nor to bother with injecting a nationalism into his work. It was because he loved those melodies. My point is exactly the same.

I have lived among these folk-songs of the West and South; they have interested and delighted me, and their inexhaustibility has as-

---

[6]Henry T. Finck (1854–1926) was, at the time Farwell wrote this, music editor of the New York *Evening Post* and *The Nation* and author of several musical studies, including the two-volume *Wagner and His Works* (1897).

tounded me. It is as natural for me to think along these lines as it is for our critical friends not to. I use these melodies because they arouse my enthusiasm. They are filled with vigorous and delicate poetic suggestion; they bring up the glorious memories of daybreak and dusk over forest and plain, which make one despair while he still strives to transmute them to music. They are worth while for their own sake; they do not need their nationality to recommend them,—their intrinsic beauty is sufficient. Yet neither need they blush for their nationality, nor can they escape it,—but, for that matter, neither can the truly creative work which is not based upon folk-songs. Art is good or beautiful, not because of its nationality, but in spite of it. It should bear with it and carry it off as easily as a man does the color of his hair or the shape of his nose.

Folk-song is the natural source of melody. It is dangerous for musical art to get too far out of sympathy with it. The greatest historians of music have known this. Beethoven, Wagner, and Tschaikowsky knew it. We are fortunate to have such an abundance of new and unexploited folk-song in America, to keep us mindful of the source and quality of natural melody, whether we actually draw upon this supply or not. I draw upon it from time to time for the same reason that I would gather nuggets if I had the freedom of a gold mine. If I can make a beautiful use of it, that is sufficient justification. I do not use "American" folk-songs for the sake of insisting on nationalism. I do not believe that they are the basis of American music to be, although they have lent and will lend their force and charm to many individual compositions. I spend a part of my time studying and developing them because they appeal to me strongly and intimately; and to do this is not a propaganda for nationalism, but a part of the *national work*.

The entire matter of the folk-songs is now distinctly a side issue, a personal matter for each composer to work out for himself. There they are, after the discussion of the past few years,—those that are entitled to the name of "American folk-song," and those that are not,—for the composer to take or leave as he chooses. The battle that has been waged about them has served to call attention to their existence, and that is perhaps the greatest good that has come out of the matter. The composer is to settle this question in his private workshop, while matters of much more immediate importance are to come before the public.

I do not see how I can explain my position more clearly. It is not often worth while to speak thus personally, but since my position has been called personally into question, I feel that it is time for a word of explanation and truth, for the sake of any who may be interested. We cannot be for or against "nationalism" any more than we can for or against the color of our skin or the language which we speak. The need of the hour is that we shall do the national work that is to be done,— and that is to organize throughout the country for the testing of the works of our own composers.

A Glance at Present
Musical Problems in America[1]

The pace at which musical evolution is hurling itself along, more or less blindly, in America at the present time, is likely to be terrifying to one who gets a standpoint from which he can view it broadly. It is like a tide sweeping in from an old world to a new, its torrents rushing with equal force and equal sightlessness into open courses where they may advance, or blind bays where they may be hurled back with their force spent and broken. Thousands of musicians, trusting themselves to these blind tides of evolution, mistaking mere motion and activity for real advance, come to unproductive and even tragic ends.

Witnessing this torrential and haphazard evolution that brings so many lives to an unsuccessful conclusion, those among us who seek any genuine accomplishment in the world of music are guilty of folly if they do not stop and take thought.

We need to think whether or not there may be highways to follow, or broad principles to adhere to, which shall lead us to a securer ground, truer to American needs and inevitabilities, and more certain to make us, each in his own sphere, stronger and greater personalities in the world of music.

Let us face American facts. What have we to start with? An enormous, mixed and musically unregenerate population on the one hand, and a high degree of specialized musical cultivation, the possession of a few, on the other. There is also a supposition abroad—a kind of fixed idea—that this musical aristocracy and the democracy of Amer-

[1]Appeared in MA 14 (14 October 1911): 137–38.

ica have nothing in common; that taking the people into consideration necessarily involves a lowering of the artistic standard.

Those who succumb to such a belief quickly arrive at a pessimism and despair which paralyzes them, killing not only their own power for helpfulness, but their own capacity for individual growth as well. Or, if any courageous ones succeed in resisting so hopeless a belief, they are apt to take what seems to them the only remaining tenable position, that the people as they are should be educated up to music as it is. In other words, they suppose that the only possible thing to do to help the situation is to lead, or force, the people of America to accept the music of Europe.

Suppose, however, that this is a false idea. It may be written in the destiny of things that America is not to gain its great musical uplift by familiarizing the masses with music as it is. Perhaps the masses are, all unconsciously, waiting for something else, or for some other means of the presentation of music that the conventional ones of concert, recital, or opera.

Let us examine the musical culture of the present, as practised in America, and see if it points the final direction for American progress. It may be that there is much of it that must be got rid of before we can advance. It is well that young persons, universally, should be taught to sing, or play, or compose, and be afforded the opportunity to hear good music. The difficulty comes a little later on, when certain ideas and ideals begin to be held up before the pupil, as to the ends to be sought and gained by his study.

After the period of the classical Germanic obsession in America, the romanticists were admitted to the student's ken. He could safely study a little Schumann and Chopin, so long as he did not forget that the only *real* music was that of Beethoven. It was not as warriors, fighting for the further liberation of musical expression, that the romanticists were presented to him, but rather as lesser though still somewhat worthy lights, appearing after night had fallen upon the world's day of music. Wagner, at work altering the face of the world, was chiefly anathema.

This order has passed, at least for the larger cities of America, although it is a condition of thought still existing wherever the broad dominion of the old-fashioned German music teacher has not been encroached upon by modern ideas. During all this earlier epoch, no hint was thrown out to the army of musical aspirants that American conditions might one day radically alter the nation's attitude toward these older ideals.

Then Wagner dazzled the world. American composers changed their style, but not their attitude toward their nation. The nation, to be saved, must still rise to meet the European idea of music and musical presentation. The people, the very strength of the nation, out of whom must ultimately come all its powers, musical and every other kind, were regarded from the isolated heights of musical culture precisely as the French commune was regarded by the aristocracy before the revolution.

For the musical aristocracy the people in America possessed one very desirable quality—they could be taxed. The public served well for the predatory flights of virtuosi. These fleeting appearances of the message bearers of the world's musical geniuses had little to do with the solid popular cultivation of music.

The virtuoso merely skimmed the cream from each community and went his luxurious and parasitical way.

Such is virtuosodom, and this is the ideal still held up to our gifted young people today. What has the would-be American virtuoso to look forward to, even if he be successful? At the outset, to compete with the genuine imported article in appearance, he must make himself a laughing-stock to his fellow men. The remainder of his life is largely consumed in a more or less undignified advertising propaganda and a fight for engagements. In the end he has a little glory, for which he pays the enormous price of an ever-present sense of the vapidity of such an existence. It is safe to prophesy that the brilliant young instrumentalists of America to-day with leanings toward virtuosity will perceive their error in time to make of themselves good and useful *artists*.

America's latest achievement in the pursuit of musical culture is the discovery of modern France. Here was a tremendous acquisition of fresh supplies by the faithful little band of those devoted to true musical "culture." Here was refinement beyond refinement—musical culture carried to the nth power, and into the fourth dimension. Its exaggerated antithesis to the crudity of America constituted its very virtue. The *noblesse oblige* of the cultured aristocracy in America today is to lift oneself out of a sympathy with the rough, wholesome and dramatic facts of American life into the radical atmosphere befitting the latter-day Parisian. The more completely one can do this, the higher the approval he can win from the leaders of the cult, and from critics who make it their business to put musical fashions and exotics before the facts of national development. Pride thus draws the guileless neophyte, who thinks himself to have found the true path of musical culture, further and further into the toils. He would deem it a far higher honor to achieve even an instant of actual "atmosphere," however faint in a composition, than to have written the national hymn. He is lost in a maze of false standards. If he has gone too far in his folly he is ended as far as any usefulness to America is concerned.

For those to whom the school of the augmented fifth[2] is unsympathetic, and who still require musical culture (placing that before musical evolution) there is Richard, with his ultra-refinements of realism.[3] Eastward Ho! is forever the cry of the musical culturists. Once in the clutches of the educator, the young man is forever shown what Europe has done. He is made a historian, when he should have been a prophet. Never is he made to ask—What does America want?

America is saddled, hag-ridden, with culture. Those who have it have something that cannot reach the people. Those who have not got it fear that it *will* reach them. America's problem is to get rid of musical culture and put musical evolution—creative musical evolution—in its place. To do this it is necessary, not to give up studying music, but to study the country as well. And to study the country is to study the people. They are the final arbiters, the final appreciators and the source of power and honor. Their deepest nature and sympathies are also the mould in which the future forms of American music and musical presentation in general shall be cast.

Let no one suppose that the people are satisfied with what they have. Their popular music reaches them broadly and keeps them amused, keeps the superficies of their nervous system busy, but it does not satisfy them. They themselves put the brand *ephemeral* upon it. New York "kills" a new popular song now in three months. Moreover, the people are *aware* that they are not satisfied with their popular music. Their own word "ragtime" has become in their own mouths a term of derision, and they have invented the term "shoo-fly music," of similar significance. Great is the reward of the one who shall give them what they really want. It will not be measurable by the dollar sign alone.

---

[2] The augmented fifth, whether in an augmented triad or in passages of whole tone writing, provides a characteristic and atmospheric sonority in the music of Claude Debussy and other followers of the so-called Impressionistic school.   [3] Farwell refers to the German composer Richard Strauss (1864–1949), whose symphonic poems in particular were noted for their extramusical depiction. For more on Farwell's regard for Strauss, see p. 123, n. 11.

Now—a word for (or against) the culturists. They hold at present a monopoly on something which the people need; namely, the conceptions of musical genius, by which is not meant particular works of genius. In these very works of intensified culture already referred to are the rhythmic, the melodic, the harmonic inventions which it is the province of genius to conceive. But it is not always given to genius to see beyond these details of invention, to perceive the greatest use to which they could be put. Especially when the American genius is caught young and persuaded that an appeal to the people is necessarily a lowering of the standard, is he to be wheedled and petted into applying his ability to the creation of imitations and exotics.

The American people need to be given something which is more broadly and deeply their own than anything which they already have. It has already been shown that musical "culture," as practised by many in America, leads in precisely the opposite direction. Now it is to be seen that that which is to be more broadly and deeply the people's own cannot by any possibility come through any lowering of the creative capacity of American genius. It is to come, in fact, by an enhancing of that genius, by a growth in its power of vision until it sees the broad musical form or mould which shall be the acceptable vehicle to carry its multitudinous inventions to the people. In such broad musical conceptions the genius can dissolve as much "culture" as he desires, and it will not trouble any one, not even the *people*. Let him but find a form fittingly large or congenial of acceptance by the people, and no one will quarrel with him if he chooses to employ such details as doubly altered dominant thirteenth chords.

What is to be the nature of such American forms? The question is not merely one of musical form, as commonly understood. It is rather one of the form of presentation, the manner in which music shall be given to the people. It may be that the symphony concert, the opera, the recital, in their traditional forms and methods of presentation at least, are not destined to constitute the central pathway of music's advance in America. It may be that other methods of the presentation of music to the people are to draw forth the heart of the creative musical genius of America. The music by which America is to find itself among the nations of the world, or ahead of them, may perhaps take its rise in new kinds of musical events, better suited to the temper and the numbers of the people than the conventional system of concert and opera. The task of the creative musician in America is to liberate the creative spirit from the fetters of old-world usage and ideals, and apply it to uses and ideals better fitted to America's humanity. To do this will produce the great man in American music. It is not so much a new palette that is needed as a new canvas.

There is a conventionalism, a cynicism, a self-consciousness, in symphony concert, recital, and opera, as practised, that is already felt by cultivated audiences, and which militates against a thoroughly confident promotion of these musical enterprises, from both the artistic and commercial standpoints. America needs something in which it has greater faith. That deep universal sense of music's inmost nature which makes music almost a religion, is gone from these usual forms of its presentation. The composer who tries to reinject it there seems strangely out of place. The whole system is too much in the hands of technicians, professionals and traders. The people have no part in it. Humanity is banished from the temple.

Where, then, are the new forms to be looked for? Chiefly in those events in the production of which the *people* have a share. These forms may be growing up, through their early and experimental stages, under the protection of semi-privacy, or inevitable obscurity, until they are strong enough to stand boldly forth before the nation in their own right. The country is full of indications of such a gestative process. And the events thus in process of formation are stamped with one invariable stamp—*the participation of the people.*

Such a development is to be seen in the annual Forest Festival of the Bohemian Club, near San Francisco;[4] in the Peterboro Pageant; in the so-called "Norfolk Festival";[5] in such events as the Boston Civic Pageant, the Thetford (Vt.) Pageant, the Rochester Summer Festival, the celebration of national holidays in New York and elsewhere, and other events of a similar nature. There is an intensity of popular belief behind such undertakings, and an intensity in the popular enjoyment of them that augurs well for their future.

No music can be too good or too highly inspired for these events. The popular enjoyment of the best music is dependent only upon a sufficient familiarity, as the Summer symphony concerts in Central Park, New York, alone would prove, did not the results of these primitive democratic art forms in themselves afford ample proof of it. In the latter this familiarity is gained in the best possible way—by active

---

[4]In regard to the Bohemian Club's annual productions see also pp. 111f., 124ff., and 177, n.19.
[5]Farwell lauds the "communal enthusiasm" of this annual festival in Norfolk, Connecticut, in his "Noted Composers Honored at Great Norfolk Festival," *MA* 14 (17 June 1911): 1, 3–4.

participation. A popular comprehension of what music means—that is, the art of music—is thus fundamentally implanted. Here the untrammeled, unfettered creative musical spirit and the people can meet on a common ground, and the farther such development is carried the more perfectly they can meet. These events have often, though not always, in the past, involved a throwing together of incongruous musical material. They should be created all of a piece, as the San Francisco Forest Festival is created, that the composer may have full scope for his powers. When composers throw themselves into the composition of the music, on a large scale, for national celebrations, America will no longer lack for national hymns.

The ordinary music festival does not take rank with such events. The hired orchestra and hired soloists from a distance, together with a more or less moribund chorus rehearsed in one or two of the old war-horses of the choral répertoire, the audience remote from it all and unprepared for its appreciation, do not combine to make a living art-organism.

The indoor stage may well play a large part in such developments as those suggested. There is virtually nothing involved in any of these democratic art forms that may not be made conformable to the ordinary stage. It does not follow that because a certain kind of thing has been done on the stage in the past a different thing will not be done on it in the future. It does not follow that because old-fashioned opera and Wagnerian music drama have held the musical stage for a century or so, that a national American music-drama, presenting wholly new features of conception, may not occupy it in the future.

It is not implied in these considerations that there may be no future for the symphonic form, or other existing forms. Probably there must always be a standard of pure music, to show what the medium is capable of in the abstract—a forum for debating the possibilities of pure music. Reasons already given must incline us to think, however, that the symphonic can never be the great popular form in America.

It is more than possible, it is probable, that music will assume a new relation to humanity in the artistic unfolding of American life and genius. Our minds should be ready for such a phenomenon. Certain it is that at present we need less "culture" and more creative musical evolution, less retrospect and more prophecy.

Individual Advancement[1]

I

We are to-day upon the threshold of a new era of musical life, as of life generally, an era that shall be marked by startling and momentous changes, by new ideals, new beliefs, new conditions and new powers. The extent of past achievement and the recent rapid progress of the world's thought have brought us by an irresistible evolution to this point. No further real progress, but mere continuity and repetition, is possible along the familiar lines of the past and present, in musical education of all kinds, in artistic development, in composition. Our personal perceptions and beliefs will undergo so radical a change that we shall see in most of the activities about us a mere endless circling, without progress, which must continue until we shall lay hold of mental principles hitherto little generally understood, by which we shall lift ourselves into a new set of conditions.

The extraordinary developments which are pending in the mental world are reflected in the world of physical science. Professor Soddy, one of the chief experimenters, with Professor Rutherford and Sir William Ramsay, in the field of radium and radio-activity, said at the last meeting of the British Association that the problem of influencing the action of radium is bound up in the larger one of breaking apart the atoms of all elements and extracting therefrom energy of the same order, a "million times greater than any at present utilized."[2] He said

---

[1]Included here are the first two installments of a three-part article appearing in *MA* 19 (20 December 1913): 18; (27 December 1913): 32; and (3 January 1914): 32. The final part of the article omitted here is a fairly theoretical investigation of the relationship between an individual's "personal subjective mind" and a "universal creative spirit," a relationship that Farwell touches on more practically in the first two sections.   [2]Frederick Soddy (1877–1956), the English chemist, would receive the Nobel Prize for Chemistry in 1921 for his investigation of radioactive substances and for his work on the theory of isotopes. His mentor and colleague,

that such power as we now control is "but a secondary and insignificant offshoot of the primary tide," and added, "the main streams which vivifies and rejuvenates the whole universe passes by our very doors, and to its ultimate control it is now legitimate to aspire."

This is the same as saying, "heretofore we have dealt with limited forces; hereafter we shall deal with infinite Force." The statement is a staggering one to those who have not already foreseen its possibility by the recognition of the corresponding truth on the mental plane, as the possibility of wireless telegraphy could be foreseen by the perception of telepathy. It serves, however, the important purpose of showing us, by comparison of known forces with knowable Force, the relation which exists between the mental capacities with which we have been familiar in the past and those which we are beginning to perceive as the capacities of the future. It is the difference betweeen limited mental powers and infinite mental Power. Physical science and mental science are racing for the goal, and when they reach it they will find it *One*.

Illusory Progress

In the light of such an evolution, which means changes in the scheme of life deep as Existence itself, it is certain that the activities of the present, however busily pursued, will not look much like progress to us. Insight into the principles and possibilities of the coming order are, however, by no means lacking to-day, for knowledge is being rapidly increased, and many persons are recognizing the startling truths which are ripe for revelation at the present time. The geographical extension of musical life and musical influence has been progress, in one sense, and must still continue, though, in America to-day, it is a small village indeed that has not partaken of the crumbs, at least, that have fallen from the table of the masters of music. But in merely adding to the number of persons reached by music, there lies no actual evolutionary progress; such activity, however desirable and necessary, represents merely a further dispensing of the products, and a perpetrating of the conditions, of the past.

It is different with the colossal national work which remains to be done, in the eradication of fundamental and general superstitions and

---

the physicist Sir Ernest Rutherford (1871–1937) is said to have set the foundation for the development of nuclear physics with his studies of radioactivity. Soddy studied under the noted British chemist Sir William Ramsay (1852–1916) in London. Both Ramsay and Rutherford also received Nobel Prizes for their work, in 1904 and 1908, respectively.

evils in our musical life. The way must thus first be cleared, in America, for the unhampered manifestation of the new era and the principles upon which it shall be based. Such evils are the slavish imitation of the past and the alien, the lack of proper recognition, in a material way, of native talent and genius, and the graft and charlatanism which have thriven in our midst. The work of combating these is in strong hands, and is already starting upon its last and most far-reaching phase.

Generic and Individual Evolution

Thus far, in our American musical progress, the advance has been on *generic* lines. It has been a question of national collective issues. First came the general implanting of musical culture, then the general acceptance of the American as composer or interpretative artist. Later follows the general crusade against the vices and abuses of our national musical world. The great fundamental difference between the existing era, which is fast drawing to a close, and the era which is to come, is that while the past and present have represented such *generic* movements, based, as they are, upon the law of averages, the coming era will arise from the special development of the individual, from a higher knowledge and use of his individual powers, through which he will lift himself above the law of averages. How such a thing is to be done is about the most important matter to which anyone can devote himself in these days, when competition is degenerating into a scramble, and effort into an insane rush. And because of the heightened power of the individual, the coming era will be characterized by a great increase of originality, of the exercise of the creative power, both in public and private enterprise. For in the first place only by a conscious invoking of the higher creative powers within himself can anyone rise out of the generic condition of mankind into the higher condition of individual control, and when one has done this he has discovered the source of all originality.

The times are hungry. We crave new light, new power, new and surer ways of accomplishing things, in accordance with the higher evolution for which through centuries we have struggled. We weary of the grinding of the mill of chance, of the petty things to which we have stooped to attain our ends—the things which have made cynics of us. Something within us makes us refuse to believe that so miserable a destiny has been mapped out for the soul of man. It is not a tragedy, it is an absurdity, that a dead star should sweep unswervingly upon its orbit, and that a man should flounder and cringe. Never was there a time when the human mind was so dissatisfied with its circumstance, so weary of it, or so eager, so receptive, so ready to believe in its own higher powers, could it but become plain what these powers are, and how set in action.

In the world of the arts it is the same as in the world at large. The monstrous unrest of the present, the lack of anchorage for mind or soul, the insane rushing from school to school, from ism to ism, the forest of irreconcilable ideals in which humanity wanders aimlessly about— these are conditions which cannot last indefinitely. We tire of the endless repetitions in the old round, of the long succession of arid novelties and the presentation of the inept. The academies are complacent enough, with their infallible rule of three for artistic salvation, and so are those who, under the laws of chance, with a good pinch of shrewdness or chicanery thrown in to tip the balance, have *chanced* to succeed. Like the shadows which are thrown before coming events, there are individuals here and there, nevertheless, who in measure greater or less have grasped the laws of conscious control and have found a more dignified and substantial success. In a world where about ninety per cent of all business ventures are failures, it cannot be said that the understanding of such laws is very prevalent as yet, and the statistics concerning artistic enterprises, both in their artistic and business aspects, would be likely to prove vastly more discouraging. The occasional individuals who are born so gifted that they cannot possibly fail, even if they try and those others, apparently equally gifted, who cannot succeed, even by their most heroic efforts, are too few in number to serve as a basis for the deduction of general laws. As the laws of being and evolving are better understood they enable us to explain such exceptional cases as the known laws of electricity enable us to explain why one electrical apparatus works while another will not.

We shall not have any help in our search for true progress out of the existing condition of things by merely seeking to do more and more artistically that which we or others have already done well. That is refinement only, and no jugglery can turn it into that which we most need, which is a new influx of truth, of vision, of the spirit. The end of refinement, if it be taken as an end, is uncreativeness, ennui and despair.

Beyond Chance

The great step before us is in the nature neither of a mere extension nor a refinement of our present activities, but in the lifting of activity altogether out of generic, or chance conditions, into conditions of conscious and special control in accordance with laws acting on a higher plane. The accomplishment of this is intimately bound up with the devoting of our efforts to broader and worthier ends, for any use of higher laws not in harmony with universal Law must be destructive to the user. It must be very clearly understood that it is not expansion, but elevation, which constitutes the step to be taken in passing from the present to the coming era, and this not by any law of average development, but by the conscious and particular action of individuals who perceive the law.

What is required is to find the law the exercise of which will destroy once for all the superstitions, false beliefs, prejudices that hold us back, individually, in our material and artistic development, and at the same time provide the power and condition for our advancement upon the new plane. Some of these superstitions and false beliefs are that financial success depends upon a lowering of artistic ideals; that a "struggle for existence" is a necessary condition of life; that we cannot rise above the sphere where the law of chance is operative—that the outcome of our efforts must depend upon chance; that we know what is impossible of accomplishment, by ourselves or by others, and especially that we can determine future possibility by existing precedent; that we can advance in a material sense only in competition with, or at the expense of others, or that the stress of modern competition lessens a man's opportunity for success; that progress through sharp dealing is actual progress; that anybody or anything can stand in the way of one's individual advancement; that getting is more important than giving; that the traditional or accredited ways of artistic advancement, or any advancement, are the best or only ways; and that there is any limit to one's growth or the power at one's command.

If any set of beliefs as deeply rooted as most of these are in men's minds is to be destroyed, it must be seen that it can be only by some absolutely radical change of direction in the general mental tendency of the race. It is plain that no mere rearrangement of outward factors could accomplish such a thing; it is not the power to *rearrange* that is needed, but the power to *create*. Along the ordinary and understood lines we have gone as far as we can, and without a greater *science of the mind* we can only go around forever in the same old circles. And we have reached the period in the development of the race when it is inevitable that the law of the creative operation of the individual mind should be made known to all, whatever the consequences, for the sake of the many who are now ready to apply it in the right way. The authoritative general presentation of the subject is to be found in two books, *The Creative Process in the Individual* and the *Edinburgh Lectures* by T. Troward.[3] These should be read in connection with my writings on the subject, which will concern themselves more with the relation of the matter to our world of music and allied arts. I shall go into the matter more deeply in a forthcoming article.

II

Every artist to-day knows that the utmost confusion of ideas exists as to how the artist, who must be before all else the seeker for the ideal, is to meet the conditions of life in a real world. Leander's puny achievement becomes insignificant beside the Hellesponts of materialism, cynicism, disbelief in all ideal effort, and actual hardship, which the struggling and sincere artist stems to reach his beloved, the Ideal. This loyalty to the ideal, by which the nobler souls of art lift themselves to the commanding place which they occupy, is nothing more than a profounder belief in the law and order of the universe. They look farther than others, and beneath the eternal flux and shifting shadow-play of visible phenomena, they sense and believe, even if they do not actually see, the one Law of all phenomena. On the steady tide of that Law, whether by mere belief or actual perception of it, they move steadily onward and upward, while others pin their faith only to what they can see by day or lock in a vault by night, and the law of whose lives is the same law of eternal change without progress which governs a drop of water forever toyed with by the forces of the natural world.

Such nobler souls can regard only with horror those wretched beings—the innumerable crawling larvae of the art world—who have harkened to the false testimony of the world against their own first vision of the true and the beautiful, and who, with befogged minds and envious eyes, can see in the successful and the noble only those who are luckier than they.

The only reason why this confusion should exist as to the true relation of the seeker of the ideal to this real world, and his best course in it, is that the world generally does not understand the laws which govern the relation of such a one to his environment. If it did understand them there would be no more difference of opinion or argument about the matter than there could be as to how an aeroplane should be

---

[3]See p. 21.

constructed so that it would rise, instead of flopping on the ground. And as there is "a light that lighteth every man that cometh into the world," and since this guiding gleam of mind and soul for any man, whatever may be his particular bent, is no different in essence from the ideal which animates the artist, there will not be found one law for the idealist and another for the non-idealist. Natural law is natural law, and if one person rises to the point where he perceives and directs it in its higher aspects, it is no more than any other person can do on the same terms, be he bricklayer or poet.

Revelation of Law

It has been the intention, in what has been said above, and particularly in my first article on this subject, to prepare the mind of the reader to expect a revelation of the working of some natural law hitherto little understood, which shall place the individual, man or woman, upon a higher level of evolution, where, instead of blind struggle or mere hopeful effort, he shall have a conscious and unlimited control over his condition and environment in every respect. Astounding as such a leap in a our mental powers appears, it is no whit more astounding than the latest declaration of physical science upon its plane, which referred to in my first article, namely, that the problem of controlling the action of radium is bound up in a larger problem involving the liberation of energy "a million times greater than any at present utilized." And unprecedented as such a mental achievement appears, it is no more unprecedented than the recent achievement of human flight for the first time, so far as we know, since the beginning of the world. To take a mental parallel, it is no more unprecedented than the invention, or discovery, of speech, of the spoken and written word, by primitive man.

It is most important to get out of our minds the idea that a thing cannot be done because it has not been done before. Moreover, in the matter in hand, the knowledge at which we are arriving is not new, although not until now has there been a sufficient general increase in knowledge and experience to provide a basis for the promulgation of it as a broad movement. Also it should be said that between the discovery of such unsuspected forces, physical and mental, as those we are considering, and the violent and sudden overthrow of existing conditions which we might expect as the result of such discoveries, there intervenes the "law of growth" which provides for the gradual understanding and employment of the laws and forces discovered. What the ascent to such a plane of control of circumstance as that pictured would mean to the artist who strives, and yet who feels himself powerless, or unduly or fatally restricted in power in this material world, may well be imagined, especially by the artists themselves.

As one more preliminary let me say that I am not talking about theories, but about the results of my own experience during a period of fourteen years of conscious exercise of the principles involved. The first four of these years represented the merest skirmishing on the outskirts of these principles; the next seven a more definite and frequent practical application of them, involving a certain working knowledge, but not a full realization of their scope and meaning; and the last three years have represented in question, in the full knowledge of their infinite scope and significance, my own experience and perceptions having been met and completed, as a result of this practice, in the illuminating writings, far more profound than their author would at first allow his readers to suspect, of Judge Troward.

Solving Problems

To begin with the most salient and graspable aspect of the law of the mind's action along the lines indicated, though without conveying the slightest hint of the immense potentiality of the law in its fulness, I may say that beginning with ordinary auto-suggestion for the improvement of physical and mental states, I long ago learned that certain problems, which I could not solve through any exertion whatsoever of my objective mind, my "subconscious" or "subjective" mind would solve for me entirely without effort, especially when I called upon it to do so, and allowed a space of time to intervene. Such a process requires no more knowledge of the subjective mind than is to be had by watching a hypnotized person respond with his "unconscious" mind to the suggestions of the hypnotizer, while his conscious mind is asleep. If that experience is lacking, a simple belief in a mind below the conscious mind is quite sufficient for practical experimentation. If the conscious mind of another can suggest ideas to my subjective mind (which is the most obvious result of hypnotism) by getting my otherwise interfering objective mind out of the way by putting it to sleep, certainly it is to be assumed that my own objective mind, which could have interfered by staying awake, is in even a better position to suggest ideas to my own subjective mind.

This is the simple basis of auto-suggestion, the action of which within a certain restricted sphere has long been familiar to scientists and physicists. What these scientists have not recognized is the natural and universal law of most far-reaching importance for the evolution of the individual, and ultimately of the race, which is bound up with this apparently simple little phenomenon of auto-suggestion.

First Experiments

My first applications of the law involved in it were simple enough and consisted in the rectification of a persistent tendency to despondent moods by devoting a few moments a day, for a time, to the auto-suggestion of the opposite. Then I found that the exact ideas required to solve complex problems and provide necessary bars to overcome snaggy and obstinate places in musical composition could be had by propounding these problems to the subjective mind by a species of meditation, and giving it time, untroubled by any conscious thought on the matters in question, to work them out. The answers usually came instantaneously, when least expected, though I have since learned to provide properly for receiving them.

On one occasion I was wholly unable to find the precise cause of my dissatisfaction with a certain place in a composition which had otherwise gone very much to my satisfaction. While I did not work at the problem I propounded it earnestly to my subjective mind and went about my affairs, which kept me wholly away from composition for some time. After two weeks, when I had for all immediate practical purposes forgotten the matter, two bars of music suddenly obtruded themselves upon my consciousness, while I was talking with a friend on a matter wholly unrelated to music. I thought of the troublesome composition. The two bars went exactly into place, fitting the complicated chromatic harmony at both ends, maintaining the color scheme and rounding out the sense of rhythmic completeness, the lack of which, while I had not recognized the fact before, had been at the bottom of the whole difficulty.

Shortly after this the necessity arose of giving a great many lecture recitals. Not having touched the piano until after my twenty-first year, my playing was not only crude, but I was never certain of being able to play a composition through in public, however much I might have practised it. The result was that I endured terrors before and during every performance that were making a nervous wreck of me until it occurred to me to have recourse in this matter to the subjective mind.

I accordingly practised regular advance auto-suggestion for each recital for several weeks to come, devoting a little time to it each day. My suggestive thought took somewhat this form: "On such and such a day and hour, at such and such a town and hall, I shall play a recital consisting of such and such compositions. I shall play them all perfectly, with absolute confidence and without a break or a hitch." That ended my difficulties in this respect at once, and after that my slight normal nervousness in beginning to play passed directly into eagerness and confidence. In other words, I played all my recitals perfectly, *in advance*.

Discovery of Power

In these experiences, then, I had discovered within myself a power that, at my direction, would cure despondency, compose music, and bestow confidence in public performance, all absolutely without so much as stirring the will power by a hair, except for the slight initial effort of the few minutes' meditation per day required to present these matters clearly to my subjective mind. In this and many similar matters, the subjective mind did all the actual work; all I did was to indicate the direction in which it should work.

It now became apparent to me that there was here a natural law of wide application, if one could but get to the root of the matter and discover the whole significance and reach of it. It may interest some of my readers to know that I was engaged at this time in writing an elaborate article against mental science "as she was taught," because of my disgust with the numerous writers on the subject, whose treatment of the matter was infected with the spiritual anemia of the puritanical heritage of New England, and who appeared to regard the mind as a curious insect on a pin, to be inspected through lorgnettes, rather than as an instrument through which a man was to do red-blooded work in a real world. As I had certain Boston influences in mind, the article was to have been called "The Huntington Avenue School of Philosophy."

Finally it occurred to me to attempt the solution of this problem of the subjective mind and its true significance and operation, *by placing the whole problem itself with subjective mind*, and directing it to give me the answer. To meditation upon this in various ways, in all earnestness, I devoted an hour a day for two months, in the summer of 1910, at the end of which time there were placed in my hands the two masterworks on the subject by Judge Troward, to which I have referred. This was my first experience, and by no means my last, of observing the action of the law with relation to the influencing of material affairs outside of myself. With what I now learned, the fulness of the law, which in its lesser issues I had been invoking, became plain to me with its infinite vista of tremendous consequences. With this I shall deal in another chapter.

The New Gospel of Music[1]

The New Gospel of music is this: *That the message of music at its greatest and highest is not for the few, but for all; not sometime, but now; that it is to be given to all, and can be received by all.*

Let no one get the false impression that this is merely a pretty dream or a vague altruistic fancy. The New Gospel of Music stands upon established fact and principle, and its full meaning is a thing to be grappled with by everyone who sets out to lead in musical matters from this time forth. The fact upon which it rests is that its successful practice is arising and becoming established in many places, as will be shown; and the principle upon which it rests is that which I have called "mass-appreciation," the spontaneous response of the human mass to the substantive reality in all music, however great, without previous education in musical appreciation.

Fact and Principle

The *fact* is beginning to be somewhat broadly appreciated in America, as is witnessed by the emulation of the communities which have been most successful in their experiments, and the corresponding constant advance in the movement to bring the best music to the people through various channels. The immense significance of the *principle*—its potential capacity to give birth to the most stupendous developments of music in its relation to humanity in the future—has not as yet been dreamed

---

[1] This is the first of a two-part article that appeared in *MA* 19 (4 April 1914): 32 and (11 April 1914): 36. In the second part Farwell expands on his theory of "mass appreciation" of music that he has set forth in the first, discussing more fully the conditions that help to create this phenomenon.

of by our present civilization. Our method of growth by emulation and experiment in America is a healthy one, but nevertheless in a large measure blind. Many of our American cities set out to build a system of municipal music, or other means of bringing the great message of music to the people, very much as a child sets out to build a house of blocks. The child imitates and endeavors, without any thought of inquiring into the principles of construction, or its purposes. The time has come when we must improve on such primitive hit-or-miss methods, and proceed in accordance with understood principles, which cannot be violated without a diminution in the efficiency of the undertaking, or perhaps without actual failure. The principles of universal musical distribution which we are now discovering, such as "mass-appreciation," bear the same relation to our completed communal musical enterprises, as the electrical principles of resistance, induction, etc., bear to the completed dynamo. These principles ignored or violated, an impairment of the result necessarily follows; but the understanding and fulfillment of the conditions fixed by them brings the most complete possible efficiency which those principles, by their nature, are capable of yielding. We must first discover what the principles in any question are, and then provide such conditions as will enable us to get the most out of them.

My first great experience of "mass-appreciation" of music of a high order was at the performance of *The Hamadryads*, one of the "Grove Plays," of the Bohemian Club of San Francisco, given on the natural stage in the club's giant redwood grove on the Russian River, in August, 1904.[2] I purposely omit reference to Bayreuth, which I had visited at an earlier date,[3] as the audiences there are drawn in large measure from those to whom music has always been an object of special study or interest. Except for a small proportion of persons from various parts of the world, the audiences at the "Grove Plays" are made up, in the main, of business and professional men of San Francisco, who give little thought to music during the rest of the year, especially to music of symphonic caliber. At the time of which I write, San Francisco was without a symphony orchestra. Nevertheless the response of these audiences to these impressive and seriously conceived music-dramas, on the occasions of this annual pilgrimage, is phenomenal in the reality of its fervor. The hearers, as a mass, and wholly irrespective of individual musical training, never fail to respond more ar-

---

[2]See p. 124ff.   [3]See p. 46.

dently to the more powerful of the music-dramas produced, and never forget them through the years, while not even the romantic conditions and association of the Grove can cause such a response to an inferior work.

An Enduring Tradition

So profound was the emotion produced in the hearers by *The Hama-dryads*, that the memory of it has taken on the character of an enduring tradition. It was the first of the "Grove Plays" to step forth from an earlier and more primitive phase of the evolution of these festivals, into a fuller beauty and more complete realization of the elements composing them. Certain it is that the audience at *The Hamadryads* had experienced no previous special education of a nature to enable it to take the forward step in artistic appreciation demanded by the superior character of this work. And yet the reaction was instantaneous. Neither did this reaction have any relation whatsoever to any analytical or other intellectual appreciation of the drama and the music. It manifested itself in a spontaneous and glowing sense of *joy*, universally felt. It was a reaction to sheer *beauty*. It was *mass-appreciation*, a principle inherent in the psychological and spiritual constitution of man—an intellectual process "short-circuited" by a spiritual process. If this immediate human phenomenon is to be thought of as related in any way to the idea of the education of the mass, it can only be to what I may venture to call *Education by Revelation*, and to which I hope to have an opportunity of referring in greater particular at another time.

Perfect Conditions

The conditions at the Grove are singularly perfect for the manifestation of mass-appreciation. The audience, *en masse*, has left its usual occupations behind, and has gone up to the Grove *already united* in a definite spirit and intent (namely, the "burial of Care," following upon his being slain in the drama). This spirit and intent is one of *festivity*, of festive ceremony. The ceremony which the audience is to witness (the Grove Play and Burial of Care) is created out of and by itself, and is thus community self-expression, which means *community joy*. The creative artists who have been the immediate makers of the ceremony have given themselves utterly to their highest vision of beauty. The ceremony is a *regular periodical* event. The place of its observance is one of great natural beauty. Each one of these matters enumerated is related to a particular principle having a bearing upon the general principle of mass-appreciation. The more completely these several particular principles are fulfilled, the more complete will be the manifestation of the general principle of mass-appreciation.

Question of Abstract Music

Such an effect as that described, it may be thought, may well be expected from a *drama*, which has all the elements of a "show," and can make an appeal not only through its music, but through scenic effect, through dramatic action and the spoken word, as well. But what of music alone, in its higher phases? What of abstract symphonic music, divested of all that an accompanying dramatic presentation can bring to its aid in making an appeal to the average human mass?

Does not such music represent a refinement of art which must lift itself beyond the sphere of any general appeal? This is undoubtedly what most persons still believe, especially those who attend regularly the symphony concerts of the winter season in the great cities. For our refined concert, supporters have become hardened in the illusion that the great composers wrote especially for their superior culture, whereas the truth is that those musical giants wrote for their common humanity—for that within them which they share with all, rich and poor, cultured and rude, by virtue of human birth.

The only thing proved by the fact that symphony societies exist only among the cultured and wealthy, is that we have not got as far away from the monarchical and aristocratic civilization of our ancestors and old-world neighbors as we had thought. It proves nothing about the nature of a symphony, or a dollar or a doughnut, that the prince has it, and the pauper hasn't it. That the few have for themselves alone the benefits of the music which was created for all—though, happily, in far less measure than formerly—is merely an indication that we are, in externals at least, still in a crude phase of evolution as to human brotherhood.

Fortunately, the spiritual ferment is now far advanced and spreading rapidly. The soul of man no longer accepts what the eye is compelled to see. It needs but the enkindling into living flame of the accumulated general aspiration already awakened, to change the facts of an older age into the facts of the New Age, and throughout America this is beginning to be accomplished.

Principles in Practice

Sure as we may be, through intuition, of the truth of principles, our joy is not full until we see them unfold into material operation. And if they deeply concern ourselves, we can not rest until we have guided them to such an unfoldment. With reference to the immediate relation of abstract or symphonic music to the human mass, however prolific the country may have been in earlier demonstrations of it, my own first experience was gained in 1910, through my connection with the then newly installed orchestral concerts as a definite institution in Central Park, New York, and as the chief feature of the system of municipal concerts planned by the then incoming city administration. Nothing more conclusive as an answer to the question concerning abstract music could have happened. At the "Grove Play" spontaneous mass-appreciation was produced in a body of men of good general education (the type of non-artistic man commonly known as a "philistine" in the art world), by music of a high order aided by its conjunction with drama. In Central Park this same spontaneous mass-appreciation was produced in a vast mass of the "common" people far below the "Grove Play" audience in average culture, by pure symphonic music unaided by any agent external to itself. A very great proportion of these people had never heard an orchestra, or any music of symphonic character, in their lives, or in fact any except the popular music of the streets. Nor was their musical awakening a matter of education through these concerts during the subsequent years;—*it was an established fact in the first concert of the first year.*

At the meetings of the Litchfield County Choral Union at Norfolk, Conn.;[4] the Bach Festivals in Bethlehem, Pa.; in the spreading institution of municipal music and of popular price concerts by American symphony orchestras; in the phenomenal spread of the custom of Christmas trees with light and music for the people; wherever community self-expression has begun to appear, the principles of the New Gospel of Music are becoming the realities of American life. Those principles hold the seeds of a flowering splendid and wonderful beyond all reach of present imagining. In chapters to follow I shall seek to suggest in some faint way the trend of the present evolution.[5]

---

[4]See p. 209, n. 5.   [5]In the weeks after the two-part "The New Gospel of Music" had appeared, Farwell continued with his theme of democratic music in a new age, producing (between 18 April and 11 July 1914) eight articles in *MA* that dealt with his vision for a musical genre which he called "community music drama."

Community Music Drama:

Will Our Country People in Time Help Us to Develop the Real American Theater?[1]

Two years ago, up among the hills of Vermont, I found myself one summer afternoon in circumstances which quite unexpectedly produced within me a surprising emotion which, in beauty, in joy, in humanity, above all in a sense of upliftedness and blessedness—a fusion of self with the great heart and soul of all mankind, and of God—surpassed all other of the emotions and experiences of life. At the same time I became aware that I was not alone in what I felt. Among the many persons about me there were, in the eyes of the younger, looks of wonder, and in those of the older, tears. Together with all else that I felt, I seemed to feel within the region of wonder and tears myself. There was something strangely inexplicable in it all, something that all familiar logic and reason failed to explain. It was like a dream or a miracle.

All that these people, seated with myself on an out-of-door grandstand, were witnessing, were incidents from the history of their own and some allegorical scenes, rather crudely acted, and some novel but not very extraordinary dances, all done by a number of their townsfolk whom they were quite accustomed to seeing every day of their lives in the ordinary routine of affairs. There was music of a simple and effective, but in no sense of a remarkable character, composed by a young

[1]Appeared in *Craftsman* 26 (1914): 418–24.

man of the town and played by an orchestra, which he had mustered from among the townspeople; and there was a chorus similarly procured. The actors and dancers were in costumes which, though appropriate and picturesque, were made of cheap and ordinary materials. The stage was Mother Earth,—a hillside with "wings" of forest to frame it, and at one side, in view of all the people, the town itself, with its little river in the valley below. The people had come up to this spot to see, but more than that, to *give*, a "pageant."[2]

Still the miracle of the emotions which had been produced did not seem to be explained. The amateur acting and dancing which the people had seen could not compare in point of skill with that which they could see almost any day in the theaters in their town. The same could be said of the music in comparison with the artists from the Metropolitan centers who visited the town to give concerts. Neither was there here any attempt at scenery or scenic illusion, the familiar hillside, forest and view of the town serving as the prospect throughout; while in the town theaters could be seen all the wonders of illusion which may nowadays be achieved upon any modestly equipped stage. Nor was there here, as frequently upon the professional indoor stage, any noted actor's or actress's name to give glamour to the occasion. The actors were local carpenters, farmers, merchants, blacksmiths—the everyday people of the town, and their wives, sons and daughters. None of the things shown or done on this outdoor stage were extraordinary or wonder-provoking in themselves (the wonder was that they were being done at all!), or anything beyond what any American town or country community could do proportionately to its own size. And yet these things brought together and put into a certain order were capable of gripping the attention of several thousand persons for two hours and a half, and of producing in the multitude one of the most powerfully exalting and humanly moving emotions which life can afford. If some profound tragedy were being enacted, or if some unimaginably splendid spectacle were presented, the matter would not appear so inexplicable. But such extreme measures for making an emotional appeal proved

---

[2]The pageant that Farwell witnessed took place in Thetford, Vermont, on 12, 14, and 15 August 1911. Farwell had been appointed to an "advisory committee" for the production, which had been funded by the Russell Sage Foundation to help promote pageantry in the United States. See Naima Prevots, *American Pageantry: A Movement for Art and Democracy* (Ann Arbor, MI: UMI Research Press, 1990), 40, 43; Prevots provides further information on the *Pageant of Thetford*, including a detailed description of its plot (42-48).

here wholly unnecessary, and one had to look elsewhere for the mysterious element which produced so powerful an effect.

Every one present knew, as I knew, that the awakening and stirring of that strange deep human emotion that spread through the assemblage had its source in the event of the day. The people, going away, knew, although they had not known it before, that it was *that* they had come for. But it was the last thing spoken of. Men and women with lumps in their throats and moist eyes shook the hand of the "pageant master" and muttered a few inadequate words, or went away silently. They all felt more emotional ecstasy than they had ever felt before, though they could not have said why. Perhaps the inexplicable pathos that mingled with the emotions of beauty and joy came from that very thing—that they had long carried in their hearts uncomprehended dreams of a life realized in forms of order, of rhythm, of beauty and joy, of brotherhood, and here in some mysterious way they had suddenly found themselves in a world where the dream had come true; here the dream was outside of themselves, shared by all, instead of being carried lonelily within—they could see it with their eyes and hear it with their ears, instead of having merely to imagine it deep in the solitary recesses of heart and mind. And it was not somebody else's dream put before them to wonder at or admire, it was their own story, how they and their town, their families and their friends, had come to be what they were, then and there—what they might become in the future—that the pageant had spread out in living reality before them. And best of all, they had not *bought* the thing that had touched them so deeply and given them such great joy—they had *made* it.

If, being new at such a thing, they had had to call in a teacher, a "pageant master," to guide them, that is nothing more than any student does who is learning how to begin his work. And if they entrusted to the pageant master the labor of writing out the dialogue for the spoken scenes, they had had to teach him what to say and tell him what their fathers and mothers had done, and the generations before them, to make their town what it then was; and so, using the teacher as an instrument, they themselves made the "book" of the drama through him. When a community has gone to school in these matters for a little while, it will quickly enough learn how to stand entirely on its own feet. But these people had acted the parts, danced the dances, composed the music, played and sung it, made the costumes, built the grandstand, financed and advertised the pageant, all among themselves. And the months of preparation of these matters had stimulated the study and practice of all these things among the people and had implanted such joyous activities in the midst of their everyday lives; many happy gatherings had been brought about, and a stimulating sense of activity and expectancy had brightened the entire life of the town.

And then when at last all was ready, and the days of the pageant arrived, and all these hosts were marshalled on the outdoor stage in scenes of interest and beauty, of rhythm and order—then, the wonder happened, and the unseen Spirit of Life and Joy descended upon all the people, stirring within them deep and long-slumbering emotions and dreams, revealing to them the marvel of a life—their own life—uplifted and freed at last from perpetual bondage to a ceaseless round of sordid and despairing routine. Joy, crushed, blotted out for a time by the grinding machinery of the age—Joy was found again!

Such is the miracle of the pageant, when its secret is understood. The pageant—*community drama*—has shown a bright pathway up and out of the blighting grind and joyless routine of this present mode of life with which our nation is becoming at last so profoundly dissatisfied. Metropolis, large city, town, village or country-side; it is all the same; community self-expression and self-dramatization in forms of beauty and joy are showing us the way forward and through. In these activities life throbs again, no longer with the dull pounding machinery, but with the beating of the heart.

Why should so important an issue, the inspiring of so life-giving an emotion, hang upon this matter of community expression in the pageant or community-drama? A moment ago I told you how comparatively simple were the different elements of the pageant, and yet how great an effect was produced upon the people when they were "brought together and put in a certain order." But think for an instant how great a meaning lies hidden beneath the surface of these simple words. To "bring together" for such a common purpose implies no less a thing than *human brotherhood*; and to "put into a certain order" means nothing less than *art*. And so, at a stroke, we have the Brotherhood of Art! How mighty is such an idea for our democratic land of America—how simple and how new!

With this come the glad tidings of the new gospel of art, that its joy and beauty, its pleasure and refreshment and inspiration are not for a favored few in some distant metropolis, in musty museums or stifling concert halls and theaters, but for all the people in any and every corner of the land—not in some far-away day of hoped-for wealth and "culture," but now, for the making, and with materials that are immediately at hand.

Art is not something you buy and hang on a wall. It is not something you *get*; it is something you *do*. Its prize of joy is not for the buyer, but for the maker. Every one knows that the real happiness of art belongs to the one who creates it—to the artist himself. But, you say, not every one can be an artist—only the exceptional person has such gifts. But stop a moment and think; there is something which may not have occurred to you before—suppose the *community* becomes an artist! Suppose the community does what the individual artist has done in the past!

When the community does this, it must have, as a whole, the same experience that the individual had before. All the inspiration and exaltation that the individual artist had alone will now suffuse the whole community. And how much greater is a joy thus shared than one which must be borne in solitude! When the community becomes the artist, every individual becomes a part of a mighty artist. Each does that part of the art-work which he can, knowing that the whole can be perfect only by his doing his share, however little that may be. It may be only the making of a costume or a part of one, being one of fifty "nature spirits," tending some electric signals to call certain groups on to the pageant stage, or something equally simple. Or it may be the taking of an acting part, unpretentious or prominent, playing or conducting the music, even composing it, or perhaps guiding the whole pageant force through the performance. Through this brotherly work of art, every community in the land can thus become an artist.

The little talents of individuals, bound together in one common effort, make the genius of the people. It is my experience, in the production of pageants, that every community, no matter how remote or obscure, is rich in unsuspected ability and talent of innumerable sorts, and is, in fact, chiefly made up of people who have not done what they can do either for lack of opportunity or from lack of any experience which shows them that they can do it. I have seen village blacksmiths, farmers, ministers, schoolteachers, students, not forgetting wives, mothers and sisters, blossom out into creditable and even very excellent actors with but the slightest coaching, although they had never before stepped out of the orbit of their usual routine of work. And I have not failed to notice the happiness which it has given them to find that they could do so, and especially to find that they were forming an indispensable part of a great spectacle of dramatic art such as they had never before seen or dreamed of.

This acting can often be made very natural to people by "casting them in their own parts," or in parts similar to their actual trade or profession. If to carry out a certain scene a constable, a newsboy or a mayor is needed, get a constable, a newsboy or a mayor to take his own part, and all he will have to do to act is to be himself. If a certain family played a very important part in the history of a community, get the present members of that family to take their ancestors' parts. Probably they will have some of the original clothes of the earlier generation to use as costumes. I know one case of a man whose family had degenerated since the days of his prominent ancestors, who was rehabilitated in self-respect and in the regard of the community by taking the part of his grandfather in a pageant. A sense of shame at first prompted him to refuse to take the part, but once he was led to consent the family dignity reasserted itself and made a new man of him.

The art of the Brotherhood of Art is the broad and noble art of the *drama*. But it is no longer the commercialized "play" written to lure the dollars out of the pockets of a jaded, neurotic and sensation-hunting throng in a garish Broadway theater. It is a thing infinitely more thrilling—the representation of the history, the present life and even the future of the people of a community prepared and enacted by the people themselves. The eminent American pioneer of the pageant, Mr. William Chauncy Langdon, calls the pageant "a drama of which the place is the hero and its history is the plot."[3] In Europe chiefly a "spectacle," in America the pageant has become a veritable drama, a play, given on a stage like any other play, except that the stage is usually, and certainly preferably, out of doors. The idea of "procession" has wholly vanished from our pageant of today, and its dramatic aim and end has led us to rename it "community drama."

So strongly has this form of drama appealed to our country, so perfectly has it fulfilled the great need of the American people to engage in joyous artistic activity, that it is undergoing very rapid and striking developments. Above all else it is giving a constantly greater place to music. Music, at first a merely incidental thing in the pageant, is at least given dominion over entire scenes. Mr. Langdon, and myself as composer of the music for his recent pageants, have experimented with the broadest and freest use of music in community drama, with

---

[3] W. C. Langdon (1871–1947) was one of the best known pageant directors in the years before World War I when pageantry flourished in the United States. Farwell and Langdon collaborated on the *Pageant of Meriden* [New Hampshire] and the *Pageant of Darien* [Connecticut], both produced in 1913. Farwell also worked with him to further pageantry through the American Pageant Association, which Langdon founded in 1913 in Boston.

the happiest results, and it may be confidently predicted that from now on music and drama will go hand in hand in the making of the most desirable form of community drama. So our pageant, even if not devoted to solo singing, becomes at last as musical as opera itself! But since Wagner converted opera into "music-drama," our new American product we call *Community Music-Drama*.

The little Pageant of Meriden, New Hampshire, and the large one of Darien, Connecticut, in the production of which Mr. Langdon and myself have been associated, may thus be regarded as steps in the making of such an American community music-drama. The Pageant and Masque of St. Louis, produced in May of present year,[4] by Thomas Wood Stevens, Percy MacKaye and Frederick Converse, in collaboration, bears out the same tendency.[5] But large or small, the wonder and the beauty of the matter is (and practical experience in many places is constantly bearing it out) that there is not a community in the whole broad land, from countryside to metropolis, that cannot have for itself the joy and the benefit of engaging in this new art-life of the people, and making this community music-drama for itself. In fact, it is precisely the national need of such a thing that has brought it to birth.

How easily choruses may be organized and drilled in any kind of a community I have learned for myself. But until some such need of them as community music-drama brings about, there is little reason for organizing them. Band or orchestra in at least a simple form can be developed practically anywhere. We are, as a nation, not spending six hundred million dollars a year for music and musical instruction without its showing some results! Setting forth to make such a community music-drama calls forth as if by magic every such possibility that a community has within itself. And so this new people's drama, with its art-needs of every kind, is setting athrob the art activity of the whole people in every corner of the land and giving them *one* of the greatest things of life, which they had thought belonged only to great critics, to

[4]Farwell published an article on the pageant, "The Pageant and Masque of St. Louis: A People's Drama on a National Scale," *American Review of Reviews* 50 (1914): 187–93.   [5]The drama director Thomas Wood Stevens (d. 1942) was involved with other pageant-like works, including his masque *The Drawing of the Sword*, given during World War I at the Metropolitan Opera House. The dramatist and poet Percy MacKaye (1875–1956) was a strong advocate of community theater; he and Farwell collaborated on the masque *Caliban by the Yellow Sands* produced for the Shakespeare Tercentenary in New York City (1916) as well as another community work, *The Evergreen Tree* (1917). Frederick Converse (1871–1940) is distinguished as the first American composer to have an opera produced at the Metropolitan Opera (*The Pipe of Desire*, 1910).

far-away centers of fashion and wealth. The fact is, that the old, narrow, conventional and over-commercialized art-life of the few great centers is growing stale, is failing to meet the national need, and is paling and withering before the new and various-aspected art movement of the people. The people are waking up to the fact that there is something which they want, and which they have not been able to get, and so, from their own need, they are *making* it.

And even with all that has been expressed, nothing has been said of the stimulation of commercial, educational, religious, agricultural and other interests of the community through the "pageant," or of the wonderful way in which such united effort brings about a new order of social and spiritual progress in a community. The organization of the Pageant of Thetford, Vermont, encountered particular difficulties at the outset through the existence of long established social and religious cliques. It united them in the end, and at the close of the pageant, when most of the townspeople together were massing for the final scene and exit, an old farmer on the grandstand was heard to exclaim, "Huh! that's the first time the town of Thetford ever did anything all together!"

For this new condition of creative art and joy of art in America, the people are ready. All they need is to be shown how to make a beginning. The creative force is in themselves, and the materials are in their hands. The community itself is the artist, its people are the medium which the artist uses (as a painter uses his paints), and the dramatic representation of these people's own life in forms of beauty and order is the art-work. It is in order that the people may be shown how to set about it that the leaders of the "pageant movement" have arisen. Their function is to serve the people to this end, and teach them how to stand on their own feet.

Over all rise the two great spirits of Brotherhood and of Art, proclaiming a new gospel of more abundant life and joy for all.

Evolution of New Forms
Foreseen for America's Music[1]

The present moment of dazzling and manifold national musical activities in an external and distributive way, and the almost total eclipse of spiritual bearing and direction in the creative art of music itself, would appear to be an interesting moment, whether it can be profitable or not, in which to consider the outlook upon a hypothetical real creative culture of music in America. A sufficiently deep faith in music and its capacity for development, together with an equally deep faith in the United States of America as a nation of high and unique destiny, must necessarily result, it appears to me, in a conviction that America will eventually effect a fundamental change, and an upward-aiming one, in the whole course and direction of the evolution of the art of music. Such a conviction, springing from these causes, I confess to having entertained from earliest years of pre-analytical musical enthusiasm.

An evolutionary phenomenon of this nature would, however, necessarily have to await a more vital contact of musical evolution with American life than then existed, a profounder grappling by our nation with the idea of music. This contact and grappling has since taken place in a slight degree which admits of the beginnings of analysis, and sug-

---

[1] Appeared in *MA* 45 (19 March 1927): 3, 13. A companion article, "Dramatic Ceremony and Symphonic Song Visioned as New Form in Development of True American Art," appeared in the same publication a week later. The thrust of the essay reprinted here reiterates that of another Farwell article which appeared only a couple of months before this one: "The Zero Hour in Musical Evolution," *Musical Quarterly* 13 (1927): 85–99.

gests, even if faintly, the direction of prophecy. It is, at base, a question of the American spirit and world-view remoulding to their particular needs the plastic medium of music, as well as shaping musical activities and institutions to correspond. This implies nothing less than a new musical epoch, a culture, and this is a matter not of a few decades, but of centuries.

Distinct creative cultural epochs are the spiritual flowerings of particular racial or national groups which have struck their roots deeply into certain spots of the earth favorable to their life and growth. Such cycles, in their characteristic creative expression, are confined to their own nations and races, in their own locale. While they may export their product and affect the taste, artistic activities and certain imitative pseudo-creative efforts elsewhere, as the Grecian culture in Rome or the West-European in America, they do not, as authentic creative movements, cross their own proper frontiers, still less bridge oceans. New vision is predestined and unescapable in a new continent. It would be folly to suppose that a true creative musical epoch in America could be a direct continuation of European musical evolution, resting upon the principles of that phase of an evolution.

Individual Vitality

Already, before we have put forth an impossible "American Beethoven," the trite dictum of a quarter of a century of our not having developed a characteristic music is rapidly losing its veracity. Leaving the notoriously characteristic quality of our popular music wholly aside, the mass of our more vigorous musical expression in America today has its own tang, its own terse vitality, which may be felt even through widely different styles and personalities. Under all this American music a fresh spirit is at work.

Just at this time, however, at the end of the first quarter of the new century, there exists a kind of hiatus, a lacuna of our general progress toward a bold and outstanding continental achievement. Up to the World War we were animated by a naive and youthful national enthusiasm in our musical creativity, the result of the first dawning of something resembling a national musical self-consciousness. Out of that period there issued a number of works of clean-cut, definite American aim, which the intervening years have by no means cast into oblivion, although transient exotic styles may have caused them to be neglected. The question of a characteristic Ameri-

can musical art had been broached at various times in the last half of
the nineteenth century, but it was not until the new century that those
events occurred which launched a more widespread conscious national
creative endeavor, and brought the matter to the status of a national
issue.

In these developments it was my fortune to play a not inconsider-
able part, in the establishment of the Wa-Wan Press, at Newton
Center, Mass., in December, 1901.[2] During a period of more than ten
years the progressive and experimental work given out by some
twenty American composers through this medium, which as part of its
program made for the first time a concerted practical application of the
suggestion given out by Antonín Dvořák in 1893, made this enterprise
at the time the center of a national issue and debate on this question,
which reached its height in the years 1904 to 1908.

Since the War chaos has overtaken the artistic ideals of the
world. Europe has been diverting itself with the mad sensationalism
of futurism and post-futurism, which has stimulated a feeble imitation in the United States. The latter, incapable of so profound a
cynicism as that which has prevailed in Europe, has been sincerely
seeking proficiency in the employment of the "modern idiom." The
progress has in general been one of technical advancement, with
virtually no sense or inner indication of spiritual direction, certainly
nothing comparable in this respect with the pre-war decade. With
the war-shocked mentality of the world, it has been difficult for the
individual to believe ardently in anything, especially with respect to
those great spiritual currents which in the end must always determine the direction of the evolution of art.

Seek National Ideals

From this war-shock and its aftermath of confusion, doubt and
hesitancy, we would be nationally reprehensible if we did not at this
time make a determined effort to extricate ourselves. In the roughest
terms, to do this, in the sphere of music, means that we shall cast off
the pretense and self-delusion that the great traditional European
ideals and forms, now passing to their decline, are to be our ideals
and forms, to cease dallying with ingenious imitations of the despairing post-futurists of Europe whose work can mean nothing to our

---

[2]See p. p. 87ff.

people, and to seek out the ideals and aspirations of America as the only promptings and subject matter to which we can apply the art of music if we are to enter upon a significant American musical culture in the twentieth century. Such an American achievement and epoch must stand upon a new formulation of principles and bear a new relation to the American people.

At this time, therefore, a quarter of a century after the inauguration of the Wa-Wan Press, I offer this necessary and directly sequential contribution to the evolution of the art of music in America, in essaying in some sort the formulation of the principles which must govern this new epoch. This essay comes to birth, now that the fact of musical composition is established in America through the imperative need of seeking to discover the spiritual direction and the principles which must determine the matter and forms of our creative musical art if it is to embody truth to the spirit, aim, the message and processes, of the American nation and the new world. This, it should be needless to say, must be in accord with the most complete individual artistic liberty. The exercise of this liberty, however, will remain sterile so long as it does not align itself with the deeper spiritual currents of the new world. The currents alone can yield the sources of power which will give that liberty real force in action. With this introduction we will pass to the presentation of principles, some comments upon which will be made in a second article.

1. New Spiritual Direction

That the art of music can live and proceed toward a great new creative fulfillment and epoch in America only as it takes to itself spiritual purpose and direction, by identifying itself with the life of the whole people, with their deepest sympathies and aspirations and the most central qualities of their character; that it can realize itself only as it finds and unites itself with sentiments and emotions of nation-wide validity and of a depth equivalent to that of religion; that it shall only thus free itself and lift itself out from under the old-world decadence, the present loss or confusion of ideals, and the spiritual bankruptcy of the old traditions.

2. Inclusion of the Whole People

That music, the musical life, shall be regarded as a normal function of the whole people, in its highest use as a power for the unification and liberation of the people in the light of their greater racial ideals, and, as such, its maintenance for the whole people, the events and ceremonies constituting the public musical life and the central channel of creative progress under the new order being practically available to all, and not improbably open to all without admission fee, and maintained by the community for the community.

3. Restoration of Song

That song, the singing of the people, shall be restored as the foundation of all musical development, and essential to its further normal evolution, and shall constitute the basis of the new type of musical events as well as of all festival events of the movement.

4. Evolution by New Forms

That the creative evolution of music in the new culture shall, as always with new cultural epochs, proceed through new forms; that such forms shall be determined in the creative vision of the artist by the essential elements of the new time-spirit, involving the needs of the people, the matters and ideals now demanding expression, the restoration of song, new institutions and the new modes of musical presentation.

5. Origin in Community Music Movement

That the new movement shall be understood to take its rise from the beginnings made by the "community music" movement, as being the one spontaneous American musical movement by and for the people as a whole in response to imperative national needs, but that this movement must be lifted into its higher possibilities and true estate as the vehicle of a new evolutionary cycle through the application of American poets, composers, other creative artists, and culture leaders generally, to the development of its characteristic and appropriate forms.

6. A New Vehicle

That a new type of public musical event, with regular meetings and special festivals, apart from the sphere of the traditional pay concert and commercial musical enterprise generally, on a new and democratic basis, manifesting and developing the principles and musical forms of the new epoch, shall be established as the vehicle of the new movement, and shall constitute the central feature of the general musical life of the people, and the main theater of creative musical activity and evolution; and that the various "community" and other democratic musical movements of the time indicate the point of departure and elementary form of such a vehicle.

7. Secondary Place of Instrumental Music

That the symphonic and other instrumental music, while forfeiting none of the powers which it has gained in modern times, shall in the new epoch find its chief employment in works presenting definite poetic conceptions and appropriate to the new type of public musical events, and in which voices take an equal or predominant part; that such instrumental music shall primarily serve the larger needs and ideals of the time, as expressed in part through the people in song, ceremony and drama, departing from a chief attention to the working out of abstract musical problems.

8. The Ceremonial Principle

That the ceremonial principle shall have an integral place in the development of the new movement, to make possible the more intimate participation and the more effective unification of the people in the expression and celebration of appropriate ideas and national, seasonal or other festivals having a meaning for the whole people; and that such ideas and festivals shall be given concrete practical artistic form by creative artists.

9. The Dramatic Principle

That the dramatic principle shall be of outstanding importance in the new evolution, because of its unique and needed power in the representation of ideas, its wide appeal and comprehensibility, and its adaptability for the participation of the people, and that a new and freer musical dramatic form shall be sought as one of the principal paths of the new movement.

10. The Recording of Technical Advance

That the technical development of the musical medium in general must follow and be re-shaped by the needs of the major forms of a new culture of new purpose and direction; that the spirit of the new epoch, and the necessary factor of comprehensibility by the people, as well as their participation, will dictate normal styles of musical expression devoid of extravagance and sensationalism, while still seeking the wonder of new beauty; that no advance is to come from a further abnormal and disproportionate forcing of harmony and orchestration, and that among the valid factors of technical advance will be the invention and development of new forms of wide appeal, the continuing liberation of the elements of musical composition from traditional restrictions and relations, the seeking of a truer balance of these elements, and the compelling of the powers of modern harmony to the service of a wider conception of scale and melody.

11. New Type of Musical Artist

That a new type of musical artist shall arise who will be the living embodiment of the principles of the new epoch, animated by the deeper aspirations of the time and understanding the need of the service of the whole people, who shall be the leader of the public events and festivals of the new movements, qualified in the knowledge of musical history, in the conducting of the higher developments of vocal and instrumental music as well as of communal singing, and in dramatic direction.

12. New Economic Condition of Music

That creative musical evolution, as essentially a spiritual movement, cannot exist or proceed as an activity primarily commercial, or through a distributive medium as greatly dependent upon its commercial aspect and private commercial enterprise as the existing system; that the relation of music to the people in the new epoch will necessarily require and create a new economic condition of music, in which the events centrally constituting the public musical life shall be maintained in a non-commercial and democratic manner similar to that in which government, religion, libraries and art museums, or the various community music movements of the time are supported by funds derived from individual contributions, municipal or other appropriations, endowments, gifts, collections, and in other available and possible ways.

13. Ultimate Musical Form

That a new type of music-drama, presenting aspirational concepts of the highest evolutionary racial significance, as well as a new freedom in the employment of the elements of dramatic representation, and tending toward the aspect of a great periodic community ceremonial, will constitute the ultimate form of musical expression of the new epoch; that the American pageant, masque, "grove play,"[3] and related forms of the present, in their best and most significant examples, constitute a point of departure from which such a form may arise through the application of the proper aims and the requisite creative capacities.

---

[3]Refers to the annual musical play of the Bohemian Club of San Francisco; see pp. 111f., 124ff, and 177, n.19.

References

Manuscript and Rare Materials

Beach, John Parsons. Collection. New York Public Library at Lincoln Center, New York, NY.

Farwell, Arthur. Collection. Sibley Music Library, Eastman School of Music, University of Rochester, Rochester, NY.

Farwell, Arthur. Scrapbook entitled "Clippings and Some Programs Describing the Career of Mr. Farwell from 1903–1911." Microfilm copy, New York Public Library at Lincoln Center, New York, NY.

Farwell, Arthur. Special Collections. University Research Library, University of California at Los Angeles.

Freedman, L. A. Special Manuscript Collection. Butler Library, Columbia University, New York, NY.

Gilbert, Henry F. B. Papers. Beinecke Rare Book and Manuscript Library, Yale University, New Haven, CT.

James, G. Wharton. Collection. Southwest Museum, Los Angeles, CA.

Lummis, Charles F. Collection. Braun Research Library, MS.1.1.1288A and MS.1.1.1288B, Southwest Museum, Los Angeles, CA.

Oldberg, Arne. Collection. Music Division, Library of Congress, Washington, DC.

Parker, Horatio. Papers. Beinecke Rare Book and Manuscript Library, Yale University, New Haven, CT.

Shepherd, Arthur. Papers. Marriott Library, University of Utah, Salt Lake City, UT.

Twentieth Century Club of Boston. File of published Bulletins, Annual Reports, Programs, etc. Widener Memorial Library, Harvard University, Cambridge, MA.

University Archives. President's Files. University of California, Berkeley, CA.

Books and Articles

"American Composers Receive a Hearing." *MA* 3 (7 April 1906): 6.

"American Music Heard." *Musical Courier* 58 (6 January 1909): 11.

"American Music Heard." *New York Times*, 31 December 1908, 9.

"American Music Society." *Musical Courier* 50 (31 May 1905): 13.

"American Music Society Concert." *Musical Courier* 58 (21 April 1909): 25.

Amsden, Charles A. *Navaho Weaving: Its Technic and History*. Santa Ana, CA: The Fine Arts Press, 1939.

"Arne Oldberg." *Musical Courier* 33 (5 August 1896): 22.

Atherton, Percy. "Boston Days (1909–1922): Some Engeliana." In *A Birthday Offering to Carl Engel*, edited by Gustave Reese, 27–34. New York: G. Schirmer, 1943.

Atlas, Allan W. "Belasco and Puccini: 'Old Dog Tray' and the Zuni Indians." *Musical Quarterly* 75 (1991): 362–98.

Ayars, Christine M. *Contributions to the Art of Music in America by the Music Industries of Boston: 1640 to 1936*. New York: H. W. Wilson, 1937.

Baker's Biographical Dictionary of Musicians, 4th ed. New York: G. Schirmer, 1940.

Beer, Thomas. *The Mauve Decade: American Life at the End of the Nineteenth Century*. New York: Alfred A. Knopf, 1926.

Bingham, Edwin R. *Charles F. Lummis: Editor of the Southwest*. San Marino, CA: The Huntington Library, 1955.

Bio-Bibliographical Index of Musicians in the United States of America since Colonial Times. 2nd ed. Prepared by the District of Columbia Historical Survey, Division of Community Service Programs, Work Projects Administration Under the Auspices of the Board of Commissioners of the District of Columbia, the Pan American Union, and the Library of Congress. 1956. Reprint New York: AMS Press, 1972.

Bispham, David. "The American Idea in Music, and Some Other Ideas." *Craftsman* 15 (1909): 671–80.

———. *A Quaker Singer's Recollections*. New York: Macmillan, 1920.

Boston Evening Transcript. [Obituary, William I. Cole], 27 September 1935.

———. [Obituary, Helen A. Clarke], 9 February 1926.

Boston Globe. [Articles and reviews on opera seasons for 1895 and 1896], 25 February–9 March; 9–14 April 1895; 17–29 February 1896.

"Boston Music Notes." *Musical Courier* 33 (18 November 1896): 15.

Braden, Charles S. *Spirits in Rebellion: The Rise and Development of New Thought*. Dallas: Southern Methodist University Press, 1963.

Brewster, William L. *William Mead Ladd of Portland Oregon*. Portland: Metropolitan Press, 1933.

"A Brief Summary." *Southwest Society of the Archaelogical Institute of America. First Bulletin*. 1904, 24–25.

Chase, Gilbert. *America's Music*, 3rd ed. Urbana: University of Illinois Press, 1987.

"Concert by the American Music Society." *Musical Courier* 58 (3 March 1909): 15.

"Concert of American Music." *New York Times*, 19 April 1909, 2.

Crawford, Richard. *The American Musical Landscape*. Berkeley: University of California Press, 1993.

Culbertson, Evelyn Davis. *He Heard America Singing: Arthur Farwell: Com-

poser and Crusading Music Educator. Metuchen, NJ: Scarecrow Press, 1992.

Currier, Thomas P. "Edward MacDowell as I Knew Him," *Musical Quarterly* 1 (1915): 17–51.

Curtis, Edward S. *The North American Indian: Being a Series of Volumes Picturing and Describing the Indians of the United States and Alaska*. 20 vols. 1907–30. Reprint. New York: Johnson Reprint, 1970.

Dahlhaus, Carl. *Nineteenth-Century Music*, trans. J. Bradford Robinson. Berkeley: University of California Press, 1989.

Dawdy, Doris O. *Artists of the American West*. Chicago: Swallow Press, 1974.

"Della Thal, Gifted Pianist, Now a New Yorker." *Musical Courier* 58 (31 March 1909): 31.

Deloria, Vine, Jr. "Introduction" to Christopher M. Lyman, *The Vanishing Race and Other Illusions: Photographs of Indians by Edward S. Curtis*. Washington: Smithsonian Institution Press, 1982.

Dent, Edward J. "Hans Pfitzner." *Music and Letters* 4 (1923): 119–32.

Deseret Evening News. [Obituary, Spencer Clawson, Jr.], 7 May 1917.

Downes, Olin. "An American Composer." *Musical Quarterly* 4 (1918): 23–36.

———. "Henry Gilbert: Nonconformist." In *A Birthday Offering to Carl Engel*, edited by Gustave Reese, 88–94. New York: G. Schirmer, 1943.

Dvořák, Antonín. "Music in America." *Harper's New Monthly Magazine* 90 (1895): 428-34. Reprinted in *Dvořák in America: 1892-1895*, ed. John C. Tibbett, 370-80. Portland, OR: Amadeus Press, 1993.

Earle, Henry Edmond. "An Old Time Collector: Reminiscences of Charles F. Lummis." *California Folklore Quarterly* 1 (1942): 179–83.

Elson, Louis C. "American Composers Since 1900" in Rupert Hughes, *American Composers*. New York: L. C. Page, 1914.

———. *The History of American Music*, rev. ed. New York: Macmillan, 1915.

Engel, Carl. "Views and Reviews." *Musical Quarterly* 26 (1940): 113–21.

Evanston [Illinois] *Index* . [Article on Farwell's lecture for Evanston Woman's Club], 4 January 1908.

Falk, Peter H., ed. *Who Was Who in American Art: Biographies of American Artists Active from 1898–1947*. Madison, CT: Sound View Press, 1985.

Farwell, Arthur. "Afterword," *Land of Luthany: Poem for Violoncello and Piano*. East Lansing, MI: Arthur Farwell, 1933.

———. "Afterword," *Two Songs on Poems by William Blake*. East Lansing, MI: Arthur Farwell, 1931.

———. "America's Gain from a Bayreuth Romance: The Mystery of Anton Seidl." *Musical Quarterly* 30 (1944): 448–57.

———. "The Bohemian Club High Jinks of 1909" *MA* 10 (16 October 1909): 3–8.

———. "An Eleven Years' Adventure." *MA* 16 (14 September 1912): 9.

———. "The Coming Composer." *MA* 21 (10 April 1915): 28.

———. "Dramatic Ceremony and Symphonic Song Visioned as New Form in Development of True American Art." *MA* 45 (26 March 1927): 3, 17.

———. "Francis Grierson—Musical Liberator." *MA* 19 (13 December 1913): 19.

———. "A Hidden Race." *Tomorrow* 2 (August 1943): 41–42.

———. "How the 'Midsummer High Jinks' Came into Existence." *MA* 10 (17 July 1909): 3.

———. "The Improvisations of Francis Grierson." *MA* 19 (17 January 1914): 12.

———. "In a Musical Utopia." *MA* 8 (10 October 1908): 45.

———. "Likes His Königskinder Best." *MA* 13 (17 December 1910): 6.

———. "Music in the Abstract." *Musical World* 3 (1903): 93–95.

———. "The Music of Humperdinck's New Opera." *MA* 13 (31 December 1910): 1, 4–5.

———. "A Musical Poet of Childhood: Engelbert Humperdinck, the Composer of 'Hänsel und Gretel.'" *The Outlook* (23 December 1905): 1007–09.

———. "The National Movement for American Music." *American Review of Reviews* 38 (1908): 721–24.

———. [Memorial tribute to Thomas Mott Osborne.] *New York Times*, 6 March 1927, 10.

———. "Noted Composers Honored at Great Norfolk Festival." *MA* 14 (17 June 1911): 1, 3–4.

———. "Overtones and Sanity," *MA* 17 (3 May 1913): 26.

———. "The Pageant and Masque of St. Louis: A People's Drama on a National Scale" *American Review of Reviews* 50 (1914): 187–93.

———. "Pioneering for American Music." *Modern Music* 12 (1935): 116–22.

———. "The Relation of Folksong to American Musical Development." *Studies in Musical Education: History and Aesthetics. Papers and Proceedings of the Music Teachers National Association*, Series 2 (1907): 197–205.

———. *Songs and Music of To-Day with Special Reference to The Laurel Song Book.* Boston: C. C. Birchard, 1902.

———. "The Struggle Toward a National Music." *North American Review* 186 (1907): 565–70.

———. "Three Days at Musical Sing Sing." *MA* 22 (5 June 1915): 25.

———. "What Teachers and Pupils Could Do for American Music," *Etude* (1908): 770.

———. "The Zero Hour in Musical Evolution." *Musical Quarterly* 13 (1927): 85–99

——— and W. Dermot Darby, eds. *Music in America*. Vol. 4, *The Art of Music*, edited by Daniel Gregory Mason. New York: The National Society of Music, 1915.

Farwell, Brice, ed. *A Guide to the Music of Arthur Farwell*. Briarcliff Manor, NY: published by the editor, 1972.

"First Concert of New Music Society." *MA* 3 (17 March 1906): 11.

Fleming, Robert E. *Charles F. Lummis.* Boise, ID: Boise State University, 1981.

Fletcher, Alice. *Indian Story and Song from North America*. 1900. Reprint. New York: AMS Press, 1970.

"From Beyond the Seas." *MA* 3 (17 February 1906): 10.

Gabriel, Charles H., Jr. "Music and Colored Lighting Glorify Natural Theater." *MA* 43 (11 November 1925): 3, 10.

[Gilman, Lawrence]. "New American Music." *Harper's Weekly* 47 (7 October 1903): 1658.

———. "Some American Music." *Harper's Weekly* 47 (7 March 1903): 394.

Goshen [Indiana] *News*. [Obituary, Noble Kreider], 21 December 1959.

Hale, Philip. "In Memoriam B. E. Woolf." *Musical Courier* 42 (13 February 1901): 28–29.

Hamm, Charles. *Music in the New World*. New York: W. W. Norton, 1983.

Harvard University. [Secretary's] *Report: Class of 1898*. Cambridge, MA: Harvard University, 1904, 1913, and 1928.

Hawley, Oscar Hatch. "Musical Life in St. Joseph." *Musical Courier* 60 [30 March 1910]: 39.

———, "National Federation of Musical Clubs: the Sixth Biennial Meeting at Grand Rapids," *Musical Courier* 58 (2 June 1909): 43–45.

Hicks, Michael. *Mormonism and Music: A History*. Urbana: University of Illinois Press, 1989.

Hipsher, Edward E. *American Opera and Its Composers*. Revised edition. Philadelphia: Theodore Presser, 1934.

Hitchcock, H. Wiley. *Music in the United States: A Historical Introduction*. 3rd ed. Englewood Cliffs, NJ: Prentice Hall, 1988.

——— and Stanley Sadie, eds. *The New Grove Dictionary of American Music*. London: Macmillan Press Limited and New York: Grove's Dictionaries of Music, Inc., 1986.

Horowitz, Joseph. *Understanding Toscanini: How He Became an American Culture-God and Helped Create a New Audience for Old Music*. New York: Alfred A. Knopf, 1987.

Hudson, Wylna Blanche. "Boston." *Musical Courier* 58 (26 May 1909): 38.

Hughes, Rupert. *Contemporary American Composers*. Boston: L. C. Page, 1900.

Humperdinck, Wolfram. *Engelbert Humperdinck: Das Leben meines Vaters*. Frankfurt am Main: Verlag Waldemar Kramer, 1965.

Huneker, James G. *The Philharmonic Society of New York and Its Seventy-fifth Anniversary: A Retrospect* (N.p., n.d.).

———. "The Raconteur." *Musical Courier* 40 (24 January 1900): 28.

James, George W. *Indian Blankets and Their Makers*. Chicago: A. C. McClurg, 1914.

Johns, Clayton. *Reminiscences of a Musician*. Cambridge, MA: Washburn and Thomas, 1929.

Kingman, Daniel. *American Music: A Panorama*, 2nd ed. New York: Schirmer Books, 1990.

Kirk, Edgar Lee. "Toward American Music: A Study of the Life and Music of Arthur George Farwell." Ph.D. diss., Eastman School of Music, University of Rochester, 1958.

Knight, Ellen. *Charles Martin Loeffler: A Life Apart in American Music*. Urbana IL: University of Illinois Press, 1993.

Koegel, John. "Hispanic Music in Nineteenth-Century California: The Lummis

Collection of Cylinder Recordings at the Southwest Museum." (unpublished manuscript).

———. "The Lummis Collection of Cylinder Recordings as a Source for Hispanic Music in Southern California in the Nineteenth Century." Ph.D. diss., Claremont Graduate School, 1994.

Kravitt, Edward F. "The Joining of Words and Music in Late Romantic Melodrama." *Musical Quarterly* 62 (1976): 571–90.

Krehbiel, Henry E. "Music: A Concert of American Compositions." *New York Daily Tribune*, 19 April 1909, 7.

Lawrence, Vera Brodsky, ed. *The Wa-Wan Press: 1901–1911.* 5 vols. New York: Arno Press and the *New York Times*, 1970.

Loucks, Richard. *Arthur Shepherd: American Composer.* Provo, UT: Brigham Young University Press, 1980.

Lummis. Charles F. "Catching Our Archaeology Alive." *Southwest Society of the Archaelogical Institute of America. Second Bulletin*, 1905, 3–15.

Mark, Joan. *Four Anthropologists: An American Science in its Early Years.* New York: Science History Publications, 1980.

———. *A Stranger in Her Native Land: Alice Fletcher and the American Indians.* Lincoln: University of Nebraska Press, 1988.

Marquis, Albert N., ed. *The Book of Chicagoans: A Biographical Dictionary of Leading Living Men of the City of Chicago.* Chicago: A. N. Marquis & Co., 1911.

McNutt, James C. "John Comfort Fillmore: A Student of Indian Music Reconsidered." *American Music* 2 (1984): 61–70.

Müller, F. Max, ed. *The Sacred Books of the East.* 50 vols. Oxford: Clarendon Press, 1879–1910.

"Music and Musicians." *New York Evening Sun,* 19 April 1909, 9.

Musicians of Los Angeles: 1904–05. N.p., n.d.

"New Music Society Incorporated." *MA* 3 (30 December 1905): 1.

New York Evening Post. [Reviews of American Music Society Concerts], 26 February 1909, 5; 19 April 1909, 7.

New York Evening Sun. [Review of American Music Society Concert], 19 April 1909, 9.

New York Times. [Obituary, Arthur Depew], 25 September 1940, 27.

New York Times. [Obituary, Isabel Stevens Lathrop], 28 October 1964, 45.

Pacific Coast Musical Review. [Announcements regarding the Los Angeles and San Francisco centers, American Music Society], 16 (22 May 1909); 16 (14 August 1909); and 17 (6 November 1909).

Pincus-Witten, Robert. *Occult Symbolism in France: Joséphin Péladan and the Salons de la Rose-Croix.* New York: Garland, 1976.

Pratt, Waldo Selden, ed. *American Supplement. Grove's Dictionary of Music and Musicians,* 3rd ed. New York: Macmillan, 1934.

Prevots, Naima. *American Pageantry: A Movement for Art and Democracy.* Ann Arbor, MI: UMI Research Press, 1990.

Reynolds, William J. *A Survey of Christian Hymnody.* New York: Holt, Rinehart, & Winston, 1963.

Sadie, Stanley, ed. *New Grove Dictionary of Music and Musicians*. London: Macmillan, 1980.

Schwab, Arnold T., ed. *Americans in the Arts—1890–1920: Critiques by James Gibbons Huneker*. New York: AMS Press, 1985.

Seidl, Anton. "The Development of Music in America." *Forum* 13 (May 1892): 386–93.

Skeel, Sharon Kay. "A Black American in the Paris Salon." *American Heritage* 42 (February-March 1991): 76–83.

Smith, Catherine Parsons. "'Something of Good for the Future': The People's Orchestra of Los Angeles." *Nineteenth-Century Music* 16 (1992): 146–60.

Spanish Songs of Old California, Collected and Translated by Charles F. Lummis; Pianoforte Accompaniments by Arthur Farwell. Published privately, C. F. Lummis, 1923; and, New York: G. Schirmer, 1923.

Stoner, Thomas. "'The New Gospel of Music': Arthur Farwell's Vision of Democratic Music in America." *American Music* 9 (1991): 183–208.

Symons, Arthur. "Music and Social Flurry." *Saturday Review* [London], (21 March 1908).

Tomlins, W. L., ed. *The Laurel Song Book: For Advanced Classes in Schools, Academies, Choral Societies, etc.* Boston: C. C. Birchard, 1901.

Trapper, Emma L. "National Federation of Clubs." *Musical Courier* 62 (5 April 1911): 29–33.

Twentieth Century Club of Boston. *A Survey of 20 Years: 1894–1914*. Boston: The Twentieth Century Club, 1914.

Upton, William T. "Frederic Ayres." *Musical Quarterly* 18 (1932): 39–59.

———. "Our Musical Expatriates." *Musical Quarterly* 14 (1928): 143–54.

Waters, Edward N. "The Wa-Wan Press: An Adventure in Musical Idealism." In *A Birthday Offering to Carl Engel*, edited by Gustave Reese, 214–33. New York: G. Schirmer, 1943.

Waters, Grant M. *Dictionary of British Artists Working 1900–1950*. 2 vols. Eastbourne, England: Eastbourne Fine Art Publications, 1975–76.

Wilkinson, Ernest L., ed. *Brigham Young University: The First One Hundred Years*. Provo, UT: Brigham Young University Press, 1975.

Williamson, John. *The Music of Hans Pfitzner*. Oxford: Clarendon Press, 1992.

Yeats, William Butler. *Land of Heart's Desire*. Portland, ME: Thomas B. Mosher, 1913.

Zuck, Barbara. *A History of Musical Americanism*. Ann Arbor, MI: UMI Research Press, 1980.

Index

Page numbers in italics indicate illustrations.